Bodies Inhabiting
the World

Bodies Inhabiting the World

Scandinavian Creation Theology and the Question of Home

Edited by Derek R. Nelson,
Niels Henrik Gregersen,
and Bengt Kristensson Uggla

LEXINGTON BOOKS
Lanham • Boulder • New York • London

Published by Lexington Books
An imprint of The Rowman & Littlefield Publishing Group, Inc.
4501 Forbes Boulevard, Suite 200, Lanham, Maryland 20706
www.rowman.com

86-90 Paul Street, London EC2A 4NE

British Library Cataloguing in Publication Information Available

Library of Congress Cataloging-in-Publication Data

Names: Nelson, Derek R., 1977- editor. | Gregersen, Niels Henrik, 1956- editor. | Uggla,
    Bengt Kristensson, editor.
Title: Bodies inhabiting the world : Scandianvian creation theology and the question
    of home / edited by Derek R. Nelson, Niels Henrik Gregersen, and Bengt
    Kristensson Uggla.
Description: Lanham : Lexington Books, [2024] | Includes bibliographical references
    and index. |
Summary: "Fourteen theologians consider what it means to have a home in the world.
    Drawing on and also critically engaging with Scandinavian creation theology, they
    explore how we are at home (or are threatened with its opposite) in one's own skin,
    dwelling, community, or even the cosmos writ large"-- Provided by publisher.
Identifiers: LCCN 2023041942 | ISBN 9781666931433 (cloth) | ISBN
    9781666931440 (ebook)
Subjects: LCSH: Home--Religious aspects--Christianity. | Creation. | Bible--Theology.
Classification: LCC BR115.H56 B63 2024 | DDC 233/.11--dc23/eng/20231024
LC record available at https://lccn.loc.gov/2023041942

Contents

Acknowledgments

This book began with a conference hosted at Wabash College, finally, in May 2022. We say "finally" because it was an event, like many others, whose trajectory and eventually even its content was affected by the Covid-19 pandemic. Originally scheduled for May 2020, it became clear early in March 2020 that things might not happen as we planned. Like countless other suckers, we thought "surely this will blow over in a few weeks." Or maybe months. Or maybe not . . . When it was finally able to take place, many of us had been more or less confined in our homes for a very long time, adding new dimensions to our thinking about this key question of theology and human existence.

The editors would like to thank Wabash College for its hospitality in hosting the conversation that started this book. Its Dean, Todd McDorman, has been supportive and enthusiastic about the scholarship behind and ahead of this volume. Some financial support also came from the Early Career Pastoral Leadership Development Initiative, funded by Lilly Endowment. In thinking about ecumenically approachable but existentially vital theology while working with pastors of many different Christian faith traditions, it has become clear that the best way forward is with a carefully crafted focus question. "What is it to have a home?" is one of those questions, and we are grateful to the Lilly Endowment for helping us offer provisional answers to it. Other funds came from the Stephen S. Bowen Professorship in Liberal Arts and the Eric Dean Fund at Wabash. We also wish to thank Helga Marie Ishøy Carstens for doing the index, supported by the Danish foundation Samfonden.

The editors wish to register in this public way our deep appreciation for the authors whose work appears here. In addition to the practical difficulties alluded to above, these scholars have worked very hard to engage a multi-faceted and significant tradition (SCT) with its own questions and inertia, and yet also posed new questions to it and elicited nuanced and diverse responses. The North American theologians, especially, who were not particularly well-acquainted with SCT, did significant work to ready themselves for the debates, and many (though not all!) of them found themselves perhaps surprisingly convinced of the promise of future conversation with SCT.

This collaboration has been one in which old friendships have deepened, contemporary questions have been newly considered, and future possibilities imagined. The editors are therefore grateful for the productive disagreements we have trusted each other enough to have, and we commend to our fellow scholars the difficult but immensely rewarding approach of working together across oceans, generations, and mother-tongues to make a shared contribution to the work of theology, which remains always *soli deo gloria.*

Crawfordsville
Copenhagen
Stockholm
June 2023

Introduction

Belonging, Comfort, and Delight
An Invitation to Home and SCT

Derek R. Nelson

What is it to have home, to be at home? It's one of those things that everyone, or almost everyone, knows. But it's also elusive. No one can quite say why or how they know they feel at home. Yet when they know, they know. It's a mystery. Lichens are organisms where a dominant fungus nonetheless needs a partner alga in order to grow and reproduce. Mystery and theology are like that: mystery needs theology in order for the one who experiences mystery to understand what is or isn't known; theology needs mystery to save itself from its tendency to claim to know more than it does. In attending to mysteries like what "home" really means, theology thrives at the edges where knowing meets not-knowing.

This book invites different perspectives on the question of "What is it to have a home?" The answers—temporary, exploratory, provisional, and partial—offered here emerged from a conference I hosted at Wabash College in 2022. Proponents associated with the exciting research program sometimes called "Scandinavian Creation Theology" (SCT) met with theologians in North America to explore both the question above as well as what it would mean to continue to internationalize and modulate a particular orientation toward Protestant theology with a rich history and bright future. This introduction to the question of home, the program of SCT, and the contributions in the present volume is intended to invite you into a conversation that will—because it must—continue.

HOME AS A CONCEPT

Just to get the mystery on the table so we can encounter it, rather than be stupefied by it, I propose to discuss a home as a place where we experience belonging, comfort, and delight. Let's think about those three key terms in turn and see how our thesis fares.

Belonging

In Robert Frost's poem "Death of the Hired Man" a farm couple is debating what to do with their ailing former hired hand who has come back and knocked on their door asking for help. He left, we are made to understand, under some unsavory conditions, and now he is in need. The husband says the fellow ought to go instead to his brother's house, not so many miles away. After all the brother is rich, "a director in the bank. . . . " But the farmer's wife protests and says "he has come home to die." The husband mocks this idea, but is told, "Home is the place where, when you go there, *they have to take you in.*"

That is a powerful way to think about the social aspects of home, certainly. "Home" has a "they" who take you in. As exiles and immigrants can tell you, "home" means forming attachments with other people in a way that makes you feel (and be!) safe and secure. Migrants and refugees know that home will have to be *other* than the home they are leaving, and there is a yearning to find a new place to be welcomed and set at ease. "Home" is about relationships, and thus a sense of belonging, or one can even speak of a sense of a "longing for belonging." I have come to feel at home in new places when I formed attachments with people who knew more about the place than I did and were very different from me, yet they found ways to connect with me. To "belong" to something is both active and passive; I can actively sign up to be a part of a club or team or organization, but a sense of belonging is something that I also undergo, when others accept me as their peer. To speak theologically, belonging is in a sense both law and gospel.[1] It is law because learning to belong in a new community means learning its rules and customs. But one can never straightforwardly choose to snap one's fingers and say, "Now I belong here." It is, instead, a gospel-like mercy extended by others. In having been accepted by others, you begin to belong.

Comfort

So home is a social concept, to be sure. It requires and deepens a sense of belonging. But when I think of "home" it has to a place, a space. Yes, people and pets and various social "others" are there, too. But we have other words for that, like family, or community. Home is walls, floor, and a roof. And it exists for our comfort.[2] Like belonging, comfort is a term that has many different registers. Once I move into a new house or apartment, it might feel like a glorified hotel room until I start to know it better, and thus get more comfortable there. I learn how to control the temperature, I fix the broken screen door hinge, and in a thousand other ways make the place more comfortable.

Etymologically, "comfort" comes from Latin "*con-fortare*," which means to make stronger. When I go to my home after a long day of work, I am strengthened for other activities, including working the next day. Were I to leave my place of work to go to a broken home, one where I could not feel safe or be comforted, then I would be accordingly less able to do my work, to pursue my interests, to extend myself into the world and use what gifts I have. In that sense, "home" is both a descriptive and a normative idea. It describes places where we go to sleep, eat, and share life with others. But intrinsic to it is a notion of what a *good* home is, one where others accept me, and where I can be comforted, strengthened, for the work ahead. And it is tied to the theological notion of vocation.[3] A good home strengthens you for some purpose, some activity, and that purpose is your vocation, your calling.

A prison chaplain with whom I was speaking about this topic asked a pointed question. "Can a *prison* be a home?" I did not know how to respond when he asked, and even now I do not quite know. Surely there are places in a prison where one can (or should be able to) feel safe, and be strengthened to face another day. Surely there are friendships and a sense of community, no matter how imperfect or tenuous. But home is also something you can and should *leave*. In Genesis (quoted again in Matthew and Ephesians) we read "For this reason, a man leaves his father and his mother and clings to his wife, and they become one flesh." You leave home to become an adult. Put another way, homes are for *sending*, not just for staying comfortable. If you have to stay there, it isn't a home, not quite.

Perhaps this aspect of home has taken on a special relevance during the COVID-19 pandemic. So many were forced to stay home, and many others were desperate to be safe at home but could not be because their calling was to work in hospitals or essential services. Home means something different now to the telecommuter. You're always around your work if your living room is your office. Walking past the table to get a bowl of nighttime ice cream, you notice that stack of papers you haven't taken care of. Or desperate for elbow room, you begin to resent the others around you. Or you crave the commute you used to have and the chance it gave you to decompress. Still others were finally motivated to get their homes in better shape. The pandemic made us think about the comforts of home differently in all kinds of ways.

Delight

That leaves delight. Delight means that it feels good, feels right, to be in this place, among these people with these things. But delight isn't something we can control. Delight happens. There is a surprise element to delight, like when a loved one brings home dessert unexpectedly or the light comes in the East window just right as you drink your morning coffee. Being around things of beauty that are both surprising and yet familiar is a quintessential feature of feeling at home.

The German sociologist and philosopher Hartmut Rosa calls such feelings *resonance*. By this he means, "a form of world-relation in which subject and world encounter each other and are mutually transformed."[4] Resonance happens when you, the experiencing subject, can't merely control the world you're relating to. It's the difference between, for example, seeing a wild animal in its own habitat when you're on a walk and seeing one in a controlled environment at a zoo. Or between a genuinely pleasurable conversation among friends and a staged political debate between opponents. The conversation features people deeply listening to each other and then responding after having been affected by those spoken thoughts. The debate involves the same pattern of one person speaking, and then another, but each is seeking to control the outcome, and this is not resonant.

A resonant experience is something like what I'm calling delight. When I hike on a mountainside and thoughts come to me, and I'm surprised by them. I might end up solving a problem I've been worrying over, or suddenly understand an argument I had with a coworker. That's resonance. It's not being in control, but rather being open to be changed. Rosa notes that many technological advances we depend on to control the world have a dark side. It's nice to have a camera and email and a stock-market report on my phone, but when I do it's harder to relax at home or simply take in a show. Our technological advances open up the world for us by helping us control it, but they also capture us. Rosa talks about the snow day, when plans get canceled and we just sit in wonder.[5] That's delight.

HOME, THEOLOGY, SCRIPTURE

Being at home in your body, your dwelling, and your community happens when you resonate with the world, when your home speaks to you, tells you who-you-are, where-you-are, why-you-are. Good homes are full of delight because they contain elements of beauty, whether it is a picture of a beaming kid on her first day of school, or a treasured antique hope chest. There is, in fact, a kind of miracle that happens when a house becomes a home. We contribute to that by our living, but mostly we undergo it, receive it, experience its beauty. So delight, as well as comfort, lives in a fascinating tension between activity and passivity, between work and grace.

Home and related metaphors are actually very common in the Bible, and in the history of theology, for the God-world relation. The symbol most often used in the Bible to name this relation is, admittedly, "kingdom." Yet as many have pointed out, this presents some problems in the contemporary day. I am more or less morally opposed to monarchies actually governing countries. There is a maleness to "kingdom" that the Greek biblical word *basileia*, which it translates, does not have. But most important is the kind of subjectivity the term evokes. In a kingdom, there is little for us non-kings to do except *obey*.

And so we would be wise to look for and re-discover the many ways that "home" names God's presence on earth.[6] Here are some examples. One of the two oral sources behind the Creation stories in Genesis, the so-called "Priestly" document, maintains literary integrity all the way up to the end of Exodus when the Israelites build the tabernacle. In other words, the creation of the world is not completed until there is a symbolic dwelling place for God.[7] Then there are the texts in John about God "dwelling" with humans, that "the word was made flesh and dwelled among us."[8] And going right to the end of the Bible, the voice from the throne in the heavenly city in Revelation says, "Surely the home of God is among mortals . . . " If ever you'd expect "kingdom" language, it would be from a throne! But "home" or "dwelling place" is what we get instead.

The subjectivity evoked and elicited by "home" is richer than kingdom-language can bring about. I have some privacy in a home, some autonomy. But I also know there are house rules to be followed. House rules are different than a king's laws. They're more likely to be tied to my own well-being, and less about a ruler's whim. The kinds of things we do in homes are different than we do in public, in a government. So focusing on a different symbol can lead to a quite radical re-thinking of religious themes that may have become so familiar they're stale.

The history of theology, as well, contains more home metaphors for doctrinal loci than one might expect. In contrast to the Gnostics, whose key teaching seems to have been that the Good Earth is not our true home, Irenaeus and Athanasius begged to differ. Athanasius compares the incarnation's healing of sin to a king's intervention when a home is robbed.

Now in truth this great work (the incarnation) was peculiarly suited to God's goodness. For if a king, having founded a house or city of dwellings, if it be beset by bandits from the carelessness of its residents, does not simply neglect it, but avenges and reclaims it as his own, having regard not to the carelessness of the inhabitants, but to what beseems himself; much more did God the Word of the all-good Father not neglect the whole of humanity.[9]

Later in the same work Athanasius imagines the ennobling of humanity by the incarnation to the gentrification of a neighborhood when God builds a house and moves in.

> Just as when a great emperor has entered into some large city and dwelt in one of its houses, such city and home is naturally deemed worthy of much honor, and no enemy or bandit any longer descends upon it to overthrow it, but rather it is deemed worthy of all respect because of the emperor dwelling in one house there; so, too, is it with the Monarch of all. For having come into our region, he dwelt in one body amongst His peers.[10]

All kinds of other examples from the history of theology could be marshaled in defense of a claim that is so obvious it need only be mentioned rather than defended. To desire to be at home is so universal a human emotional longing, so factually a human physical need and, when the desire is met, so universal an experience of joy that of course Christians have associated it with the mystery of salvation and understood it to be foundational to the work of God.

ENGAGING SCT

It has become somewhat dangerous in recent decades, however, to claim too much universality of human experience as the previous sentence implies. Scandinavian Creation Theology, however, does in fact try to venture provisional answers about matters of potentially universal significance. That it does so with a *humble boldness* is the first of three reasons I have benefitted from engaging SCT, and which I will enumerate here.

For all kinds of reasons, many of them good and even persuasive ones, the opposite of a claim of universality is usually highlighted. This is termed the "turn to particularity," and it includes critiques of doctrines of sin, salvation, and conceptions of God, among many others. What Niebuhr thought of as the universal sin of pride belies the particular tendency of powerful men to overvalue themselves. What Schleiermacher thought of as the salvation of a sick consciousness belies that he in particular could afford not to think of the body or the bank account when considering liberation. What Aquinas thought of as God's aseity belies a tendency toward an idealized self-sufficiency. Yet sometimes I have worried that highly particularized theologies sell themselves short; one can and should tell the truth from one's own particularity not just to set the record straight about how complex the world is, but also with the hope that you will touch on something that is true *simpliciter*.

SCT proceeds with a humble boldness in regard to regaining a sense of universality in the midst of our pluralistic world, a world filled with contrasting voices and an ever-new search for particularity. Universality is not the same as unanimity, though, for total consensus is quite rare. Neither is the universal the same as "what is everywhere the case." Homes are vastly different across time and space. And homes are somewhat miniscule compared to the vastness of other social constructions like schools, workplaces, and train stations, to say nothing of mountains, forests, fields, oceans, and other items in the inventory of nature. Universality is rather about what can be *recognized* in the life of others. Reading literature is like entering into lives that are not our own but are nonetheless recognizable as particular examples of human longing and desires, that expand our understanding and empathy. Likewise novels, poems, and films invite us into understanding how we ourselves could be placed, had we had we lived in another age or been born completely elsewhere. They profitably cause us to ask ourselves, "How would I make myself at home there, and then?"

Jan-Olav Henriksen, in an excellent introduction to SCT, notes that SCT founding figure K. E. Løgstrup insisted that what he called "sovereign life-utterances" were phenomena across time and space that Christians could note in non-Christians and appreciate. "Perhaps the main contribution of Løgstrup is that he makes it possible to realize that Christianity is a fundamental interpretation of the conditions for human existence and experience."[11] Universality in the humbly bold sense is then not the erasure of difference nor the imposition of a false sameness, in the sense that the racist response in the United States to the mantra "Black Lives Matter" is "All Lives Matter." Instead, it is the *solidarity of recognition*, and the hope that can come from quite different people with quite different experiences nonetheless making common cause with each other in pursuit of common goods.

A second facet of SCT I have found important is its placement as a Reformation-based resource for a *post-Christian, yet also post-secular, era.* Centuries ago Martin Luther emphasized the central role of the home, or the household by arguing that it is not enough to set up a distinction between the role of secular authorities and the role of the church. Instead what is needed is reflection on the middle space occupied by home life (*economia*) between the secular political order (*politia*) and the gospel message of the church (*ecclesia*). For Luther, secular authorities only came into the world after the fall, but both family life and the conversation with God started in Paradise, and continued up to this day as life-giving centers of human existence.[12] The household is particularly important because the home is the civic institution in which children are reared to understand the values of community life, both its demands (law) and its promises (gospel). This same approach shaped N. F. S. Grundtvig's (1783–1872) work as a hymn writer, pastor, member of parliament and general Great Dane, regarded as the father of modern Denmark.

In a secular age, this is even more important as life in the home is not only lived by Christians and other religiously inclined people, but by all people, regardless of faith. Due to this sensitivity to the common good, some have called the Lutheran emphasis on shared everyday life, in and around the home, an example of a "third-zone" Lutheranism, which is shared by believers and unbelievers. The rules for the household, including mutual help, can neither be relegated nor reduced to the task of the civil government, nor to the particular role of the church.[13] The sense for the third zone as a shared realm of human life has been particularly emphasized in the Scandinavian welfare societies, where no distinction is made between the needs of active participants in the state-aligned Lutheran churches, on the one hand, and those of non-religious or even anti-religious residents, on the other.

A significant question becomes, then, how to explain the core concerns of SCT for audiences not particularly interested in Scandinavia. I once challenged Niels Henrik Gregersen to re-name the movement to indicate its applicability in other contexts. After considering it for some time, he proposed that "It could be called the expansive view of creation." His thinking was that the world of creation—and the divine creativity manifested in the world—is not simply a background foil for a merely human redemption that comes from the church. Humans are not redeemed *from* the world but *with* the world. If it were otherwise, there would be no redemption of individual lives and shared identities. However, the expansive view of creation is not expansionist either, since SCT does not want to reduce Christian faith to a first article-Christianity. Løgstrup, Wingren, and Prenter were all aware that the problem of death cannot be solved within an immanent framework, just as death cannot be reduced to human evil-doing. Suffering and death long existed before humanity, which was not acknowledged in the tradition from Augustine to Luther. As Løgstrup put it: "Darwin lies between Luther and us."[14]

SCT is thus a theological movement originating in Scandinavia after World War II which attends to the many facets and implications of the doctrine of creation. It is based partly on Martin Luther's theology of creation and vocation,[15] partly on the affirmative anthropology of N. F. S. Grundtvig with his principle "Human first, then a Christian," and partly through an emphasis on reflecting on ordinary life situations in the philosophical vein of Løgstrup and the theological vein of Wingren. There is otherwise nothing particularly Scandinavian about it, in the sense that its interests would only be salient there, or that it needs such soil to flourish and illuminate.

A third element of SCT I have found refreshing is its particular take on *exocentricity*. For example, Wingren's theological anthropology begins by reflecting on the ambiguously profound experience of being de-centered. This de-centering of a provisionally centered self comes in many forms by many means. There are gifts of nourishment and love that come from without. There are demands that do not originate in the thinking subject's conscious reflection on duty.

All that is truly important in one's life originated outside of oneself. Wingren writes, To live means to receive life from outside oneself. As soon as we are cut off from these external sources, life is extinguished. The resurrection life is the receiving of life from an external source, from which even now in faith man (sic) draws his sustenance. But the same thing holds true even now of the bodily life, and not just that of believers, but of all bodily life.[16]

Other theologians have emphasized exocentricity as a feature of theological anthropology, such as Wolfhart Pannenberg, David Kelsey, and Catherine Keller.[17] Yet I find myself drawn to Wingren's down-to-earth reflections on the *extra nos* character of selfhood that is not simply the constitution of a human subject by the *verbum externum* (although I am by no means opposed to such formulations).[18] It is rather the interconnectedness of humans and the rest of the world, the knowledge in one's gut that we are not our own masters, self-positing and self-controlled. Because of every human being's actual, biological gut, there are far more cells in the human body that are bacterial rather than human. Even the centers of ourselves have been selved from without.

A decentered view of the human self is prominent also in Løgstrup's anthropological construal, but here the terms of analysis are a level of abstraction removed from the earthy Wingren's understanding of food, warmth, and affection coming from outside. For Løgstrup, the self receives things like communication and stimuli to our sensation. These experiences then lead to a renewed sense of a need for a re-centering. The promise of the theme of home in testing and furthering SCT is that living in homes with human skin, and living with and by means of an openness for the more-than-human world through sensation and resonance experiences, together point to provisional senses of what it means to be *redeemed*.

THE PRESENT VOLUME

We have arranged this volume into three parts. Part I, Home and Creation: Place, Journey, and Arrival, examines ways that root metaphors for home help us understand our relationship to God. Svein Aage Christoffersen's essay, for example, identifies pilgrimage and homecoming as important metaphors for the Christian life, because alongside the metaphor of life as "dwelling," pilgrimage and homecoming imply and develop an eschatological horizon in which our true home is still, in some sense, the heavenly Jerusalem. In conversation with Pope Francis's encyclical *Laudato Si*, Christoffersen shows that creation theology and its eschatological formulations are a help for the present climate crisis, not an impediment to taking seriously the problems of here and now. Likewise, Bengt Kristensson Uggla's essay makes use of the insight that all homes have cracks, and indeed, that's how the light gets in. By developing an "alienated phenomenology," Uggla shows how stages of belonging, then rupture, then return bring human beings to understand that they are home now and will be home with God.

Ryan McAnnally-Linz and Mary Emily Briehl Duba's contributions provide fascinating counterpoints on the specificity and generality of theological reflections of home. Duba's essay uses "place" theories, which draw on geography and ethnography, among others, to describe the irreducibly particular ways in which concrete contexts like watersheds, streets, fields, and climates force us to find our homes. Yet theologies of place have some shortcomings that SCT, she finds, helps to overcome. McAnnally-Linz's essay, on the other hand, looks at histories in the neo-Platonic tradition (Pseudo-Dionysius and Marguerite Porete) that identify spiritual ascent and return to God as being the hallmark of every believer's trajectory, no matter where or when they found their earthly homes.

Part II is titled "Homes, Bodies, and Society." Trygve Wyller's and Allen Jorgenson's essays are about the body's relation to home. Jorgenson recounts the pain experienced by those whose bodies are different because of disabilities. Broken bodies upset the desire for certainty, and this interruption can be salutary. Taken from the point of view of the body's sensing skin, bodies are home, as well as horizon; they are launching pad as well as landing place—a site we leave and to which we return. In a similar vein, Trygve Wyller considers a home as a "second skin." It is porous yet protective, a site for keeping out some things and yet allowing others in. In this way, there is a kind of universal meaning of home, and reflecting the "humble boldness" described above, Wyller carefully but passionately insists that theology should strive to make sense of universal human experiences.

Elisabeth Gerle's essay makes similar points, in that "home" is always both actual and ideal, imagined and real. Experiences of not being at home are disruptive or worse, but they only make sense on a horizon of a still-deeper orientation toward being safe and cared for. Homes need to have windows to let others in, despite the risks that can come when one encounters another. Therefore trust is needed, as well as presumed. Sasja Emilie Mathiasen Stopa's essay examines the legacy of trust developed by K. E. Løgstrup from the Reformation theology of Martin Luther. Stopa argues that life on earth is exilic, but that an exile can still be at home. Attention to a transcendent God can give the Christian access to an understanding of a true world beyond the confusing, sinful, and threatening phenomenal world of present existence. Knowing that all are in the same lot can help us to care for each other in relationships of trust and nurture. And Else Marie Wiberg Pedersen's chapter considers the terrible ruptures of trust and nurture that women and girls disproportionately bear. She suggests practices for "re-homing" figures in scripture, Christian history and contemporary society who have been pulled from their homes and turned into victims of violence and loss. SCT offers, she suggests, especially strong resources to help re-home the homeless, lost and driven away.

Part III is titled "Cosmos as Home." In helpful counterpoint to the preceding chapters that identify particular experiences of particular homes, the essays in part III expand and analogize ways that all of human existence unfolds and continues on a cosmic horizon, as well. Niels Henrik Gregersen builds on his earlier corpus of writings on Deep Incarnation (the idea that the Logos is not enfleshed only in the skin-deep incarnation in Jesus of Nazareth, but in all flesh) to connect Deep Inhabitation with ecology. Deep Inhabitation refers to the ways humans make homes in and are homed by the natural world. He distinguishes three kinds of ecology: one that sees the natural world as powerful, inspiring, and threatening, one that sees it as something to be tamed and controlled, and one within which we are enmeshed and embedded and from which we cannot escape.

Ted Peters' essay is not concerned with escaping the natural world, but rather having our world be shocked by the entry of new elements to it. Can our planet be home to non-native life forms? A test case for our home-making on planet earth is whether we can conceive of this blue marble being home also for planetary travelers in need of our welcome.

Threats are inevitable, and any theology worth its salt ought to be honest about the destructive forces that harm humans and the systems we depend on for our thriving. Jakob Wolf's hard-nosed chapter considers the many forces that press in on the coziness of humans in their well-homed life (the relevant Danish word here has become an American phenomenon as well: *hygge*). If theology is to be a reliable help for real people, it must give an account of destruction and annihilation, not just of pleasant creativity and the finer things in life.

Finally, Lois Malcolm attends to the "dyschronicity" of contemporary life. This names not only the accelerations of technology and associated change that can be so disorienting and alienating, but also the atomization and isolation that come from a lack of embeddedness in lasting, stable structures, narratives, and communities. She thinks with and then past Wingren, whose own theological proposal offered parallel diagnoses and proposed remedies for the modern, as opposed to postmodern, theological project and context.

Taken together, the essays in this book invite new readers to a promising tradition (SCT) not to persuade them of its promise, but to publicly test that tradition's ability to speak past its original audiences to new issues, problems, and thinkers. What "method" to use in theology is a perennially necessary question, but rarely one that is illuminated by hypothetical discussions of "how to do theology." The proof, instead, is in the pudding. Instead of testing a theory by examining it as a theory, see what answers it gives to an interesting question, such as "what is it to have a home?" We would do well to ask: what approach to theology actually yields interesting, persuasive, faithful, edifying, and just arguments? What practices underwritten by such a theology produce interesting, persuasive, faithful, edifying, and just people? I have become provisionally convinced that in my own context and according to my understandings of the challenges the church, academy, and public face today, SCT needs to be my main conversation partner. Perhaps you, reader, will come to the same conclusion.

NOTES

1. Law and Gospel, not surprisingly, is one of the main ways that SCT founding figure Gustaf Wingren formulated theology. His two-volume systematic work divides them like this: Creation and Law; and Gospel and Church. One should not make too much of this presentation, though, as he also referred to his theological project as "Creation and Gospel."

2. The pre-eminent historian of architecture Witold Rybczynski wrote a book on the history of domestic living, making the point that the through-line for what counted as a good home was what comforted the one who lived there, but then admitted that he actually could not define what "comfort" really meant. Witold Rybczynski, *Home: A Short History of an Idea* (New York: Penguin, 1987), 217–31.

3. William C. Placher, *Callings: Twenty Centuries of Christian Wisdom on Vocation* (Grand Rapids, MI: Eerdmans, 2005). For a more SCT-centered approach, see Gustaf Wingren, *Luther on Vocation*, trans. Carl C. Rasmussen (Philadelphia: Muhlenberg, 1957).

4. Hartmut Rosa, *Resonanz: Eine Soziologie der Weltbeziehung* (Berlin: Suhrkamp, 2016), 298.

5. Hartmut Rosa, *The Uncontrollability of the World*, trans. James Wagner (Cambridge, UK: Polity, 2020), pp. 1–4.

6. In fact the very best place to go to find a harvest of these kinds of reflections is Miroslav Volf and Ryan McAnnally-Linz, *The Home of God: A Brief Story of Everything* (Grand Rapids, MI: Brazos, 2022).

7. See, for example, Jon D. Levenson, *Creation and the Persistence of Evil* (Princeton, NJ: Princeton University Press, 1988), 85–86.

8. Ben Quash emphasizes the notion of *meno,* which can mean "I remain," "I wait," or "I dwell" as "abiding" in his *Abiding: The Archbishop of Canterbury's Lent Book*

for 2013 (London: Bloomsbury, 2012). This unfortunately has the effect of diminishing the everyday experiences of being at home that the gospel of John intends to highlight as holy. An exception occurs on p. 154.

9. *On the Incarnation of the Word*, I.9.

10. *On the Incarnation of the Word*, II.9.

11. Jan-Olav Henriksen, "Systematic Theology in the Nordic Countries after 1945," in *St. Andrews Encyclopedia of Theology* (2023), 10. https://www.saet.ac.uk/Christianity/SystematicTheologyintheNordicCountriesafter1945

This understanding of universality as solidarity of recognition is the focal point of another project on Scandinavian Creation Theology, to be published in the forthcoming book, *Redeeming the Universal: Scandinavian Creation Theology on Politics and Ecology*, edited by Trygve Wyller, Johanna Gustafsson Lundberg, and Niels Henrik Gregersen.

12. See, for example, Michael P. DeJonge, "Luther, Bonhoeffer and Political Theologies," in Derek R. Nelson and Paul R. Hinlicky, eds, *Oxford Encyclopedia of Martin Luther* (New York: Oxford University Press, 2017), 1:201–3.

13. See, for example, Niels Henrik Gregersen, "From *oeconomia* to Nordic Welfare Societies: The Idea of a Third-Zone Lutheranism" in *Theology Today* 76:3 (2019), 1-9.

14. K. E. Løgstrup, *Metaphysics: Volume 1*, trans. Russell L. Dees (Milwaukee, WI: Marquette University Press, 1995), 336.

15. See, for instance, Oswald Bayer, *Freedom in Response*, trans. Jeffrey Cayzer (New York: Oxford University Press, 2007), especially chapter 7, "Nature and Institution: Luther's Doctrine of the Three Estates," 90–118.

16. Gustaf Wingren, *Creation and Law* (Philadelphia: Muhlenberg, 1961), 18–19.

17. Wolfhart Pannenberg, *Anthropology in Theological Perspective*, trans. Matthew J. O'Connell (Louisville, KY: Westminster John Knox, 1985); David H. Kelsey, *Eccentric Existence* (Louisville, KY: Westminster John Knox, 2009); Catherine Keller, *From a Broken Web: Separation, Sexism, and Self* (Boston: Beacon, 1988).

18. For a fascinating comparison of Wingren and another philosopher of the self, see Bengt Kristensson Uggla, "What Makes Us Human? The Lutheran Anthropological Link Between Wingren and Ricoeur," in *Open Theology* 4 (2018), 308-15.

PART I

Home and Creation

Place, Journey, and Arrival

Chapter 1

Home and Creation Dynamics

This World Is Not an Alien Place, It Is Where We Belong

Bengt Kristensson Uggla

In this chapter I will outline an "alienated" phenomenology[1] of what it means to have a *home* as a modern conceptualization of the Christian doctrine of creation. My aim is to explore what kind of theological resources the specific approach to Christian faith that we have come to name Scandinavian Creation Theology (SCT) can provide for our understanding of what it means to have a home.[2]

THE "HOME" OF SCANDINAVIAN CREATION THEOLOGY

SCT emerged as a critique against the "anti-liberal turn" in Protestant theology in the aftermath of the breakdown of the grand old paradigm of Liberal theology. In a situation when the methodology used for comprehensive presentations of Christian theology, by leading "post liberal" theologians like Karl Barth (1886–1968) and Anders Nygren (1890–1978), was primarily focused on the church and on isolating *the distinctively Christian*; thus, neglecting and discrediting the doctrine of creation. Against the devastating consequences of this way to achieve theological clarity, leading SCT theologians like Gustaf Wingren (1910–2000) declared a contrasting program for identity formation: "to return the Christian faith to those human situations where it belongs is perhaps the most important task for contemporary theology."[3] As an alternative to the "curious anti-liberal mania"[4] of contemporary theologians, picturing the world as a strange, alien, and hostile place, a loose constellation of young Scandinavian theologians carried by creation faith claimed that the gospel should never be considered as a message spoken into an empty God-forsaken world and comprehended if it is considered as God's first contact with human life. Furthermore, they argued, we can neither understand the theological significance of Christ, salvation nor church, if we recognize them in radical opposition to the world. The aim of Christian faith is *not* to *cut off* God's work in human life, but to *restore* creation and make us human again—*recapitulation* (Ireneaus). Thus, in contrast to both the predominant postliberal theology, and existential theology inspired by an Heideggerian understanding of the human existence as *thrownness* [*Geworfenheit*], the theologians we associate with SCT claimed that an affirmation of God's omnipresence in all life, and a theological articulation of the human condition we all share, is a prerequisite also for embracing the unique element of the Christian faith—and furthermore that a creation perspective that approaches the world we inhabit as our home is a necessary and integral part of any articulation of a trinitarian doctrine.

THE SCANDINAVIAN CONTEXT—AND BEYOND

Due to their origin, and as the name indicates, the "founding figures" of SCT, K. E. Løgstrup (1905–1981), Regin Prenter (1907–1990), and Gustaf Wingren, were all embedded in a particular Scandinavian context of grand national Lutheran churches and emerging strong democratic welfare states in the making. A common inspiration for SCT's appreciation of a lifeform associated with the "homely" atmosphere of creation was N. F. S. Grundtvig (1783–1872). His famous dictum "Human comes first, Christian comes next"[5] could almost be comprehended as "Home comes first, Church comes next," because Grundtvig provided, not only access to sources from the early church fathers (in particular Irenaeus), but also a modern interpretation of the Lutheran heritage and connections to nation building ambitions within a universal framework.

Considering this embeddedness in the Scandinavian soil, it would notwithstanding be a mistake to limit the relevance of SCT to Lutheran majority cultures of the nineteenth and twentieth centuries. Wingren often emphasized the wider significance of the historical fact the first profound Christian theology of creation was developed by Irenaeus, a theologian who was leading a tiny little congregation in an extreme minority situation where Christians were being hunted and killed. Wingren used these circumstances as an argument that the doctrine of creation, conceived as an affirmation of God's universal presence in all creatures, has a relevance that transcends the original "homelands" of

SCT.[6] I have thus defined the most extensive and consistent elaboration of SCT, presented by Gustaf Wingren, as a *post-Constantinian Lutheran theology educated by the pre-Constantinian theology of Irenaeus,*[7] which makes SCT an appropriate theology of greatest importance in a post-Constantinian era when Christians have to co-exist and cooperate with people of other faiths (or without faith) in a post-Christian society.

AT HOME IN SWEDEN

For more than quarter of a century I have lived with my family in Vasastan, downtown Stockholm, in the same area as were one of the most admired Swedish authors during the twentieth century, Astrid Lindgren (1907–2002), lived. When our children were young, we sometimes met the author at the playground in the park outside her home. The narratives in Lindgren's many novels for children circulate around homes of different kind.

The challenges associated with housing was on the top of the political agenda in Sweden during the twentieth century, and the narrative about the homeowners movement and the "millennium program" of massive activities of construction have affected the national heritage to such an extent that *being Swedish* and *being at home* have almost become equivalents. If the legendary Swedish Prime Minister Per Albin Hansson became an emblematic figure for the project of building a "people's home" with housing for ordinary people as political top priority for decades, these houses were later "furnished" by Ingvar Kamprad and IKEA—and I dare to say that Astrid Lindgren provided some of the most influential narrative configurations that tell us what it means to have a home in Sweden.

Yet, it is amazing to note that, with very few exceptions, it is not the "perfect" home that dominates the picture, rather the opposite seems to be the case, because the many homes where her intrigues are taking place seem all through to be dysfunctional, "broken" and "wounded" homes. Also, in the author's private life, the home seemed to have been an ambiguous reality, associated with such painful experiences of her own, as when she as a young unmarried girl got pregnant, was forced to move and give birth to a son, whom she had to send away. Later in life, she experienced a divorce. Thus, in Lindgren's world, *there seems to be a crack in every home—but that's also where the light comes in* (to coin a phrase from Leonard Cohen). Literary masterpieces were born out of tragedies and painful experiences in her own life. Only far out in the margin of these narratives we guess the contours of a "perfect" home—but mostly as an extraordinary boring place to be. This is also why Tommy and Annika, who live in a traditional family home next door to Pippi in Lindgren's first book, *Pippi Longstocking* [Pippi Långstrump] from 1945, prefer to spend as much time as possible in Pippi's "magic" home, where she as a child lives alone with her monkey and a horse, far away from her absent parents (her mother is dead, and her father reigns an island in the South Pacific). Furthermore, the main character in *Mio's Kingdom* [Mio, min Mio] from 1954, the young boy Karl Anders Nilsson, "Andy" [Bo Vilhelm Olsson, "Bosse"], is also part of a broken home, adopted by an elderly couple who harass and obviously dislike him. Yet, the magic light shines through the crack into the darkness and the narrative opens for an imaginary home-coming when he suddenly through a golden apple is being transferred to another world where it is being disclosed that he is the son of a mighty king and gets drawn into a fight against Kato, the evil knight. The collapse of the home in *Ronia the Robber's Daughter* [Ronja Rövardotter, 1981], culminates when Ronia's father cries out in anger: "I have no child!" Thus, instead of a "perfect" home, in Lindgren's world the home is seriously "wounded," and homecoming seems only possible through narrative imaginations where "the light comes in" through "cracks" and ordinary people capable of performing deeds of love in their daily life.

HERMENEUTIC MEDIATION: HOUSE TURNED INTO HOME

The readers imaginary homecoming in "the world in front of the text" of Astrid Lindgren's many novels introduces us to the home as an elusive and enigmatic reality requiring hermeneutic sensibility. Because home is more than a physical place, more than a house. Strictly speaking, we can neither "buy," "create," nor "have" a home—and sometimes, we suddenly no longer feel at home in our own appartement. Only houses are for sale—not homes. For the miracle to take place that may *turn a house into a home*, the physical reality of the house needs to be *refigured* by configurations and narratives that can inscribe the lived phenomenological experience of the space in the physical reality of a geometric space. This "inhabited space" (to use the words of Paul Ricoeur) is constituted by "mixed categories" and linked to a parallel kind of temporality where the true human, "historical" time requires that the phenomenological experience of lived time is being inscribed in cosmological time. This means that home must be comprehended as a fragile "third" category, a kind of space and time constituted by unstable discourses and "broken" ontologies only possible to articulate in terms of an "alienated" phenomenology. According to this hermeneutic experience of the world, home appears as an *always already* mediated reality, a dynamic, complex, and fragile "heterogenous synthesis" that we at the same time *receive* and *maintain, discover* as a given and *invent* through acts of interpretation.[8] This sensible hermeneutic membrane in the interface between ourselves and the world comes close to what Hartmut Rosa refers to when he uses the metaphor *resonance.*[9]

STAGES IN AN ALIENATED PHENOMENOLOGY OF HOME

I will now in five steps outline the fundamental structures of an "alienated" phenomenology from the perspectives of creation dynamics, in order to answer the question how we can understand the "resonance" of what it means to have a home, according to SCT.

Home as Creation and Gift

In contrast to the dominant postliberal approaches, and the "pure" Christian love of Nygren's exceptionalism, SCT does not picture the world as a cold and hostile place—instead the world is recognized as our home. This means that Christian faith does not promote the Church, the "Christian home" or the "heavenly home" as privileged places where we belong—in separation from the world we share with all living creatures. If SCT is an "interpretation of the Christian faith that integrates the human element" and starts from "the integrating function of the Christian faith in human life as a whole," it might be conceptualized as an original affirmation of *home*, a place and state in the world where we belong. Home, conceived as a state to *receive* and a place to *be received*, means a recognition of this world as a the primarily place where we belong and associated with a profound solidarity with all living creatures—in sharp contrast to *the flight from creation,* which SCT criticized as "the most profound theological tragedy of our time."[10]

The focus on creation in SCT invites misunderstandings, thus it seems necessary to stress that the doctrine of creation is neither connected to information about an historical origin nor a theology of orders (*Ordnungstheologie*) as an affirmation of *status quo* and hierarchical orders within the home. Instead, for SCT creation means *change*, transformation and becoming. Creation is primarily a *gift* and the doctrinal statement that God creates is equivalent with *the profound experience that we are alive.* To quote Wingren: "To live means to receive life from outside oneself. As soon as we are cut off from these external sources, life is extinguished."[11] Therefore, it is no surprise that the experience of home is characterized by so many vegetative activities, as a place where we can fall asleep and rest, where we eat and drink. To have a home means, from this point of view, to belong to a place where God creates—and where human beings simultaneously are being created. According to this dialectical approach, reception does not mean that *divine activity* presumes *human passivity*, as sometimes has been mentioned as a critical remark. This is reinforced by the fact that there can be no competition neither between human and divine nor between activity and passivity, because the fact that God creates and the occurrence of actions of capable human beings are considered *exactly the same reality only perceived from two different angles*.[12] The necessity of receiving life from a source that is located outside ourselves teaches us instead that the world is not to be considered as "mute" but full of "resonant" relationships—"a place where things speak to us"[13]— and that through the refiguration of a hermeneutic experience, the world as creation may be considered our home.

This leads us to the aporetic experience of what it means to "have" a home. Because in the strict sense of the word, we can never "have" a home—but only act in ways that makes it possible for us to *receive* and *be received* at home. Home is a paradigmatic place and state where someone is being *welcomed*. This means, however, that "creating" a home is an action that can never be considered solely our own work, it is always already anticipated by the experience of gift. The hermeneutic experience that can transform a house into a home is a particular kind of activity which always implies a great amount of passivity: It is a paradoxical act where production and reception meet and intersect. To be received at home presumes the capacity to act in such a way that a voice also can be heard in opposite direction— addressing ourselves. In order to understand the creation dynamics of the experience of being at home, we might return to Rosa and his elaborations on the meaning of the concept *resonance*: "Resonance is not an echo, but a responsive relationship, requiring that both sides speak with their own voice."[14] Consequently, the hermeneutic appropriation that makes it possible to imagine a house as a home—and thus experience the miracle of a dead space come alive and *approaching* and *welcoming us*—requires a capable human being that is a playful figure: the player is also *being played* when entering into the home.[15] Or, speaking the language of K.E. Løgstrup, we might say: *home is not our own making, but a given*.[16]

And Yet, There's a Crack in Every Home

The experience of a profound gift is a fundamental element in any phenomenology of what it means to have a home. Once this has been sat, we need to remind ourselves that in real life home is at the same time an extremely dangerous place to be. Home is where frequent accidents occur and furthermore a place of violence, mostly with women and children as victims, a crime scene where even many murders are committed. These "dark" aspects of the home were reinforced in a significant way during the pandemic, when many experienced how their homes suddenly were transformed into prisons.

Even though we tend to imagine the place where we come from in terms of an original harmony and security within an air of nostalgia, as adults we gradually identify more and more cracks in the walls of the family home of our childhood. In accordance with the many broken homes configured in Astrid Lindgren's novels, there seems to be a crack in every home. Most of us have to face this painful experience when our idolized memories of our original family homes are being demystified and demythologized. Ernst Bloch has captured this reality in his majestic work, *The Principle of Hope* (1959), where he teaches us that home is *always already lost*—it is "a place and a state in which no one has yet been."[17] Our original "perfect" home, the place we often are longing to return to, thus seems to be an always already broken reality. Yet, these experiences of negativity do not necessarily eliminate the original gift, ending up in nihilism. If we consider these experiences of negativity within a broader framework of creation dynamics, they may instead testify about, point toward, and even presuppose, a more profound original affirmation of life as a creation gift. The core of the theological hermeneutics elaborated by Wingren is a "grain-of-wheat-eschatology" where these experiences of negativity are interpreted in terms of a movement *through death to life*. So yes, *there's a crack in every home . . . and that's where the light comes in!*

Home as Vocation and Ethical Demand

Home as research topic came to the fore in 1942, when Wingren defended his PhD dissertation on the concept of vocation, *Vocatio* (*Beruf*, calling) in Luther.[18] In his interpretation of Luther, he deviated from the main research tradition by claiming that vocation should not primarily be associated with church ministry or priesthood within an ecclesiological context. Vocation should rather be connected to "impiety" and the many "callings" in the daily irreligious life in the world, where home may be identified as one of the important places for the practice of vocations. And this understanding of vocation was also seen as the guiding principle for Martin Luther himself, when he walked out of the monastery into—a home.

This new theological contextualization of vocation, within the daily life of ordinary people, could also be considered an integral part of the aim of Wingren's early research program where he focused on developing a theological understanding of the law, recognized as a calling that originates from the actual needs of other people. This understanding of the law is totally dissociated from eternal rules written in books—instead the law is constituted by the specific and yet ever-changing demands that we approach in concrete interpersonal relationships in daily life. This understanding of the law, and ethics in general, as something that originates from contextual ethical demands, has extensively been explicated by Løgstrup.[19]

The driving force behind Wingren's early theological project was his investigations on how the law functions as an ethical demand within all kinds of human actions as a necessary prerequisite to sustain the daily life in the world. And as such, this flexible creation dynamics, regulated by the changing ethical demand of the other, is also necessary for the sustainability of the home. In the late 1950s, at the time when he was about to outline his first dogmatics, Wingren started to elaborate more systematically on the dialectical relation between the free *gift* of creation and the ethical *demand* of the law. This creation dynamics, which relates creation and law, makes it also possible to develop an understanding of home as a place constituted by this dialectical relationship.[20] Through the law, God forces deeds of love, in situations when love does not flow spontaneously from the gift of creation. In his dogmatics, Wingren explicates how creation and law are interrelated and interdependent in very concrete ways: "Only through our work, the harvest will become bread, the wool clothes."[21] These dialectic relationships of *creation* and *law*, *gift* and *demand*, within a wider *creation dynamic,* makes home a paradigmatic place for Lutheran theologians to speak about how the law is materialized in the calling and the vocation of responsible human beings.

Home as a Place of Surplus, Grace, and Hospitality

Before modernity and before Romanticism, home was primarily identified with the smallest unit of economy, the household, *oikos, oikonomia*—and also today economic concerns invades our understanding of both the house and the home. Due to these historical connections to household and the general associations with economics, it is tempting to talk about the meaning of home in terms of private ownership, a presumably safe place of intimacy closed from the outer world, according to the saying "my home is my castle." The invasion of economic concerns may also strengthen the tendency to consider home as something that we "have" in the strict sense of the word, and furthermore to manage it as a reality regulated by pure reciprocal relationships in terms of a zero-sum-game. But a "closed" and "reciprocal" home can never be sustainable because home is not only a phenomenon based on the creation dynamics of creation and law, it is also a place that presupposes a surplus of life, grace, and forgiveness. Thus, a real home cannot survive if it completely closes the door on itself. The "resonance of home" makes it a self-transcending phenomenon, as a place potentially open to extensions in a way that makes hospitality a virtue for every home.

A home welcomes at least one person, who may be received at home as a place where s/he belong. But the existence in first personal pronoun implicates the possibility of a second and third personal pronoun, manifested by the fact that the reflexive pronoun "self" can be applicated to all personal pronouns: we are relational beings already in first person.[22] In the same way as we are dependent on generational change to exist as human being, home is built on a transcending logic where already a one-person-home presupposes the potential presence of other people: such as a partner, parents, siblings, children, neighbors, friends and according to the virtue of hospitality also the stranger (because we are also strangers to ourselves). What Wingren promptly states in an article on the meaning of work, in 1949, addressing a specific Christian audience, is something that might be as relevant for a home: "If we flee from our neighbor to God, we do not come to God. But to ourselves, to our own selves."[23]

Home as an Eschatological Reality: Hope and Promise

Our understanding of what it means to have a home is loaded with memories. Yet Bloch reminds us that home is "something which shines into the childhood of all and which no one has yet been"[24]—home seems to be where we are all headed, but where none of us have ever been. This makes home appear as an eschatological category in accordance with "the not-yet-consciousness" that Bloch is focusing on. We often underestimate how much SCT is marinated by the eschatological tension between Already and Not Yet, which makes home something that can never be complete, absolute, or perfect. Wingren's "grain-of-wheat-eschatology" and Irenaeus understanding of salvation as *recapitulatio* (becoming human again) indicate that creation faith is primarily identified with hope and courage. According to this way of thinking, home is to be considered as an eschatological reality directed toward the future and based on the power of *promise*, which seems to be the only final guarantee for sustainability when it comes to partnerships as well as homes. In the same way as Moses, who had never been at home but embarked on a journey home and was yet only able to see his home at a distance just before he died; home seems to be a "limit concept" (Kant), a "guiding image" (Bloch) and something we can only cope with in terms of hope.

NOTES

1. This kind of "alienated" phenomenology is influenced by the "broken ontology" of Paul Ricoeur's critical hermeneutics, a dialectic way of thinking which he also named "post-Husserlian Kantianism" and defined in the following way: "Husserl *did*

phenomenology, Kant *limited* it and *founded* it." Paul Ricoeur, *Husserl: An Analysis of His Phenomenology* (Evanston, IL: Northwestern University Press, 1967), 201.

2. Niels Henrik Gregersen, Bengt Kristensson Uggla, and Trygve Wyller (eds). *Reformation Theology for a Post-Secular Age: Løgstrup, Prenter, Wingren, and the Future of Scandinavian Creation Theology* (Göttingen: Vandenhoeck & Ruprecht 2017) conceived Scandinavian Creation Theology as a *constellation* of protagonists where three "founding figures" are highlighted: K. E. Løgstrup, Regin Prenter, and Gustaf Wingren—all strongly dependent on the creative mediation of Lutheran theology elaborated by N. F. S. Grundtvig (1783–1872).

3. Gustaf Wingren, *Creation and Gospel: The New Situation in European Theology* (Eugene, OR: Wipf & Stock 1979/2004), 80.

4. Gustaf Wingren, *Creation and Law* (Eugene, OR: Wipf & Stock 1958/2003), 12. Cf. Bengt Kristensson Uggla, "Gustaf Wingren as Anti-Anti-Liberal Theologian: The Contribution of Scandinavian Creation Theology to a Liberal Theology for Today." In *Liberale Theologie heute/Liberal Theology Today*. Hgr: Lauster, Schmiedel, Schüz (Tübingen: Mohr Siebeck 2019), 37–48.

5. N. F. S. Grundtvig. "Human comes first, and Christian next!" (1837). In *Living Well-Springs: The Hymns, Songs, and Poems of N.F.S. Grundtvig* (Aarhus: Aarhus University Press, 2015), 249.

6. Gustaf Wingren, *Man and the Incarnation: A Study in the Biblical Theology of Irenaeus* (Eugene, OR: Wipf and Stock 1947/1959/2004); *Människa och kristen: En bok om Irenaeus* (Skellefteå: Artos, 1983/2019).

7. Bengt Kristensson Uggla. *Becoming Human Again: The Theological Life of Gustaf Wingren* (Eugene, OR: Cascade 2010/2016), 152, 291, 343–45.

8. Ricoeur elaborated on temporality in his three-volume work, *Time and Narrative* (Chicago: University of Chicago Press, 1983/1984, 1984/1985, 1985/1988) and later he extended his discussion including also spatiality in this dialectical conception in *Memory, History, Forgetting* (Chicago: University of Chicago Press, 2000/2004). Cf: "To the dialectic of lived space, geometrical space, and inhabited space corresponds a similar dialectic of lived time, cosmic time, and historical time" (Ricoeur, *Memory, History, Forgetting*, p. 153).

9. Hartmut Rosa, *Resonance: A Sociology of Our Relationship to the world* (Cambridge, UK: Polity Press 2016/2019).

10. Gustaf Wingren, *The Flight from Creation* (Minneapolis, MN: Augsburg, 1971), 21, 15.

11. Wingren, *Creation and Law*, 179. Wingren stresses that the relationship to God is not restricted to religious experience and language, but given *in* and *with* life itself: "When the Bible speaks about God, it does not speak about a reality which man encounters in a specifically religious act and of which he has some knowledge [. . .] God is creator, and his relation to man is given in the simple fact that man lives" (p. 179).

12. Wingren. *Creation and Law*, 7, 33.

13. Rosa, *Resonance*, 359.

14. Rosa, *Resonance*, 174.

15. Paul Ricoeur, "Appropriation" in *Reflection & Imagination: A Ricoeur Reader.* Edited by Mario J.Valdés (New York: Harvester Wheatsheaf, 1991), 86–98.

16. K. E. Løgstrup. *The Ethical Demand* (Notre Dame, IN: Notre Dame University Press 1997), 18.

17. Ernst Bloch, The Principle of Hope, Volume 3 (Cambridge, MA: MIT Press 1957/1986), 1376.

18. Gustaf Wingren, *Luther on Vocation* (Eugene, OR: Wipf and Stock 1942/1957/2004).

19. Løgstrup. *The Ethical Demand.*

20. Gustaf Wingren's first dogmatics was released in two separate volumes, *Creation and Law* (1958/1961/2004) and *Gospel and Church* (Eugene, OR: Wipf & Stock 1960/1964/2003). His second dogmatics was published in *Credo: The Christian View of Faith and Life* (Eugene, OR: Wipf and Stock 1974/1981/2004).

21. Wingren, *Creation and Law*, 9.

22. Paul Ricoeur, *Oneself as Another* (Chicago: University of Chicago Press, 1990/1992), 16–17.

23. Gustaf Wingren, "Arbetets mening," in *Svensk Teologisk Kvartalskrift* (1949), 278.

24. Bloch, The Principle of Hope, Volume 3, 1376.

Chapter 2

Living on Borrowed Ground

*Inhabitation as Lived
Creation Theology*

Mary Emily Briehl Duba

Wanting to give our daughter a home, we baptized her in the Bee Branch Creek. We are transplants to the Midwestern United States, which means our roots here are shallow and tentative at best, able to keep us upright but not much else. We, like many Americans today, "have careers, not places."[1] Not only are we shallow-rooted newcomers, but the place where we now find ourselves is known as "flyover country," a pejorative dismissal of any *here* here, any meaningful reason to come to this "great, green desert" of corn and soybeans.[2] In biblical terms, this region is regarded by many as *chora*, an expanse of open country between places. In an act of defiance against our sense of placelessness, we decided to baptize our daughter in the waters of our local watershed. We meant to graft her life to Christ through the promises of baptism and also to graft her story to the story of this place. We prevailed upon our pastor, planned the liturgy, and invited the congregation to process to the creek after worship on a Sunday in autumn.

The Bee Branch is a storied waterway. Prone to flooding in heavy rainstorms, the original creek posed an obstacle to homebuilding in the late 1800s because no one but the desperate would live on the floodplain. The open land of the floodplain became a dumping ground for industrial waste, which would be washed downstream into the Mississippi River each time the waters rose. By 1885, engineers had channeled the creek underground into culverts, opening up well-drained land for construction. This worked for a time, but as more of the watershed became covered in asphalt and a changing climate began bringing more frequent storm surges, the creek started regularly overflowing its culverts, flooding streets, and backing up into the basements of this racially and economically diverse neighborhood. Remediating this watershed became a matter of public health and environmental justice. The year we arrived in town, a team of engineers and earthmovers were finishing a multi-year project to daylight the creek, reshape and shore up its banks, and create multiple retention basins along the creek to receive the city's floodwaters, stabilized by deep-rooted native grasses and sedges.

In the days leading up to Sunday, it stormed. Rainwater ran off the streets of our neighborhood, parking lot asphalt, and shingled rooftops. The rush of water filled the storm sewer drains and emptied into the Bee Branch Creek, just as it was designed to do. When the skies cleared, we went to the site we had chosen for the liturgy. The creek was swollen and cloudy, churned up from the sudden influx of runoff. In the eddies swirled pop bottles caught in the fishy-smelling suds produced by turbulence and decomposing algae. We wondered if we had made a mistake in thinking that we should wash our young daughter in this particular water, this particular story. Could waters so littered and murky with decay and land so profoundly engineered beyond what we usually mean by "nature," become a site of blessing and a foothold in something called home? We wondered if, instead, we should do what much of modern, western theology has been inclined to do: namely, to displace God from creation and ourselves from the vulnerabilities of being entangled in ordinary, complicated, even compromised places. We contemplated a retreat back to the sanctuary where Word, sacrament, and infant could be kept clean. But the need for a binding homeplace was too clear an intuition and too urgent an impulse within us to imagine any way forward other than what we did: fish out the pop bottles and wade in together.

The need and longing for home is an intuition and an impulse at the center of being human. For now, let us call "home" a place where one's human creatureliness and personhood are given room for fullness of life in bounded freedom. Home, in this sense, is not merely the house that shelters and signifies us as a natural extension of the body. Rather, home is where this particular human need and longing finds fulfillment. Such fulfillment is not found in ideals of home or in abstract hopes for eschatological consummation, I argue, but in the gift, risk, and creative task of inhabiting real places. In so far as the longing for home is fulfilled, it is fulfilled *here*—here in the bodies we have, in the places we are, among the neighbors we inherit. It is precisely in this way—in and through ordinary, partial, even compromised fulfillments—that home can be for us "epiphanic space" and our practices of inhabitation a lived creation theology.[3]

To build this argument, I set key insights from the field of place studies in conversation with Scandinavian creation theology (SCT), especially the work of Gustaf Wingren. Place studies is an interdisciplinary field that includes philosophy, literature, human geography, and architecture.[4] It lends itself to constructive conversation with Scandinavian creation theology because of their mutual attention to the phenomena of everyday life and to the shared aspects of human experience. Place, I offer, is a shared condition of human life that opens outward into other shared conditions such as embodiment, trust, belonging, and interdependence, the likes of which are key themes for SCT. Moreover, in their own ways, place studies and SCT each push back against predominant hierarchical dualisms that divorce, for example, the sacred from the secular, the spiritual from the creaturely, revelation from reason, nature from culture, the spatial from the temporal, and place from power. Finally, important thinkers within both fields write out of ecological, planetary concern, as well as with attention to questions of interdependence, privilege, and power. I hope, in this offering, to encourage dialogue between SCT and place studies on the grounds of these shared commitments.

The argument will unfold in this way. First, I will orient us to the ways place studies and theology are already in conversation by providing a brief rehearsal of theology's "spatial turn." Then, I will develop an account of the phenomena of place and home in ordinary human experience, drawing on the work of philosopher Edward Casey as well as other observers. Next, I will explore the dangers of place and home as subjects for theological reflection, giving special attention to the ways in which homeplaces can become turned in on themselves in idolatrous ways. Finally, turning to the insights of Scandinavian creation theology, I will explore ways in which creation theology can uncurl our understandings of place and home, orienting us to them as epiphanic space and sending us into inhabitory practices as a lived creation theology.

THE NEGLECT AND RECOVERY OF PLACE

Place has been a neglected, even suppressed, dimension of human life and experience for much of the history of modern, western thought. This is no benign oversight.[5] Modern, western fascination with time and the supremacy of space not only supplanted the category of place, but—by some accounts—devoured it. Modern space, as conceptualized by Newton, is absolute and infinite, homogeneous and unitary, intelligible, but not sensible. Place, by this account, is merely a mathematical subset of space and a function of time, void of meaning and identity. Thus, absolute space is "not only all-embracing but also all-consuming, remaining unappeased in its insatiable appetite for ingesting places, along with the positions and points to which places themselves get reduced in the course of . . . the modern era."[6] The great devouring of place by abstract space and time has shaped modern projects and worldviews, clearly seen in the place-conquering project of colonialism. Colonial powers not only "split open the connection of people to land and to language," writes Willie Jennings, but enacted an assaultive "disruption, even mutilation of the paths to the wisdom necessary to live in the world."[7] The loss of place and the disruption of access to the wisdom, relations, and identities held in places not only characterizes modernity, but *is* the modern project, according to Jennings.[8] The legacy of this project persists in many ways, not least in our hypermobile contemporary culture in which so many of us have careers (trajectories, mobilities, transferable skills) and not places.

The roots of Christian theological suspicions of place and impulses toward a placeless universalism are deeper than modernity, however.[9] They draw on Platonic ideas about spirit's transcendence of body and space, as well as on early Christian (and, later, Reformation-era) emphases on the universal accessibility of God in faith, rather than on the local accessibility of God's indwelling presence in holy places (i.e., temple, Jerusalem, Rome). Christian theological suspicions of place and creation came to a head following the trauma of the Second World War and Nazism's exploitations of these categories. Out of this trauma, for example, Paul Tillich writes about space and time as locked in struggle, where space is the ground of nationalism, paganism, tribalism, and tragedy, while time is the realm of God's own acts in history, for justice, and through the (Protestant) church's "prophetic negation of [. . . and] victory over the gods of space."[10] In a similar fashion, Karl Barth develops a revelation theology according to which knowledge of God breaks into creation from the outside since nothing in creation is fit to receive the Word.

Under the conceptual reign of time and history, creation is reduced to an event that happened at the beginning of time, in a well-mythologized but inaccessible past. This originating creation resulted in a world that that now serves as the *theatrum* of both sin and redemption, the stage upon which salvation history unfolds. According to this predominant, temporal narrative, Christ is the revelatory center of history, the one whose coming gives new meaning to all that occurs sequentially before and after him and, indeed, to time itself. We live now in the "already" and "not yet," awaiting the *kairos* of God in the midst of the *chronos* of creaturely life and the eschaton at the end of history. Thus, Christian theology has subordinated place to time, creation to redemption, the first article to the second. Christian theology has prioritized time and history so thoroughly that the spatial dimension of life together before God—including place, home, land, and the body—has been neglected. Indeed, when Gustaf Wingren diagnosed theology's "flight from creation," he was observing a facet of this long history.[11]

Owed in part to the globalization, hypermobility, ecological crisis, and mass displacements that characterize our time, place is being recovered as an essential dimension of creaturely life together before God. Emerging in the 1970s, theological attention to place exploded at the turn of the twentieth century, resulting in what has been called the discipline's "spatial turn."[12] It should be noted that Native Christian theologians never forgot the importance of place or divorced space from time, but long have done theology through a spatial template. Those invested in place as a key for theology would do well to learn from those who have always known that place is a relational seat of wisdom or otherwise risk presuming to "discover" theological ground already long inhabited.[13]

Preceding any conceptualization of place, theological or otherwise, how-ever, stands the phenomenon of place itself as it is given to experience. It is to a thick description of place—especially the particular place of home—that we now turn.

PLACE AND HOME IN ORDINARY HUMAN EXPERIENCE

On the grounds that we are "human first, then Christian," as N. F. S. Grundtvig's dictum proclaims, we begin by examining place and home as a natural phe-nomenon given in shared, ordinary human experience. Human beings live in and through places. We long for home. Even before they become *loci* for theological reflection, everyday experiences of place and home are inher-ently theological. Place is the particularization of a world that is God's own. Thus, it is by examining place and home in ordinary experience that we find our footing for thinking about the ways in which place and home open theologically.

To be is always already to be in place. As Edward Casey reminds us, "To be at all—to exist in any way—is to be somewhere, and to be somewhere is to be in some kind of place."[14] There is no being that is not *somewhere*, standing out in existence. "Where" is one of the ten basic attributes of being, according to Aristotle. To be nowhere is not only to be groundless and unmoored but is *not to be.* Even trying to imagine the utter placelessness of *being nowhere* elicits a surge of childlike separation anxiety and sense of *being lost*. Imagining utter placelessness may be only a thought experiment, but displacement and homelessness are well known in human experience. Displacement is so threatening to being and to personhood, Tillich observed, that there is a kind of human instinct "to resist the threat of losing one's place and with it existence altogether."[15] From the common human anxiety that "a seat that cannot be found" to the existential desperation of having *nowhere to go,* human beings are intuitively aware that place and being are bound up together.[16]

Place and being co-arise in human experience such that we cannot get behind either one to the other. Places, in this view, are not bounded containers—whether for bodies or meanings—but are constructed relationally. Consider our planet as a place. Molten iron and liquid rock, minerals and fossils and soils: our planetary place is composed of untold bodies and beings in relation that together compose core and mantle, crust and biome. These beings-in-relation not only compose this place together, but also give place to one another and give the planet its form, character, and dynamics. The liturgical poetry of Genesis 1 celebrates the relational co-arising of place and being. Light in relation to darkness, land in relation to water, beasts, birds, and human beings all in relationship to one another: a world co-arises, resplendent with life in relation. In this sense, the place called "creation" is just creatures-in-relation all the way down.

Place, this suggests, is neither a bounded container nor an inert theater, but a kind of perichoretic, room-making communion.[17] A place is not homogeneous and unitary—like the absolute space of modernity—but is a congregation of beings-in-relation who make room with and for one another in the structure of their relations. The implaced nature of our life together and the relational, room-making nature of places means that we are entangled with and dependent on one another. This is true not only of other human beings, but also of the myriad other creatures that co-create places together at multiple scales. Places are fractal, their same relational structure manifest at intimate and cosmic scales. Places overlap, interplay, and nest within one another. Places hide and appear within places and among the multiplicity of places. The scope, scale, and interplay of places reflect the magnitude, intimacy, coherence, and dynamism of the relations that form them and give them their character.

Places hold meaning and personal attachment. The meaningfulness of place is a common theme among human geographers. "Place is above all a territory of meanings," writes Edward Relph, one of place studies' pioneering thinkers.[18] Places receive their meaning both "from below" as people go about their daily lives and "from above" as places are planned, named, built, and memorialized. Places are also active agents in the formation of their own meaning. Place is no "inert, experienced scene," geographer Allen Pred writes, but is "a process whereby the reproduction of social and cultural forms, the formation of biographies, and the transformation of nature ceaselessly become one another at the same time that time-space specific activities and power relations ceaselessly become one another."[19] By human meaning-making and by the dynamic relations that continually compose the place itself, places hold meanings (sometimes multiple and contested meanings) and become sites of personal attachments over time. We come to love places and to associate and identify with them as persons and communities. They become storied and sedimented with history, memory, and meaning.

What do these observations about place mean for ordinary human experience of place? Because place extends out before us, prepared, as it were, ahead of us, and because place makes room for our being, we experience place as gift. We move between and traverse places, but everywhere place appears before, under, and around us as given. From the most personal and particular places we inhabit—our mother's kitchen, our backyard garden, a favorite coffeeshop—to the world as a whole, we experience place as a gift that we receive simply by *being there*. We are not the ground of our own being. We cannot be or make place for ourselves. "To live means to receive life from outside oneself," Wingren writes, and so, too, to live means to receive place from outside oneself.[20] We live on borrowed ground by virtue of the hospitality of others.[21]

Moreover, we experience place as a more or less *trustworthy* gift: something we rely on to bear us up, to continue out before us, and to persistently precede us as we move through the world. Even when being in a particular place comes with risks—like standing on the rotten floorboards of an old barn hayloft or wading into a creek murky with storm runoff—making that place less than trustworthy, we do not worry that place itself will betray us. Should one place collapse or come to ruin, should one house burn or one empire fall, another place appears around one to bear one up in existence. One is not—even in the rubble and ruin of one place—abandoned to *no place* at all. Despite our finitude and the finitude of any one place, place itself remains trustworthy.

Our need for place makes us dependent and vulnerable. Places are not only sites of hospitality and encounter, but also of alienation, violence, and being lost. We die in places just as surely as we live in them. Some places are traps. Some constrict and malform creaturely life with their narrowness. Some places are Golgathas. Places make room, but the character, shape, and fittingness of that room for life are owed to the particular relations that form it, the structure they create, the events that transpire there. Embodied and implaced, we are truly "in each other's hands," as Løgstrup has observed.[22] Place is not only gift, therefore, but also profound risk. The risk runs in two directions. Receiving place from others, we are vulnerable to the forms and dynamics of the place itself, to the others who are there, and to the events that unfold. Receiving us, the place and its other inhabitants are vulnerable to us. Such is the mutual vulnerability of hospitality.

Even as we receive place as a gift and risk, it calls from us a creative task. Human beings are homemakers inside the gift of place. We build forts and tree houses as children. We design and decorate houses, shape neighborhoods, plan cities, cultivate gardens, imagine utopias. We frame up dwellings that not only shelter our bodies but subtend our creaturely needs, make room for the practices of everyday life, and affectively bind our personhood to place. Like place in general, home is not merely an inert stage on which we preform our personhood, nor merely a sheltering container for our bodies. Rather, home is a place (or places) where one's creaturely needs and personhood are given room for fullness of life in bounded freedom. Homeplaces fulfill a common human longing for a place or places where this longing is fulfilled, even partially and provisionally.

Partial and provisional fulfillments do not make a place less than home. On the contrary, partial and provisional fulfillments make a home *actual*, that is, incarnational and creaturely. Anything other than an incarnational and creaturely home would not be fitting for the living of an incarnational, creaturely life and, therefore, not home. While we might fanaticize about an ideal home—perhaps one that is secure, permanent, and perfectly fitting for our creatureliness and personhood—such ideals paradoxically could not actually fulfill our longing for home. Only concrete, actual homes make room for our being. The human being experiences home among creatures, in creaturely places, characterized by finitude, or not at all. Even as home makes room fittingly for the fullness of our creatureliness and personhood, it does so as any creaturely web of relations can: imperfectly, contingently, changingly. Even at home we bump up against things, and one another! Homeplaces change, break down, leak, get mucky, come to ruin, disappear, and disappoint. The places we experience as home are not permanent, but finite and experienced as gift, task, and risk.

Home is experienced through the inhabitation of a place *as home*. We can build houses and live in them, but we experience *as home* places we have inhabited. Inhabitation does not consist in a particular set of practices (including baptizing one's child in a local watershed), but something that happens in, through, and under the ordinary tasks and rhythms of daily life: washing the dishes, casting a ballot, walking the sidewalk, celebrating holidays, getting to know the neighbors, both human and otherwise creaturely. Through such ordinary human tasks and practices, we form place-attachments, bind memories and hopes, learn the wisdom necessary to live in that place, and entrust ourselves to it. Inhabiting a place as home, we ourselves are formed and co-created by it, as much as we form and co-cocreate it. While home may be a site of personal attachment and affection, it need not be singular. Sometimes inhabitation of place as home looks like a taproot sent deep into the soil in a single place of particular commitment; sometimes it looks more like a rhizome sending runners, which pop up in multiple places. In either case, inhabitation involves becoming an integral, integrated member of the communion of that place. If home is where one receives room for fullness of life in bounded freedom, it seems that fullness of life involves not merely standing out as oneself in the world, but membership, interdependency, receiving and extending hospitality, and being continually created.

In this section, I have offered a view of place and home as phenomena of everyday life. As such, they require no "Christianization" in order to become the basis for theological reflection or to be for us a means of grace. Yet, even as we have been observing the phenomena of place and home generally, we already can anticipate ways that major features of a creation theology are close at hand. Before setting place and home into explicit conversation with creation theology, however, an observation about the dangers of home and place as subjects for theological reflection is in order.

THE DANGERS OF PLACE AND HOME

Multiple dangers arise in the development of a theological account of place and home. In this section, I set out to name two of these dangers and offer significant examples of the trouble they cause. These dangers can be understood through the lens of Luther's account of human sinfulness as a self-concern that curves us in on ourselves (*incurvatus in se*) and cuts us off from both God and our neighbors.[23] In so far as places are relationally formed, this incurvature comes to bear on places. Relationally distorted by sin, places held open in hospitality to life collapse in on themselves, so to speak. They no longer make room for life together, but for suffering, idolatry, and violence. Under the conditions of sin, the gift of place becomes a site of idolatry. Curved in on ourselves, home becomes nothing but a seat of self where we escape the neighbor and deny our interconnectedness rather than a place of membership, hospitality, and opportunity to know and love the neighbor well.

In the course of theology's spatial turn, sacred places have played a prominent role. Sacred places are sites of notable beauty, natural wonder, cultural memory, and overt meaningfulness or religious significance. They may be "thin places" where a sense of the holy seems close to the surface of things. However, theologies of place that associate God's presence and activity with places of overt beauty, power, and significance quickly become theologies of glory. This leaves theologies of place without much to say for places where litter bobs in murky floodwaters and human sin rises to the surface.

Homeplaces are often described in the language of sacred place. The sacredness of home does not depend on particular theological content or religious experience. Home is experienced as sacred precisely because it fulfills a deep-seated human need and longing and is laden with meaning and personal attachments. Homes become sites of topophilia—"the affective bond between people and place"—and as such are set apart from other places in the landscape of one's life.[24] Yet, as I will show in this section, the sacredness of place and home presents two primary dangers: a concern for the purity, preservation, and protection of homeplaces and the profanation of and disregard for places that are not-home. These dangers are at once theological-religious dangers (idolatry), conceptual dangers (they misunderstand place), and they are acute, lived dangers for those sacrificed for the sake of homeplace.

Idolatry of Place and Home

Sacred places prompt concern for boundaries and access, purity and preservation. For examples of this one need not look farther than events in the United States in recent years as white nationalists marched in the streets of Charlottesville, Virginia, chanting the Nazi slogan "blood and soil" to evoke an ideology of white supremacy and a racially homogeneous "homeland" or *Lebensraum*. Gripped by idolatry, the notion of sacred place becomes bound up with protectionist and expansionist agendas. Here place is held open not for the fullness of creaturely life and personhood, but for death and violence. Wherever walls are built, borders secured, and people harmed in the name of national purity and preservation, placemaking becomes an unholy exercise in violence and "homeland" itself becomes an idol.

Personal homes can also become sites of violent protectionism and expansionism. Consider, for example, the common law "castle doctrine," which says that people have the right to use deadly force to protect themselves against an intruder in their homes. Such laws have come into public conversation in recent years as "Stand Your Ground" variations of castle doctrine are being adopted in some states, extending the right to deadly self-defense beyond one's home to anywhere one has a right to be. Your castle, apparently, is wherever you are standing. Or it is if you are white in America, for as Kelly Brown Douglas has shown, stand-your-ground culture arises from the same racial ideologies that lead to the genocidal horrors of Nazism and Manifest Destiny. In stand-your-ground culture, she argues, one's right to place—a particular place or any place at all—is contingent on whiteness. All others are denied place and so are denied being in the world. To deny people the particular goodness of home denies the humanity from which the longing for home arises. "Home is a 'safe space,'" Douglas writes, "It is a space where a person is able to live and grow into the fullness of her or his created identity. Home is a free space. It is a space where people are free to love and be loved, and to be whoever it is that God has created them to be. The purpose of stand-your-ground culture is to deprive black bodies of homes," writes Douglas.[25] Home becomes curled in on itself—that is, distorted idolatrously—when it depends on the denial of the home-longing humanity of others.

Our ecological crisis can be understood as a result of an expansionist impulse to make the whole world home. This, too, is the task of human home-making curled in on itself. Through the subduing of creation and with technical power, human beings have attempted to make the whole world our home, that is, to make the whole world *fit* for human flourishing at the expense of other kinds of creaturely flourishing and our own flourishing together with everything else. Human beings have destroyed the habitat of other creatures in order to expand their own living space. We have forgotten that the fulfillment of home is found in bounded freedom, not free license. It is found in gestures of room-making hospitality and not colonization.

Profanation of Not-Home

Sacred places, by their very designation in a dualistic imaginary, imply the existence of profane places and set them against one another. "A sacred thing is a cipher for all the rest that is disposable or deemed disposable," writes Vítor Westhelle. "The former is protected from time while the latter is only a function of it. As long as we have sacred things, sacred places, dissociated from their epiphanic time—geography without genealogy—we will have never-ending dump sites and places or bodies to be violated."[26] We justify the maintenance and protection of sacred places even at the cost of other places. When home becomes a sacred place, homemaking co-creates places of disposability, including places known as sacrificial or "shadow places."

Shadow places are the underside of the concept of homeplace, according to environmental philosopher Val Plumwood. They are "the many unrecognized and disregarded places that provide our material and ecological support, most of which, in a global market, elude our knowledge and responsibility."[27] Shadow places lie upstream and downstream from home. They are the externalities of home the comfortable wish not to acknowledge: rare earth mines, power plants, landfills, farms, and factories. People with privilege can pretend these shadow places—and the people who live and labor there—don't exist or matter: *non-place, non-person*. This allows people with privilege to continue living in a fantasy world of consequence-free homemaking. Just as sacred places imply and so permit disposable places, certain ideals of home—including the ideal of the singular, self-sufficient homeplace—atomize the home, deny interdependency, and so curl the home in on itself at the expense of right-relationship with upstream and downstream neighbors. The shame of shadow places ought to prompt in us Westhelle's incisive question: "Whose crosses have sent us to the coziness of home?"[28]

As theology continues to make its spatial turn, then, it must ward against uncritical adoption of *incurvatus* ideals of home as "a strong hyper-separate seat of self" and, homemaking practices that value the purity, protection, and isolationism of homeplaces at the expense of other places, creatures, and peo-ple.[29] Yet these dangers are no reason to reject place and home as horizons of theological reflection. Rather, following Wingren's bidding about creation in general, they give us good reason to "widen and clarify" theological accounts of home rather than suppress them.[30] Doing so calls for renewed attention to creation theology, for it is there that we find possibilities for thinking about God's life-giving presence and creativity in the places of everyday life, including places shadowed and sacrificed, beloved and laden with power.

EPIPHANIC INHABITATION OF HOME

To resist both the idolatries of sacred space and the profanation of shadow places, a theological account of home must correspond to a well-developed creation theology. Creation theology is not a subtheme of theology nor one doctrine among others, but the "universal horizon for any Christian theolo-gizing regarding Christ and church, baptism and salvation."[31] At the heart of Scandinavian creation theology is the affirmation that the world is God's own and that God's ongoing creativity takes place in, with, and under creaturely life: this grain of wheat breaking open into verdant life, that cell dividing, this open wound washed, bandaged, and scabbing, that child fed in the lap of a loving parent. But we do not inhabit the world in whole or in the abstract, but in and through particular places, our own bodies, and in the course of every-day life. Home is where we inhabit God's world most humanly.

To inhabit is to dwell in a place as home. Inhabitation is the everyday, incarnational process of "becoming fully alive in and with a place."[32] It involves daily, ordinary acts through which we come to be at home in a place. Inhabitation of a place is both a deeply personal process (the living of one's life *as homed* in this place) and a fundamentally relational process, including ecological, civic, and neighborly practices. In both its personal and relational aspects, inhabitation is a humanizing process. As such, the practice of inhabi-tation, I argue, is a lived creation theology. It is an expression of confidence in the world as a fitting place for being and becoming human. It is an insistence that concrete and particular places are where we receive life as gift and par-ticipate in the life that God is continually creating here. Inhabitory practices crack open the idolatrous function of home as a fortressed seat of self, attune one to place as a site of God's creativity, and turn us outward in vocation. In this way, the deep inhabitation of home opens epiphanically, making manifest what the fullness of human life in bounded freedom really looks like, and what it is to become fully alive.

Inhabitation is not one activity among others but happens—even catches one by surprise—as one goes about the ordinariness of daily life in a place.

In this way it is like friendship: irreducible to one activity or another, but happening in and through every story told, confidence kept, joy celebrated, and grief shard. Inhabitation develops by the slow accretion of familiar, unremarkable moments. At the same time, one also can set out to inhabit a place—just as one can set out to cultivate a friendship—by engaging in what have been called inhabitory practices, "regular, trusted *habits* of behavior" designed to create and nurture life in that place.[33] They can be formal rituals, or the daily rites and seasonal ceremonies of life together there. Inhabitory practices deepen one's attention to, integration with, and affection for a place, as well as one's sense of being at home there, given room for becoming fully alive, fully human.

One commonly commended inhabitory practice is learning the history of one's place, from its deep geological history to its biological and social histories of inhabitation. This does not necessarily involve archival research but is a practice of paying attention to where one is, what has happened here, what remains to testify. History is borne in the visible and invisible sedimentary layers of place: the fossils in the sandstone, the blood in the soil, the redline through the city, the tears on the trail, the trauma in the system. Inhabitory practice is listening to the stories told about the place publicly and with ceremony, quietly between neighbors, and not at all.

Neighborliness is another inhabitory practice. To have a home is to inherit neighbors, some easier to love than others. Neighbors are other human beings connected to one by the ligaments of place, as well as other creatures in the ecological neighborhood: soils and waters, animals and atmosphere, trees and grasses. At first, neighborliness might mean learning names: Roger, Alice, Bee Branch Creek, bur oak, blazing star, little blue stem. Gradually, knowing one's neighbors means attunement to *their* longing for home, for a place where their own full human and creaturely lives can be lived at full stretch. It means bearing their stories of suffering in narrow places. Inhabitory practices of neighboring cultivate a desire for the conditions necessary for *their* fullness of life in bounded freedom, such that one's own experience of home is bound up with that of one's neighbors. Thus, the inhabitory practice of neighboring decenters the self and opens epiphanically: becoming human is becoming a member. Fullness of life is not self-actualization, but life together in room-making communion. Inhabitory practices of neighborliness thus debunk the myth of home as a fortressed seat of self. They push back against visions of "fullness of life" or exercises of freedom that cut against the life of the neighbor. Inhabitory practices of neighboring undermine a false consciousness of place that suggests one can have a home at the expense of the profanation, shadowing, and sacrifice of other places and neighbors.

Despite such neighborly recognitions, the inhabitation of a place as home situates one concretely and undeniably in systems of injustice. Homes are not built in a clearing, but on storied ground and connected to myriad other places through a global economy of extraction and disposal. Creation theology is not utopian about creation, but acknowledges "the powers of death, illness and decay no less than [the] hope, human flourishing, and regeneration" present within it.[34] Inhabiting home is inhabiting a world rent by sin. Moreover, putting down roots into such ground with the brazen hope not only to live here, but to *become alive* there only deepens one's complicity. My own home situates me on the traditional lands of the Sauk and Meskwaki peoples, down the pipeline from several hydraulic fracturing operations, and upriver from the dead zone in the Gulf of Mexico. Home situates one in complicity, yet paradoxically also frees one for being human. The paradox of home thus opens epiphanically: becoming human means being forgiven, homed on the borrowed ground of mercy. Forgiveness allows one to inhabit the world as one set free, opened outward, and called to tend the plot of creation entrusted to one and to seek the neighbor's own good.

Overtime, inhabitory practices attune one to the ways life is continually arising and changing in one's homeplace. As a tourist, one experiences a place at a given time. Like the photographs one takes, this experience of place is thin and static. By contrast, inhabitants experience a place through seasons of change and witness newness arising within it. Inhabiting home is inhabiting a world continually recreated and vivified by God. Home is where we bear witness to and participate in God's healing and renewal of all things. Becoming human is everyday participation in the new life which is continually arising in place: watering the growth, welcoming the newcomer, witnessing the healing.

Inhabitory practices not only deepen one's attention to and familiarity with one's homeplace. They also enable us to know ourselves as inhabitants of home and, therefore, as recipients of God's own hospitality. Home opens epiphanically: Becoming human means receiving life and place from outside oneself. We live on borrowed ground. God makes room for creaturely life not simply as a matter of originating creation, but as continual creation and hospitality. God is ever making room in the perichoretic communion of God's own life. This is the "primary wonder" that poet Denise Levertov describes when she writes:

[. . .]

once more the quiet mystery

is present to me, the throng's clamor

recedes: the mystery

that there is anything, anything at all,

let alone cosmos, joy, memory, everything,

rather than void: and that, O Lord,

Creator, Hallowed One, You still,

hour by hour sustain it.[35]

Place—and life in it and through it—is a gift because, hour by hour, God creates and sustains it. God holds open room for the fullness of creaturely life, not in space ceded by the retreat or diminishment of God, but in the thick relationality and deep sedimentation of God's own eternally life-giving presence. In short, the particular home we inhabit—and the world we inhabit by way of it—is saturated with divine presence and sustained by God's continual hospitality.[36] This quiet mystery is indeed present to us in and through the ordinariness of home, amid the clamor of daily life. To inhabit home is to inhabit the life of God, a place that casts no shadows. This is why home—even in its limits, finitude, and imperfections—is experienced as the fulfillment of a longing to be received, fully alive, and free.

Practices of inhabitation are a lived creation theology. This is so, even without explicit theologizing about home and place. How we inhabit home is how we inhabit the world. They situate human life in creation and in community. They elevate everyday responsibilities—domestic, civic, neighborly, and ecological—as vocations. They decenter the self and the home, and locate full humanity in membership, forgiveness, and participation in God's continual creativity. Moreover, these practices attune one to the epiphanic wisdom that arises from creation itself, inclining our ears and eyes to the Word and wisdom through which creation comes into being every moment. Unlike concepts of revelation as knowledge that breaks into the world from elsewhere, epiphany arises incarnationally within a world that is God's own from the ground up. In fact, the content of such epiphany is not primarily a matter of knowledge, least of all cognitive knowledge, but life itself—forgiven and set free, integrated in membership, and participating in God's life-giving work.

CONCLUSION

Wet with the waters of the Bee Branch, our daughter was not simply initiated into churchliness, but welcomed into full humanity. Baptism is a rite of inhabitation. This ordinary washing—even in storm-stirred waters—is a full immersion into a world that is God's own. In baptism we receive the gift of home—not merely the particular site of the liturgy—but the promise of room held open for life together in the trustworthy hospitality of God's own life. We receive freedom for life in places sedimented with the accretion of deep time, deep wounds, and God's own deep inhabitation of the world in Jesus Christ. We receive the inheritance of neighbors—the water in which we are washed, the creaturely others who find a home there, and the human beings who draw life from its banks. Their lives and longings for home decenter our own. They call out in us a vocation of neighborliness, of room-making hospitality, and of holding them well in our hands, for the sake of the life of the world. We do not know how this rite of inhabitation will form our daughter's own sense of home, humanity, or vocation, but with the whole company of witnesses, we entrust her to the continual creativity of God.

NOTES

1. Alan Thein During, *This Place on Earth: Home and the Practice of Permanence* (Seattle, WA: Sasquatch Books, 1996), 4.

2. This phrase comes from Ryan Griffis and Sarah Ross' *A Great Green Desert* (School of the Art Institute of Chicago, 2017), an experimental documentary project that showcases how mechanized agriculture and settler colonial ideologies have led to the desertification of the US Corn Belt and Brazil's Soy Frontier, transforming what was once described as "a great, green sea" of prairie grasslands in https://art.illinois.edu/work/post/a-great-green-desert/

3. On "epiphanic space," see Vítor Westhelle, "Wrappings of the Divine: Location and Vocation in Theological Perspective," *Currents in Theology and Mission* 31:5 (October 2004).

4. Formative to my own thinking about place are philosophers Edward Casey, Jeff Malpas, and Val Plumwood, geographers Doreen Massey, Edward Relph, and Yi-Fu Tuan, and bioregional writers Gary Snyder and Barry Lopez.

5. On the absence (even the "demise" and "suppression") of place in modern western thought, see Edward Casey, *The Fate of Place: A Philosophical History* (Berkeley: University of California Press, 1998).

6. Casey, *The Fate of Place*, 193.

7. Willie James Jennings, *The Christian Imagination* (New Haven, CT: Yale University Press, 2010), 58.

8. Ibid., 58.

9. For a fuller account of the absence of place in the history of Christian theology, see Oliver O'Donovan, "The Loss of a Sense of Place," *Irish Theological Quarterly*, 55.1, January 1989, 39–58; John Inge, *A Christian Theology of Place* (Burlington, VT: Ashgate, 2003).

10. Paul Tillich, "The Struggle Between Time and Space," *Theology of Culture* (London: Oxford University Press, 1959), 38, 39. On the struggle between time and

space in the work of Paul Tillich, see Vítor Westhelle, *Eschatology and Space: The Lost Dimension in Theology Past and Present* (New York: Palgrave MacMillan, 2012).

11. Gustaf Wingren, *The Fight from Creation* (Minneapolis, MN: Augsburg Publishing House, 1971).

12. Sigurd Bergmann, "Theology in its Spatial Turn: Space, Place and Built Environments Challenging and Changing the Images of God," *Religion Compass*, Vol. 1, Issue 3, May 2007, pp. 353–379.

13. See, for example, Vine Deloria, Jr. *God is Red* (New York: Dell Publishing, 1973); George E. "Tink" Tinker, *American Indian Liberation: A Theology of Sovereignty* (Maryknoll, NY: Orbis, 2008); Josiah Baker, "Native American Contributions to a Christian Theology of Space," *Studies in World Christianity* 22.3 (2016): 234–246.

14. Edward S. Casey, *The Fate of Place: A Philosophical History* (Berkeley: University of California Press, 1998), ix.

15. Paul Tillich, *Systematic Theology*, 3 vols., vol. 3 (Chicago: The University of Chicago, 1963), 315.

16. Psychologist Paul Tournier writes about what he observes is a common, anxiety-ridden dream among modern people that "a seat cannot be found," in *A Place for You: Psychology and Religion*, trans. Edwin Hudson (London: SCM Press, 1969) p. 10.

17. The Greek verb *choreo* is directly related to the noun *chora*, meaning *space, place, or region*. Thus, the transitive use of *choreo* means *to make room for something* or *to cede a place*. On the etymological and theological history of the concept of perichoresis, see Slobodan Stamatović, "The Meaning of *Perichoresis*," *Open Theology* (2016), 2.

18. Edward Relph, "Modernity and the Reclamation of Place," in David Seamon (Ed.), *Dwelling, Seeing, and Designing: Toward a Phenomenological Ecology* (New York: State University of New York Press, 1993), 25–40.

19. Allen Pred, "Place as Historically Contingent Process: Structuration and Time-Geography of Becoming Places," *Annals of the Association of American Geographers* 74(2), 1984: 279, 282.

20. Wingren, *Creation and Law* (Philadelphia: Muhlenberg, 1961), 18.

21. David Kelsey describes the human being as "living on borrowed breath" and on "borrowed time" in *Eccentric Existence: A Theological Anthropology* (Louisville, KY: WJK, 2009), and I thank him for the gift of this formulation.

22. K. E. Løgstrup, *The Ethical Demand* (Notre Dame, IN: Notre Dame University Press, 1997), 15–16.

23. See, Luther, "Lectures on Romans," *LW* 25: 291, 345, 346, 351–352.

24. Yi-Fu Tuan, *Topophilia: A Study of Environmental Perception, Attitudes, and Values* (New York: Columbia University Press, 1990), 4.

25. Kelly Brown Douglas, *Stand Your Ground: Black Bodies and the Justice of God* (Maryknoll, NY: Orbis Books, 2015), 131.

26. Westhelle, *Scandalous God: The Use and Abuse of the Cross* (Minneapolis, MN: Fortress, 2006), 152.

27. Val Plumwood, "Shadow Places and the Politics of Dwelling," *Australian Humanities Review,* 44, March 2008, 139–50. http://australianhumanitiesreview.org /2008/03/01/shadow-places-and-the-politics-of-dwelling/

28. Westhelle, *Scandalous God,* 159.

29. Plumwood, Ibid.

30. Wingren, *Creation and Gospel* (Eugene, OR: Wipf and Stock Publishers, 1979), 64.

31. Niels Henrik Gregersen, Bengt Kristensson Uggla, and Trygve Wyller, "Reconfiguring Reformation Theology: The Program of Scandinavian Creation Theology," in *Reformation Theology for a Post-Secular Age: Løgstrup, Prenter, Wingren, and the Future of Scandinavian Creation Theology* (Göttingen: Vandenhoeck & Ruprecht, 2017), 22.

32. Peter Berg and Raymond F. Dasmann, "Reinhabiting California," in *Home! A Bioregional Reader,* ed. Van Andruss, Christopher Plant, Judith Plant, and Eleanor Wright (Philadelphia: New Society, 1990), 35.

33. Daniel Kemmis, *Community and the Politics of Place* (Norman: University of Oklahoma Press, 1990), 80. Gary Snyder writes in a bioregional key about practices of "reinhabitation" in Synder, "Reinhabitation," *The Old Ways* (San Francisco: City Lights, 1977).

34. Gregerson, Uggla, Wyller, "Introducing Scandinavian Creation Theology: Past and Present,"

35. Denise Levertov, "Primary Wonder," *The Collected Poems of Denise Levertov,* ed. Paul A. Lacey and Anne Dewey (New York: New Directions, 2013) p.1063.

36. That "the world is God given and imbued with a divine presence" lies at the center of Scandinavian creation theology; see, *Reformation Theology in a Post-Secular Age,* 15.

Chapter 3

Coming Home to God

Procession and Return in Pseudo-Dionysius and Marguerite Porete

Ryan McAnnally-Linz

Scandinavian Creation Theology (SCT) holds that "Christians are not to be considered as aliens in the world, nor as pilgrims on their way to another world."[1] Those who are neither aliens nor pilgrims (nor, I suppose, tourists) are at home. Why are Christians neither aliens nor pilgrims? Well, Christians are humans. But humans are creatures and so belong among creatures in a shared creaturely world. Thus, Christians belong in the world. "The world is not a strange and alien place—this world is God's own creation, and it is our home."[2] The ambivalences of life on earth nuance this central claim but do not efface it.[3]

As presented by Gregersen, Uggla, and Wyller, SCT arose in reaction to what its seminal figures saw as "post-liberal" theology's excessive focus on the distinctively Christian. Understandably, given its roots in lands that adopted Luther's reformation, SCT's chief theological reference points have been the Pietism opposed by Grundtvig and the anti-liberalism of Nygren and Barth. Gregersen, Uggla, and Wyller admit that Pietism and even Barthianism are not among the most influential theological perspectives today.[4] They insist, however, that the fundamental theological debates to which SCT speaks are still alive today. I would like to sketch out one facet of one such debate by discussing two figures who in at least some respects are clearly much more marginal today than Barth or even the Pietists, namely Pseudo-Dionysius the Areopagite and Marguerite Porete. (The two, it should be noted, are not and were not marginal in the same way. He was received for centuries as a para-apostolic authority was burnt at the stake.) Their relative obscurity notwithstanding, these two serve in distinct ways as exemplars of a powerful stream of Christian theology, which identifies God as the ultimate aim of human existence. This broad way of understanding the final end of human life was and is an exceedingly common Christian rendering of the story of everything. Such theologies often, but not always, construe the world as having come forth from God in creation and being destined to return to God in consummation. God is thus our true home.

When Miroslav Volf and I sketched our own proposal regarding "the home of God," we had this strand of Christian thought very much in view, but we never put it squarely on the page.[5] I think it is at least as relevant a conversation partner to SCT and its current interpreters and advocates as it is to Volf and me.

GOD ALONE AS FINAL END

Strong currents in Christian theology have assumed that human life has an aim—a purpose or fulfillment toward which it is oriented and for which it yearns. Some theologians have elaborated intricate accounts of this aim in dialogue with the teleological theories of antique philosophers, most notably Aristotle. It is not, however, the influence of those philosophers alone that pushes Christian thought to consider the aim of human life. A number of features of the biblical witness and credal articulations of the faith push in the same direction: the apparently unfinished character of the gospel stories, which leave open the expectation of an ultimate return of Christ at "the end of the age," echoed in the Apostles' and Nicene Creeds; Paul's identification in Romans 6:21–22 of different final ends of life enslaved to Sin ("The *telos* of those things is death") and life enslaved God ("The *telos* is eternal life"); the prophetic and apocalyptic visions of a new and everlasting age to come; and so on. The question arises quite naturally from within Christian theology: just what is the end towards which human life aims, for which we yearn and hope and perhaps strive?

Among the most common answers in the history of theology are *God, union with God, the vision of God, enjoyment of God,* and *glorification of God.* To give just one example of each: Bonaventure says that God, as Being, is "the ultimate end [. . .] and the consummation."[6] John Calvin says that "union with God" is humans' highest good.[7] Nicholas of Cusa claims that "the mind exists for the sake of seeing *Posse* itself [i.e., God]."[8] The *Westminster Shorter Catechism*'s well-known first question can pull double duty here: "What is the chief end of man? The chief end of man is to glorify God, and to enjoy him forever."

While these different formulations do not simply reduce to one another, and while each raises a whole host of further questions, they form a distinct set of Christian answers to the question of humans' final end. For one thing, it is not uncommon for one thinker to appeal to multiple of these expressions. For another, they are all highly theocentric. Even when it is not God as such but a state (e.g., union) or an activity (e.g., enjoyment) that is identified as humans' final end, God is the key term in the state (union *with God*) and the object of the activity (enjoyment *of God*).

In several highly influential cases, including Augustine and Thomas Aquinas, theologians have followed Aristotle and identified "happiness" as humans' telos, which might appear to diverge from the theocentric consensus.[9] But as Aristotle acknowledged, "to say that happiness is the chief good seems a platitude, and a clearer account of what it is is still desired."[10] To say that humans desire happiness for its own sake and not for the sake of anything else is not to say much unless we go on to say what happiness is. And when theologians have given their "clearer accounts" of what happiness actually means—which is to say, of the *content* of humans' final end—a great many of them have come back around to theocentric formulations.[11] Thus, Augustine says, "the fullness of our happiness, beyond which there is none else, is this: to enjoy God."[12] And Aquinas distinguishes between the "thing" that is humans' last end, and in this sense "God is the last end of man," and "attainment or possession, the use or enjoyment of the thing desired," which for humans is happiness and consists in "the vision of the Divine Essence."[13] Similarly, Calvin: "to enjoy the presence of God is the summit of happiness."[14]

There is, then, a weighty chorus of voices that give theocentric answers to the question of humans' final end. But what about the question of home? What paradigms for human homemaking and/or homecoming accord with these theocentric approaches to humans' final end? Of the several common possibilities, I will focus, for reasons of space and the value of a certain degree of polemical starkness, on one: the Neoplatonist-influenced pattern of "procession" and "return," which tends to suggest that God (and God alone) is not only our final end but our true home.

PROCESSION AND RETURN

For Christians, the basic shape of this pattern is suggested by both Paul's compact formulation, "From him [God] and through him and to him are all things" (Rom. 11:36), and by the divine self-identification in Revelation, "I am the Alpha and the Omega, the beginning [*archē*] and the end [*telos*]" (Rev. 21:6; 22:13). All creatures exist only as their existence is given by God, sustained by God, and directed toward God. God is their beginning and their end. While they may now be displaced from God, at the end, God, who is to be loved above all things, will be "all in all" (1 Cor. 15:28), and the pure in heart will "see God" (Matt. 5:8) eternally. The arc of the story runs from God to God. Using Thomas Aquinas's terminology, theologians often refer to this type of story as one of *exitus* (procession, coming forth) and *reditus* (return, turning back).[15] I will generally use "procession" and "return" as the key terms.

In order to sketch the stakes of an engagement between this way of thinking and the more "worldly" theologies of home suggested by SCT as well as Volf and my "home of God" proposal, I will consider two exemplars of the procession–return pattern. The first, Pseudo-Dionysius the Areopagite, is the formative thinker of this stream of thought. The second, the 14th-century beguine Marguerite Porete, represents what I take to be a characteristic (although not inevitable) theological extreme to which conceiving of God as humans' final end according to a pattern of procession and return can lead.

Pseudo-Dionysius the Areopagite

While earlier authors such as Origen hint and lean and take partial steps in this direction, the procession–return paradigm finds its clearest and most influential ancient expression in Pseudo-Dionysius, who puts it at the heart of his theology.[16] God, Dionysius argues, radically transcends all being. And since "whatever transcends being must also transcend knowledge," God is absolutely unknowable and un-nameable.[17] Through God's revelation, however, we can see that this "transcendent Goodness transcendentally there" is that upon which all being and knowledge depend.[18] We can, in other words, know that God is the *cause* of all.

Precisely because God is cause of all beings, God is also their end or goal: "All things revolve around him, *for* he is their cause, their source, and their destiny."[19] Attribution of sequences like this (cause—source—destiny) to God pervade Dionysius's works.[20] They stretch, almost without exception, from "source" (*archē*) or "cause" (*aitia*) to a term designating an end, goal, destiny, or objective (*peras* and *telos*, for example). For modern readers, this might appear strange. Why should a cause or source also be a goal? To make sense of Dionysius's tight linkage of beginning/cause and end/goal, we need to take note of the philosophical theories of causality that he draws on.

Dionysius's procession–return account of causality draws on two philosophical sources. On the one hand, he makes appeal to Aristotle's category of the "final cause," or "that for which" something is. On Aristotle's understanding, something's end—what it is for or what it aims at—just is a form of cause. So cause and end are partly overlapping categories. One type of end is a species of cause. "The Preexistent," Dionysius says, "is the Source [*archē*] and the end [*teleutē*] of all things. He is their Source, for he is their Cause [*aitios*]. He is their end, for he is the 'for the sake of whom' [*telos de hōs tou heneka*]."[21] Dionysius's "for the sake of" is a direct reference to Aristotle's most common explanation of what a *telos* or final cause is.[22] He quite clearly means to say that God is the final cause of all things, in Aristotle's sense. In other words, precisely because God is cause in the fullest possible sense,[23] God is that toward which all things aim. On the other hand, Dionysius's pervasive use of the term "return" (*epistrophē*) follows Neo-Platonic vocabulary common in Plotinus and Porphyry and formalized by Proclus, the fifth-century head of the Athenian Academy: "Every effect remains in its cause, proceeds from it, and reverts [*epistrephein*] upon it."[24] Given this understanding of causality, if God is the preeminent cause of each and all, then all creatures must return to God.[25]

Dionysius's pattern of procession and return operates at two levels.[26] On the one hand, it is synchronic. It names a structure of created being that is always and everywhere there. Creatures are always at once proceeding from and returning to God. Procession and return name two aspects of what it is to be a creature. This is the fundamental sense, grounded in Dionysius's late-Platonist account of causality. On the other hand, creaturely life is temporal, and Christian teaching tends to suggest that there is a diachronic arc to that life, both individually and universally. Procession and return operate at this level too. While it is not foregrounded, Dionysius does have an eschatological hope, or at least, he looks forward to a future consummation for the soul ("But in time to come, when we are incorruptible and immortal . . . "), and he contrasts that future with the present ("But as for now . . . .").[27] There is, so to speak, a return yet to come.

On the level of the creature's internal constitution, the dynamic of return to the cause involves what Dionysius calls a desire, or love, for God.[28] Each kind of creature has its own particular form of this desire: "All things long for it [i.e., for the supra-essential being of God]. The intelligent and rational long for it by way of knowledge, the lower strata by way of perception, the remainder by way of the stirrings of being alive and in whatever fashion befits their condition."[29] The object or goal, however, is the same for all. Indeed, God is "the real object of all desire."[30] At the synchronic level, this means that creatures are always structured by their origin in God and their orientation to God. They are always turning in *erōs* to their source. But Dionysius's procession and return must also be read as diachronic. The result at this diachronic level is a story in which creatures arise from God, yearn for God throughout life, and return to God in consummation. God is the determining focal point at each moment of the story, "the creative source, middle, and end of all things."[31]

What this looks like for human creatures in particular becomes clearer in Dionysius's short *Mystical Theology* and his two works on sacred orders, *The Celestial Hierarchy*, which is the founding work of Christian systematic angelology, and *The Ecclesiastical Hierarchy*, which discusses the liturgy and the orders of believers and clergy. The goal of a hierarchy, Dionysius says, is "to enable beings to be as like [*aphomoiōsis*] as possible to God and to be at one with him."[32] This is "union" (*henōsis*) or "deification" (*theōsis*).[33] That this should be the goal accords with the procession–return structure of causality. In returning to its cause, the pagan Neo-Platonist Proclus writes, an effect desires to have communion [koinōnias] in [its cause] and be bound to it.[34] While he prefers the stronger language of union, Dionysius can also follow Proclus and cast return to God in terms of communion: the desire of intelligent beings is "a hunger for an unending, conceptual, and true communion [*koinōnias*] with the spotless and sublime light, of clear and splendid beauty."[35] But, Proclus continues, "all communion and conjunction ιο through likeness [*di' homoiotētos*]," and so "all reversion must be accomplished through likeness."[36] The Neo-Platonic account of causality thus gives Dionysius a logic to connect his reference to the "likeness" of God (Genesis 1:28) to the final end of return and union with God. Yearning for return to God is thus yearning to be like God so as to be in communion or, in Dionysius's predominant language, to be one with God.

A passing phrase in one of Dionysius's characteristic lists of divine roles suggests how the Dionysian pattern of procession and return might relate to the question of home. Explicating what it means for God to be cause of all, Dionysius relocates the Pauline eschatological "all in all" to the present. "He is 'all in all,' as scripture affirms," which means that God is "for all things the creator and originator, the One who brings them to completion, their preserver, their protector, *and their home* [*hestia*], the power which returns them to itself."[37] Since God as cause spans from beginning to end of created being, God is properly creatures' hearth and home. Thus, while Dionysian procession and return does not entail the undoing of creatures' creation, it does yield a vision of our ultimate home quite distinct from the worldly focus of SCT.

Marguerite Porete

Marguerite Porete presents a bold theological vision that pushes (or perhaps stretches) the logic of Dionysius to a stark conclusion: the annihilation of the creature in a "union of indistinction" with God.[38] Porete's *Mirror of Simple Souls* is among the great literary and theological achievements of the women's spiritual movement known as the beguines, which flourished in thirteenth- and fourteenth-century France, Germany, and the Low Countries. The beguines were (and, in small numbers, still are) lay women vowed to celibacy and a communal rule, who devoted themselves to contemplative spiritual life and service to others in community with one another.[39] Their relative independence from (male) ecclesiastical authority brought them under intense suspicion. Many, perhaps including Porete, were associated, rightly or wrongly, with the "heresy of the Free Spirit" that the Councils of Vienne in 1311 and 1312 condemned. Porete herself had been condemned and killed in Paris a year prior to the first of those councils.

Porete's theological story, like Dionysius's in its own way, begins "before" creation. In this moment, humans have a sort of pre-existence in the plenitude of God.[40] God is all, so humans as such are nothing. "You must not forget who you were when He first created you," Love tells the Soul.[41] At this pre-created point, humans are, insofar as they can be said to be at all, exclusively what they are in God. Then, with the act of creation proper, God gives a free will to humans. But (almost?) coincident with this gift is its misuse in sin, which is to will apart from God's will. In sinning, the creature separates itself from God, constituting itself as a paradoxical something that is not the (paradoxical?) nothing it was in union with the God who is all.[42] Mired in sin, humans are both something and, precisely as such, lost.

There are, in Porete's schema, two routes out of the mire. The first, lower path follows virtue toward an earthly paradise, which remains distinct from and less than God. The second, which is traveled only by an elite few but which is the only one that Porete cares about, leads back to the soul's primeval non-separation in God.[43] Porete gives a seven-stage account of this second path of the pious soul (six steps in this life and the final seventh in the next). It begins with intention to keep all of God's commandments and ascends by way of the soul's increasing love of God alone for God's own sake and diminishing self-involvement.[44] The aim in all of this is annihilation of the soul insofar as it is anything other than God, such that "she is what God is," just as was so "before she flowed from the Goodness of God."[45]

In a pivotal image, Porete compares the soul to a river that flows from the sea and returns to it:

> And therefore she loses her name in the One in whom she is melted and dissolved through Himself and in Himself. Thus she would be like a body of water which flows from the sea, which has some name, as one would be able to say Aisne or Seine or another river. And when this water or river returns into the sea, it loses its course and its name with which it flowed in many countries in accomplishing its task. Now it is in the sea where it rests, and thus has lost all labor. Likewise it is with this Soul.[46]

We do not call the water that flows from the Seine into the sea "Seine." Rather, the waters "have the name of *sea* because they are wholly sea as

soon as they have entered into the sea."[47] Michael Rea has argued that we
can plausibly read Porete not to be suggesting the undifferentiated absorption
of the soul into God.[48] There was at least one roughly contemporary understanding of mixture (Thomas Aquinas's) according to which the elements in
a mixture retain their own existence "virtually," which is to say according to
their proper power. We might think of the river and sea (and thus the soul and
God) in the same way. This strikes me as the wrong background. Saltwater
and freshwater are not distinct elements in Aristotelian physics. They are both
essentially water. And Aristotle agrees with the ancient consensus that the sea
occupies the natural place for water, from which all water comes and to which
it returns.[49] Thomas concurs.[50] Which is to say, it is at least as plausible to
suppose that Porete imagines river water as belonging in the sea and totally
dissoluble therein without any remnant of its particular riverine virtues.

Juan Marin has insightfully compared this passage from Porete with a
metaphor from Bernard of Clairvaux: a drop of water that *"seems* to disappear completely" when infused in a large amount of wine.[51] The water, in
Bernard's imagination, remains water.[52] It did not come from wine, so its
immersion in wine is not a return. Porete, in contrast, says multiple times
that the water "returns into the sea" as to its proper home[53] It is, and always
has been, properly of the same stuff as the sea. Real union with God, Porete
is saying, is a matter of being "dissolved by annihilation into that prior existence" one had in God "before" creation.[54]

The unmitigated character of this union is where Porete carries the logic of
God alone as the beginning and end of creatures beyond Dionysius. Elsewhere
we see that the *soul itself* is the mirror referenced in Porete's title. And it is
God who gazes into the mirror. It is not enough to eschew all other creatures
and find one's end in God. Rather, what true fulfillment requires is to abandon
even one's *own* createdness. It is not enough merely to *see* oneself only as
one is in God. Porete insists that one *be* only what one is in God, which is to
say, nothing that is not God. The acting agent of the beatific vision is not the
human being, not even the soul, but God: "This soul, thus pure and clarified,
sees neither God nor herself, but God sees Himself of Himself in her, for her,
without her. . . . . All is properly His own, and His own proper self."[55]

All this happens at the sixth, penultimate stage in Porete's schema. She
says relatively little about the seventh stage, the final, glorified state of the
annihilated soul. Indeed, she holds firmly to the position that we cannot
understand it, much less express it verbally, in this life.[56] That said, there are
good reasons to conclude that Porete imagines that final end of the soul to at
least match annihilation's level of absorption of the soul into God. For one
thing, Porete consistently belittles those souls who seek (and, her text suggests, will find) "a created paradise."[57] But since the soul itself is a creature,
any paradise that includes it as a creature distinct from God—even one in

which it beatifically gazed upon God and all else in God—must be a created paradise. For another, it is hard to imagine that after the six stages of the pious soul in this life push incessantly toward annihilation and a union of indistinction, Porete would mitigate that union. "The soul who has completed the journey has completed the cosmological pattern of *exitus* and *reditus*, coming from God and returning to Him, while still embodied on earth."[58] How much more so, then, when, as Porete puts it, "our soul has left our body"?[59] Rea has ably argued that we must read Porete's annihilation as neither a "union of indistinction" nor "ontological erasure."[60] What she has in mind is rather the state of being a creature with no "practical identity apart from God's."[61] It may be that he is correct. Even so, the logic of the river metaphor remains. The human's "natural place" is God. One's true home holds no place, not only for other creatures, but even for one's own self.

RECIPROCAL CHALLENGES

From even these brief and rather narrow discussions, it should be clear that Pseudo-Dionysius and Porete occupy theological terrain quite far afield from the home turf of SCT. The differences in perspective are so stark that it can be difficult to know where to begin a fruitful conversation. One avenue worth exploring is to let each perspective level a challenge to the other to clarify both the shape and stakes of disagreement.

Dionysius or Porete might, for instance, charge SCT and its various comrades with insufficient theocentrism, with effectively not treating God *as God*. The procession–return paradigm offers itself as a faithful theological elaboration of the confession of God as Alpha and Omega, the one from whom and to whom are all things. Does not the command to have no other gods than the LORD entail that God be the source and term of all our good? Does not the command to "love the LORD your God with all your heart, and with all your soul, and with all your might" entail something like Dionysian single-minded theological eros? To speak in the register of home, they might say that home is the site of rest. If, as Augustine prays, "you have made us for yourself, and our heart is restless until it rests in you," then would not all of our living be not rest but journey until we complete what that other great Christian Platonist Bonaventure called our mind's journey into God (*itinerarium mentis in Deum*—the accusative makes quite a difference!) and thus arrive home?[62]

On the other hand, advocates of SCT might propose that the procession–return paradigm can muster only a half-hearted affirmation of the goodness of creation. It seems in its limitedness, its definition and materiality, to appear first and foremost as something to be left behind. Moreover, might there be a tendency here toward effectively atomistic accounts of us creatures? Dionysius was a monk who thought in intricate detail about the ontological social structures of the cosmos and the church, and Porete belonged to a tightknit lay sisterhood. And yet there seems little to no place for those communities in their members' final ends. What resources do Dionysius and Porete have to say that they are anything other than waystations to be left behind on our journey to something infinitely better? Are we not knit together in one creation, and do we not belong with one another, not only for the time being but intrinsically?

I suspect each perspective could develop, or might even have ready to hand, thoughtful replies to these challenges. I am convinced that the theme of home is a vital one for the current cultural moment, at least in my home context. I am thus eager to see dialogue develop between these alternative views and to see respective theological interpretations of home put forward for consideration and mutual challenge and enrichment.

NOTES

1. Niels Henrik Gregersen, Bengt Kristensson Uggla, and Trygve Wyller, "Reconfiguring Reformation Theology: The Program of Scandinavian Creation Theology," in *Reformation Theology for a Post-Secular Age: Løgstrup, Prenter, Wingren, and the Future of Scandinavian Creation Theology*, ed. by Gregersen, Uggla, and Wyller (Bristol, CT: Vandenhoeck & Ruprecht, 2017), 14.

2. Gregersen, Uggla, and Wyller, "Reconfiguring Reformation Theology," 12.

3. See Bengt Kristensson Uggla, "Home and Creation Dynamics," and Jakob Wolf, "'At Home in the Universe'?" in this volume.

4. Gregersen, Uggla, and Wyller, "Reconfiguring Reformation Theology," 30.

5. See Miroslav Volf and Ryan McAnnally-Linz, *The Home of God: A Brief Story of Everything* (Grand Rapids, MI: Brazos, 2022).

6. Bonaventure, *Itinerarium mentis in Deum* 5.7, trans. Ewert Cousins, in *Bonaventure: The Soul's Journey into God, The Tree of Life, The Life of St. Francis* (New York: Paulist, 1978). The Latin is *finis ultimus [. . .] et consummatio*.

7. Calvin, *Institutes of the Christian Religion*, trans. Ford Lewis Battles (Louisville, KY: Westminster John Knox, 1960), 3.25.2. *Summum hominis bonum esse eius coniunctionem cum Deo.*

8. Nicholas of Cusa, *On the Summit of Contemplation* 22, trans. H. Lawrence Bond, in *Nicholas of Cusa: Selected Spiritual Writings* (New York: Paulist, 1997). Nicholas specifies that by *Posse* he means the Triune God in §28: "per posse ipsum deus trinus et unus . . . significatur." (*De apice theoriae / Die höchste Stufe der Betrachtung*, ed. Hans Gerhard Senger [Hamburg: Felix Meiner, 1986], 40–42.)

9. In *De Trinitate* 13.8, Augustine says that "all men want to be happy . . . yearn for other things simply for the sake of this one thing," echoing Aristotle's characterization of the final end as that which is desired for its own sake and for the sake of which

all else is desired (*Nichomachean Ethics* 1.1 1094a). (Augustine, *The Trinity*, trans. Edmund Hill, O.P. [Hyde Park, NY: New City Press, 1991].) Cf. *Confession* 10.20.29; *De Trinitate* 11.10; *City of God* 19.1. So also Thomas Aquinas, *Summa Theologiae* I-II, q. 1, a. 8: "man's last end is happiness *[ultimus finis hominum est beatitudo]*," trans. Friars of the English Dominican Province.

10. Aristotle, *Nichomachean Ethics* 1.7, 1097b, trans. W. D. Ross, rev. J. O. Urmson. Julia Annas discusses the function of happiness as "a thin specification of our final end" in ancient ethics in *The Morality of Happiness* (New York: Oxford University Press, 1993), 43–46.

11. One significant shift in modern thought is the decoupling of happiness from such theocentric formulations and its identification with a (mental or affective) state of the subject with no intrinsic reference to any particular source. See Ryan Darr, *The Best Effect: Theology and the Origins of Consequentialism* (Chicago: University of Chicago Press, 2023).

12. *De Trinitate* 1.18. I take the *plenum gaudium* in this passage to be synonymous with *beatitudo* elsewhere. Cf. *Confessions* 10.22.32: "This is the happy life [*beata vita*], and this alone: to rejoice [*gaudere*] in you, about you and because of you."

13. *ST* I.II, q. 1, a. 8; q. 3, a. 1; q. 3, a. 8.

14. John Calvin, *Institutes of the Christian Religion* 3.9.4, trans. Ford Lewis Battle (Louisville, KY: Westminster John Knox, 1960).

15. See Thomas's *Commentary on the Sentences*, bk. 1, dist. 2, q. 1: "For which reason, in the first part, he [i.e., Peter Lombard, the author of the *Sentences*] defines divine things according to their coming forth from their principle; in the second, according to their return to their end." (*Unde in prima parte determinat de rebus divinis secundum* exitum *a principio; in secunda secundum* reditum *in finem*.) The terminology of an *exitus–reditus* theological schema became popular after Marie-Dominique Chenu used it to describe the structure of Thomas's *Summa Theologiae* (M. D. Chenu, "The Plan of St. Thomas' Summa Theologiae," trans. Ellen Bremner, *CrossCurrents* 2 [1952]: 67–79).

16. The author whose texts bear the name of Dionysius, the Athenian who, as Acts 17 tells it, converted upon hearing Paul's sermon in front of the of the Areopagus, wrote in the late-fifth or early-sixth century somewhere in the Eastern Roman Empire. For brevity's sake, I will refer to the author simply as Dionysius.

17. Pseudo-Dionysius, *The Divine Names* 1.4 (PG 593A), in *Pseudo-Dionysius: The Complete Works*, trans. Colm Luibheid and Paul Rorem (Mawah, NJ: Paulist, 1987). Subsequent citations given as DN followed by chapter and paragraph numbers, with reference in parentheses to the column number in Jacques-Paul Migne's *Patrologia Graeca*, vol. 3, which also allows reference to the critical edition, *Corpus Dionysiacum*, ed. Beate R. Suchla (Berlin: De Gruyter, 1990–91).

18. Pseudo-Dionysius, *DN* 1.5 (PG 593C).

19. Pseudo-Dionysius, *DN* 1.7 (PG 596C), emphasis added.

20. E.g., Pseudo-Dionysius, *DN* 4.10 (PG 705C).

21. Pseudo-Dionysius, *DN* 5.10 (PG 825B). On the Aristotelian account of causality it follows from God being cause that God is source because "all causes are sources" (*Metaphysics* V.1, 1013a).

22. See, e.g., Aristotle, *Metaphysics* V.2, 1013a; *Eudemian Ethics* II.11, 1227b; *Physics* II.3, 194b.

23. When Dionysius says that all *archai*, "whether exemplary, final, efficient, formal, or elemental," exist "for the sake of," "because," and "in" the Beautiful and the Good, he is identifying God as the transcendent ground of the fivefold elaboration of causality found in Seneca (adding "exemplary" to Aristotle's four), while leaving off the "instrumental" cause found in Proclus, and also substituting in "elemental" for the more common "material." Note that Dionysius speaks here of "final source" (*archē . . . telikē*). See Carlos Steel, "Why Should We Prefer Plato's *Timaeus* to Aristotle's *Physics*? Proclus' Critique of Aristotle's Causal Explanation of the Physical World," *Bulletin of the Institute of Classical Studies, Supplement* 78 (2003): 175–87.

24. Proclus, *The Elements of Theology* §35, ed. and trans. E. R. Dodd, 2nd ed. (Oxford, UK: Clarendon, 1963). Cf. Dodd's notes, as well as Stephen Gersh, *From Iamblichus to Eriugena: An Investigation of the Prehistory and Evolution of the Pseudo-Dionysian Tradition* (Leiden, Netherlands: Brill, 1978), 45–47, 217–229.

25. Dionysius tends not to make creatures the active subjects of their return to God. He speaks rather of God returning all things to God (e.g., *DN* 4.4 [PG 700A], 10.1 [PG 937A]) or uses the passive voice and says that all things *are returned* to God (e.g., *DN* 4.4 [PG 700B], 4.10 [PG 705D], 13.3 [PG 980C]). Presumably this is the theological passive.

26. I am grateful to Ross McCullough for underscoring the importance of this point and resisting my tendency to occlude the primary synchronic sense.

27. Pseudo-Dionysius, *DN* 1.4 (PG 592B–C).

28. "All things must desire, must yearn for, must love, the Beautiful and the Good." *DN* 4.10 (PG 708A). More literally translated, "The Beautiful and the Good is [the verb is singular] to all things desired [*epheton*], yearned for [*ereton*], and loved [*agapeton*]." The first two of these three terms, *ephesis* and *erōs* belong to the pagan philosophical tradition. *Ephesis* means originally the act of throwing something, and it came to be a technical legal term indicating an appeal to a different legal body (see Aristotle, *Constitution of Athens* 45), but Aristotle uses it for the intentional object of emotions (*Rhetoric* II.4, 1382a), and it is common in Plotinus and subsequent Neo-Platonists. *Erōs* receives its seminal philosophical treatment in Plato's *Symposium*. *Agapē*, in contrast, appears frequently in the Bible.

29. Pseudo-Dionysius, *DN* 1.5 (PG 593D). This point is repeated, with much of the same language, in *DN* 4.4 (PG 700B).

30. *To ontōs epheton*. *Celestial Hierarchy* 2.4 (PG 144B), trans. Colm Luibheid and Paul Rorem, in *Pseudo-Dionysius: The Complete Works*.

31. Pseudo-Dionysius, *DN* 5.8 (PG 824A).

32. Pseudo-Dionysius, *Celestial Hierarchy* 3.2 (PG 165A). He uses the exact same wording in *Ecclesiastical Hierarchy* 2.1.1 (PG 392A).

33. For use of the two in conjunction, see for instance, Pseudo-Dionysius, *Ecclesiastical Hierarchy* 1.2 (PG 373A), trans. Colm Luibheid and Paul Rorem, in *Pseudo-Dionysius: The Complete Works*. Elsewhere (*Ecclesiastical Hierarchy* 1.3 [PG 373D]), he says that union is one facet of deification.

34. Proclus, *Elements of Theology* §32.

35. Pseudo-Dionysius, *Celestial Hierarchy* 2.4.

36. Proclus, *Elements of Theology* §32.

37. Pseudo-Dionysius, *DN* 1.7 (PG 596C), emphasis added.

38. Joanne Maguire Robinson, *Nobility and Annihilation in Marguerite Porete's* Mirror of Simple Souls (Albany, NY: State University of New York Press, 2001), 79.

39. For a brief overview with references to further reading, see Helen J. Swift, "Beguines," in *Women and Gender in Medieval Europe: An Encyclopedia*, ed. Margaret Schaus (New York: Routledge, 2006).

40. Scholars, including Robinson, sometimes borrow Meister Eckhart's language of a "virtual existence" (*esse virtuale*) of creatures in God to describe Porete's view. On this idea in Eckhart, see Edmund Colledge and Bernard McGinn, "Introduction," in *Meister Eckhart: The Essential Sermons, Commentaries, Treatises, and Defense* (Mahwah, NJ: Paulist, 1981), 40–41. There are significant continuities here with the idea of the divine ideas as the exemplary cause of creatures in Christian Platonists like Bonaventure and ultimately with the whole set of traditions stemming from Plato's doctrine of the forms. See Junius Johnson, "The One and the Many in Bonavanture: Exemplarity Explained," *Religions* 7 (2016).

41. Marguerite Porete, *The Mirror of Simple Souls*, trans. Ellen L. Babinsky (Mahwah, NJ: Paulist, 1993), chap. 34.

42. Robinson, *Nobility and Annihilation*, 67.

43. It is telling that Christ's highest significance, for Porete, is that he totally gave over his will to God the Father. Porete, *Mirror*, ch. 109.

44. Porete quite clearly thinks that only relatively few souls are actually able to follow this path. Many more will be saved within the world that is separated from God and receive a merely created paradise. (She says relatively little about damnation, except to insist that the soul that has ceased to will cares neither for paradise nor reprobation.) Robinson argues that this elitism is at the heart of Porete's vision and traces the image of a hereditary nobility of soul through the *Mirror*. See Robinson, *Nobility and Annihilation*. For our purposes, the important point is that the story that Porete cares about is that of the pious souls who are annihilated.

45. Porete, *Mirror*, ch. 135. Porete's text is complex, and there are points where it might be taken to resist the reading I am offering. She suggests, for example, that there might still be a difference of "natures" between God and the soul after the "transformation by Love" leaves "no difference" between them (Porete, *Mirror*, ch. 23.) She also speaks regularly of God dwelling in the soul, not merely of the soul dwelling in God. My claim is that the accent in her theological story is on the soul's return into God from whom it came.

46. Porete, *Mirror*, chap. 82.

47. Porete, *Mirror*, chap. 83.

48. Michael Rea, "Self-annihilation in Marguerite Porete," *Religious Studies* (2023): 6. [doi:10.1017/S0034412523000094]

49. Aristotle, *Meteorology* 2.2.

50. Thomas Aquinas, *Commentary on Aristotle's Meteorology* 2.2.

51. Juan Marin, "Annihilation and Deification in Beguine Theology and Marguerite Porete's *Mirror of Simple Souls*," *Harvard Theological Review* 103 (2010): 100–1; the quotation is from Bernard of Clairvaux, *On Loving God* 10.28.

52. Rea argues that Aristotelian physics (again, taken to be a reasonable supposition as to Porete's rough views) would hold wine to be just a mixture of water with other elements, just as seawater is, such that wine–water and seawater–fresh water are functionally equivalent analogies. Against this reading stands a point that Ross McCullough has pointed out to me: Bernard's image is liturgical, and when the priest adds water to the wine before consecration, his prayer references the incarnation, wherein there is mingling without mixing or dissolution, a distinct humanity preserved throughout. That is to say, Bernard has theological reasons to insist that the water stays water and the wine remains wine. Unless it can be shown that Porete has similar exogenous theological reasons with regard to the river metaphor, there is no reason to assume that her reasoning follows Bernard's.

53. Porete, *Mirror*, chap. 83.

54. Porete, *Mirror*, chap. 137.

55. Porete, *Mirror*, chap. 118, emphasis added.

56. Porete, *Mirror*, chap. 118.

57. Porete, *Mirror*, chap. 69.

58. Robinson, *Nobility and Annihilation*, 84.

59. Porete, *Mirror*, chap. 118.

60. Rea, "Self-annihilation," 3.

61. Rea, "Self-annihilation," 7.

62. Augustine, *Confessions* 1.1.1, trans. Henry Chadwick (Oxford, UK: Oxford University Press, 1992), 1.

Chapter 4

Pilgrim's Homecoming

Svein Aage Christoffersen

In the following, I will focus on three life metaphors conveying a basic understanding of what life is all about. These metaphors are life as pilgrimage, life as homecoming, and life as dwelling. The link between these metaphors is of course the word "home," explicit in the second metaphor and implicit in the other two.

PILGRIMAGE AS A METAPHOR

Pilgrimage or "the sacred journey" is known in ancient Christianity from the second century onwards and played a significant role in religious life in the Middle Ages. The motives for these journeys, individually and collectively, were of a different kind. Christian pilgrimage was and still is a multifarious phenomenon and may be difficult to define. A relevant definition becomes even more difficult when we take into account that "sacred travelers" were a widespread phenomenon in Graeco-Roman antiquity as well, long before the birth of Christianity. No wonder scholars of ancient religion have been resistant to using "pilgrimage" as an all-encompassing term for a "sacred journey" regardless of religious context.[1]

Jay Elsner is well aware of the problem in his introduction to *Pilgrimage in Graeco-Roman Antiquity and Early Christianity*. He still wants to use the term, but basically in line with Alain Morinis' minimalist definition: "Pilgrimage is a journey undertaken by a person in quest of a place or state that he or she believes to embody a sacred ideal." Elsner suggests that we add "or a group" to Morinis' "person," in order to avoid too strong an emphasis on the individual. A pilgrimage may be undertaken both as a group and as an individual. A notable point is that Morinis' definition avoids any mentioning of motives or reasons for the journey.[2]

The reference for "pilgrimage" understood as a metaphor for "spiritual journey" is of course the physical pilgrimage to sacred places like Jerusalem, Rome and Santiago de Compostela. However, the metaphor is not just invoking these physical pilgrimages in order to say something spiritual about life in general. The metaphor is also an interpretation of the physical pilgrimages, pointing to the essence of these journeys to sacred places in this world. The ultimate goal is the heavenly home, and the physical journey is a way of processing the soul's rebirth. The physical pilgrimage is eschatological, transcending this world. This understanding of man as *Homo Viator* "conjures up an image of a man on a journey through terrestrial life as an exile, estranged from the world, headed towards the final destination of a heavenly home."[3]

Although the Middle Ages was the age of glory of the pilgrimage, and the Protestant criticism of pilgrimage was massive, the metaphor still lived on after the Reformation. The understanding of life as a pilgrimage and man as *Homo Viator* has left its mark on protestant Christianity as well, especially in devotional literature. A paradigm for *Homo Viator* in Protestantism is John Bunyan's *Pilgrim's Progress* (1648). Presented as a dream or a vision, Bunyan tells the story about Christian and his journey through temptations and tribulations in this world towards his hometown in the world to come. This spiritual pilgrimage is eschatological, transcending this world. It is a story about the transformation and rebirth of the soul into another world.

ODYSSEUS' PILGRIMAGE

However, as the French philosopher Pierre Hadot has pointed out in his article "The Genius of Place in Ancient Greece," there is also another reference for the understanding of life as pilgrimage:

> The first sacred place in Antiquity is the "home," that is to say, the hearth of the house; not the fire of the kitchen, but the sacred altar where the fire consecrated to the gods smoulders continuously. This is where the goddess Hestia is present, 'seated at the center of the house' as the *Homeric Hymn to Aphrodite* says. The hearth is thus in some way rootedness in the earth, which is itself Hestia, the immobile center of the Universe. But the hearth is also the point of contact with the higher gods, the point from whence the smoke of the incense or the sacrifices rises. Hestia is, nevertheless, not solely the figure of the earth, but the figure of the women who remains by the hearth, whereas the man will work outside. Our civilization has perhaps been profoundly marked by the poem, *The Odyssey*, which describes the pilgrimage of the exiled man who strives to come back to

the hearth where the women whom he loves awaits him: return to the native land, which is at base a return to oneself.[4]

The Odyssey is a story about an exiled man who quite literally is on his way home. However, home is not just a random place where Odysseus happened to live in a distant past. Home is a sacred place and life as it ought to be. If we stick to Morinis' definition, Hadot is right in defining Odysseus' journey as a pilgrimage.

Odysseus' pilgrimage also included physical journeys to sacred places in this world as a context. In antiquity, people traveled to Delphi, Delos, Eleusis, and Ephesus in order to worship the gods and find solutions to a wide range of problems ranging from health to wealth. The visit to these sacred places may also and especially in Eleusis have brought with it an "out of this world" or "otherworldly" experience, but it would not be relevant to refer to these journeys as eschatological pilgrimages. Their goal was not in a world to come, but in this world here and now.

The home of Odysseus is entirely within this world, physically as well as metaphorically. As a metaphor, "home" is the essential, authentic way of being human, of being oneself as a human being. The paradigm presupposes that this way of being human is lost. For this reason, life is a pilgrimage back to an authentic way of being human, which at the same time is a rootedness in the earth and a life in contact with the higher gods. While a Christian's pilgrimage is a rebirth, Odysseus' pilgrimage is a return. This return has religious connotations, but its ultimate goal is not eschatological, it is a confirmation of what life in this world ought to be.

According to Hadot, our civilization has been profoundly marked by Odysseus' paradigm. A main reason for this is the paradigm's plasticity. The paradigm can be molded; it can be twisted and turned in a variety of different ways and conveys no definitive answer to the meaning of life. The paradigm is open-ended. It just invites you to a restless search for the true *telos* and meaning of life.

A MODERN ODYSSEY

One—among many—interesting examples of how *The Odyssey* can be used as such a paradigm in modern times can be found in the Swedish Nobel Prize-winner Eyvind Johnson's book *Return to Ithaka*. The subtitle of the Swedish edition is very telling: "A Novel about the Present."[5]

The book was published in 1946, a year after World War II ended. Odysseus is the pilgrim, *Homo Viator*, but he is not primarily a wanderer. He is more of a sailor who is tossed around on a wild and unpredictable sea by forces he cannot fathom. He is exposed both to dangers and to temptations, but in the end the pilgrim comes home. However, life at home is not life as it should be. Odysseus comes back to a home filled with conflict on the brink of collapse. Courters who would prefer to see Odysseus dead surround his wife Penelope. Odysseus must kill them in order to win back his home. Thus, he has brought the violence of war home with him. He is a marked man, affected in mind and body by the war. The present is not "home" in a qualitative sense. It is not a holy place where one can just be. «Home» must be recreated after the ravages of war and evil in The Trojan War and World War II. Can it be done without violence? The pacifist Eyvind Johnson leaves us with the question. The return of Odysseus is a mixed blessing.

Another Nobel Prize winner who was preoccupied with wandering as a life metaphor was the Norwegian Knut Hamsun. The figure of the wanderer is a constant presence in his writing. In the books that are called novels of wandering, wayfaring or wandering has become a metaphor for life. Life is wandering, and the individual is a wanderer. This wandering, however, does not have a goal. The vagabond is not a pilgrim.[6]

In contrast with the vagabond in Hamsun's writing is the farmer. The farmer is the earthbound person who lives in a pact with nature and who cultivates it. It was the depiction of the earthbound person in his monumental *Growth of the Soil (Markens Grøde)* that won Hamsun the Nobel Prize in 1925. Here living and taking root in the earth becomes a metaphor for what it means to be human. Humans belong on earth.[7]

TO BE AT HOME IN THIS WORLD

Indeed, Martin Heidegger's enthusiastic appreciation of Hamsun applied to Hamsun's depiction of being close to the earth, to the landscape, to the instincts and to the elementary. Heidegger regarded Hamsun as a philosopher without philosophy getting in the way of art.[8] Even though Heidegger did not see himself as a pilgrim, his philosophy can be interpreted as a lifelong struggle to come to terms with life in this world, understood as a journey back to an authentic, genuine way of being at home in the world.

In Heidegger's philosophy, there is no heavenly home. We are earthlings who have lost sight of our homeland in this world. Exiled, like Odysseus, we are lost in the wilderness, struggling to find our way home. Or even worse, we have forgotten what it is to have a home, what it is to be at home in the world, and we have forgotten that there is a way home.

The reason for this catastrophic oblivion is complicated, according to Heidegger, but it stems, among other things, from Plato and not least, Christianity. Christianity has emphasized life in the world to come at the cost of life in this world and drained away its meaning. Creation theology is, in Heidegger's mind, a metaphysical veil burying the truth of things in this world in complete darkness.

Heidegger's ideas concerning home and homeland had a nationalistic bent with an anti-Semitic edge, and in the 1930s his pilgrimage resulted in a pronounced political output when he joined the Nazi Party (NSDAP). In Heidegger's view, modernity had rendered man rootless. Modern man had lost contact with the origins of life and become esranged and alienated from earth, soil, place, the native, and people. Modernity had rendered most people homeless, anemic, and utilitarian. In the eyes of Heidegger, the Jews were the ultimate representation of moderniy and obstacles in his philosophyical pilgrimage toward an authentic homeland. Heidegger was not anit-Semitic for opportunistic reasons; he was a convined anti-Semite.[9]

After the war, Heidegger did not show any sign of remorse for his anti-Semitic behavior and statements in the 1930s. Instead, he made efforts to throw a veil of oblivion over his former political *raptus*. He redirected his pilgrimage in a more "spiritual" direction, toward a change of mentality that would make it possible to live on this earth according to the earth's inherent truth. "Dwelling"—"wohnen"—is a basic metaphor for what an authentic way or mode of being in the world is now as in his "Letter on Humanism" and his essay "Bauen, Wohnen, Denken"—"Building, Dwelling, Thinking."

In the ruins after World War II, a shortage of housing was an urgent problem in Germany. A great number of homes and houses lay in ruins. However, the basic question according to Heidegger was not how to get a home, but how to understand what it is to be at home in this world. And to be at home in this world is, in accordance with Hölderlin, to dwell poetically on this eart— "dichterisch wohnet der Mensch auf dieser Erde."[10]

Diana Aurenque, in her article about Heidegger's understanding of man's dwelling, states that "dwelling poetically ultimately means sensitive attention to things. This dwelling is a stance 'in the presence of the divinities,' a stance of solemnity 'towards the nearness of things' essence.'"[11] It is only by dwelling poetically man can be brought to accord with his own essence. Aurenque also points out that dwelling poetically receives prominence in poetic speech.[12]

Hence, "To dwell poetically" means to feel at home in and to make peace with this world as it in truth is. "To dwell poetically" means to live and die reconciled to this world. Is Heidegger's dwelling a return or a rebirth? I think it is both. What is needed in order to dwell poetically is a transformation of the soul as a return to man's own poetic essence.[13]

Does dwelling imply any kind of ethics? The ethics of Heidegger is a disputed theme. Heidegger himself denied that his ontology implied any normative ambitions. He did not want to prescribe how people ought to live.

However, there is an unmistakable smell of normativity in Heidegger's dwelling. Being-in-the world as dwelling is the ultimate goal for human existence. It is a life in accordance with the truth, and truth has a normative status. This ethos, on the other hand, has nothing to do with ethics and morality in the traditional sense. "To dwell poetically, one has to forfeit the very domain of the moral, a domain in which good and evil have already been decided upon."[14]

ON CARE FOR OUR COMMON HOME

A more recent text where "home" is a key metaphor is Pope Francis' encyclical letter *Laudato Si.*[15] This encyclical is of course a most remarkable document in many respects. It is not just the first encyclical devoted entirely to the climate crisis and ecological questions. It is also an encyclical in which environmental, political, economic and cultural perspectives are woven together in what the Pope himself calls an "integral ecology."[16] There is a harsh critique of capitalism in this encyclical, and there are obvious links to liberation theology in the way the Pope takes sides with the poor against the rich.

Usually, an encyclical is addressed to all men of good will. This address is found a couple of times in *Laudato Si* as well.[17] However, the main address is "all people" and "every person living on this planet"[18]—for the simple reason that environmental deterioration affects everyone. We are all in the same boat, regardless of good or bad will.

However, perhaps the most remarkable thing in this encyclical is the language, which deviates from encyclical traditions. Paul Lynch has called the Pope's language in *Laudato Si* non-modern, as far as it transgresses the modern borders between the language of religion, science and politics.[19] This transgression is not just accidental, but a deliberate choice in *Laudato Si.* It is the Pope's deepest conviction that we have to transcend the language of mathematics and biology and technology and finance if we are to handle today's climate crisis. We need a language that takes us to the heart of what it is to be human, and in this regard, Franz of Assisi has been an inspiration and a guiding star for the Pope.

Non-modern does not mean pre-modern. The Pope's language is modern, but it is not the language of theological and philosophical dissertations. It is the language of literature, novels and poems. His language is poetic, loaded with metaphors, and perhaps the most important metaphor is in the subtitle: "On care for our common home." The world we live in, the planet we live on, is called our home. And in the first paragraph, this home is called both our sister and our mother.

When this planet—*Tellus, Gaia, Mother Earth*—is referred to as "our home," this is, as we have seen already, at odds with a more traditional way of speaking in a Christian context. Of course, Christians too have to live on this planet like everybody else and have to find a home on this planet. However, according to traditional language, our home on this planet is just temporary. Our true home is in heaven. According to the pilgrimage paradigm, the heavenly Jerusalem is our home, and life in this world is a pilgrimage towards our heavenly home. We ought to be pilgrims, heading for the heavenly Jerusalem.

At first glance, the understanding of life on this planet as a pilgrimage is not a basic metaphor in *Laudato Si.* It occurs just once. However, this occurrence is significant:

> Everything is related, and we human beings are united as brothers and sisters on a wonderful pilgrimage, woven together by the love God has for each of his creatures and which also unites us in fond affection with brother sun, sister moon, brother river and Mother Earth.[20]

This pilgrimage is not the soul's rebirth into another world. Nor is it Odysseus' struggle to return to Ithaka. On the contrary, The Pope's pilgrimage seems to be a wonderful journey, uniting all human beings as brothers and sisters, together with the whole universe. It is the Pilgrim's happy homecoming. The individualism usually connected to the pilgrimage paradigm is gone. Pilgrimage is a collective journey.

If we consider the context more closely, a less joyful background comes to the fore. In practice, we are not united. We tolerate some people considering themselves more worthy than others and more human than others, as if they were born with greater rights.[21] Hence, our concern for the environment needs to be joined to a sincere love for our fellow human beings and an unwavering commitment to resolving the problems of society: A sense of deep communion with the rest of nature cannot be real if our hearts lack tenderness, compassion and concern for our fellow human beings.[22]

The pilgrimage as a collective enterprise presupposes a tender heart, a new mentality, a conversion of the hearth in order to return to deep communion with our fellow human beings and the rest of nature. However, this mentality is not an eschatological rebirth, but a return to an authentic, genuine, simple way of life, life as it ought to be on this planet.

The Pope's pilgrimage toward "home" is more in accordance with Odysseus' pilgrimage and Heidegger's "dwelling" than with the eschatological perspective in Bunyan's pilgrimage towards the heavenly Jerusalem. The Pope and Heidegger are sharing the desire for a simple life, the wish to be reconciled with Mother Earth and the harsh critique of modern technology, utilitarianism and reductionism. There is also an interesting affinity between the Pope and Heidegger in their deliberate use of poetical language in order to come "home."

That the Pope can refer to life in this world in a way that has connecting links both to Odysseus' homecoming in Eyvind Johnson and to Hamsun's and Heidegger's "poetic dwelling" can be accredited to Creation theology. The Pope sees Creation theology as the basis for the church's view on ecology and the climate crisis. Creation theology accounts for the idea of the pilgrim receding into the background in favor of seeing this world as our common ground. This does not of course mean that the Pope has written off the heavenly goal for our wanderings here on earth. The heavenly home is common ground for Pope Francis as for all of his predecessors on the Papal seat. The point is that creation theology prevents eschatology from emptying this world of its immanent value and meaning, as Heidegger and many others have accused Christianity of.

The Pope's creation theology is, on the other hand, also the basis for his disagreement with Heidegger regarding ethics. The Pope's pilgrimage is loaded with ethical concerns that are absent in Heidegger's pilgrimage. The "homecoming" is not just a return; it is also a social reconstruction, and from this point of view, the Pope has more in common with Eyvind Johnson than with Heidegger. However, unlike both Johnson and Heidegger, the Pope's "homecoming" is based on the belief that world and universe belong to God, and not to us. In order to return home, we have to rebuild it in accordance with the will of God.

The tension between return and rebuild in *Laudato Si* is interesting. The Pope's aim is to restore Mother Earth to her former glory and to make us see and recognize how beautiful and wonderful Mother Earth still is. The keywords in this attempt are "beauty" and "beautiful," The world's beauty testifies to its unchangeable goodness.[23] In the view of these paragraphs, the Pope seems to be longing for a return to a Paradise lost where life is in a social and ecological equilibrium, and different forms of life are in a beautiful balance.

However, according to modern evolutionary biology, life has never been in balance. Life is change, life is evolution, and the driver in this evolution is a battle for food and reproductive opportunities. One species gains life opportunities at the cost of others. One species wins, another loses. One man's meat is another man's poison. Eat or be eaten. Extinction is a basic principle in evolution history, and this has nothing to do with man's sin or reckless way of life. It is just life.

Man is no doubt deeply responsible for some of today's disastrous climate changes, but climate changes as such are not a man-made phenomenon. There have always been and will always be climate changes. Today's changes are threatening to our way of life and perhaps life on this earth as we know it. However, Mother Earth could not care less. Forms of life today stem from yesterday's climate crisis, and today's climate crisis will create new forms of life tomorrow. We will always have to face climate changes and fight against them, man-made or not.

SCANDINAVIAN CREATION THEOLOGY AND THE PILGRIMAGE PARADIGM

In Scandinavian Creation Theology, K. E. Løgstrup and Ole Jensen have explicitly dismissed pilgrimage as a tenable paradigm for Christian life. According to K. E. Løgstrup, the pilgrimage paradigm has drained life in this world of meaning and thus contributed to modern secularization. Thus far, Løgstrup is in line with Heidegger. However, contrary to Heidegger and in accordance with the Pope, Løgstrup does not see Creation theology as the problem, but as the solution.

Løgstrup studied in Germany in the first half of the 1930s. He went to Heidegger's lectures, and he was blown away by Heidegger's philosophical approach. Løgstrup subscribed to Heidegger's understanding of man's existence as "Geworfenheit"—we are "thrown" into the world. However, "being thrown" meant according to Løgstrup, that we are thrown into a battle between good and evil. Life is a battle between forces of life and forces of death. There are no spectators in this battle. All and everyone are part of the battle from the very beginning and have to choose sides and be committed in one way or the other. The conflict between forces of life and forces of death is not a secondary addition brought into the world by man. We are thrown into a world that is morally qualified with an ethical demand to fight against evil, death and destruction. This is the essence of Løgstrup's Theology of Creation in the 1930s. The world is God's creation, it belongs to God, and our obligation is to take care of and protect the life God has put in our hands. This obligation is the ethical demand, given in and through our interpersonal life.[24]

In the 1950s and 1960s, Løgstrup develops his Theology of Creation as ontological ethics and ethical phenomenology. He explores how the ethical demand is deeply rooted in the givenness of life and how life is sustained and renewed again and again without our awareness through sovereign expressions of life like trust, mercy, and the openness of speech.[25]

Then, in his late metaphysics in the 1970s, Løgstrup becomes increasingly preoccupied with ecocritical perspectives. Linking to his works in the 1930s Løgstrup criticizes the modern understanding of man as standing outside and above the world as spectator and manipulator. The universe is not our surroundings, it is our origin. Due to our corporeal existence and our metabolism, we are intertwined with the universe. Vitality and zest for life are received both physically and mentally through sensory impressions of color, sound, sight, physical touch etc.[26]

However, at the same time Løgstrup also takes into account destruction and the existence of evil in nature as well. The Universe, Mother Earth is both good and bad, both merciful and cruel, life sustaining and life destroying. Mother Earth creates, and she annihilates. Death is an integrated part of the created world and cannot be explained away by man's sin.[27]

From this point of view, the ethical demand is not just a demand to combat sin and the consequences of sin, but to combat death, destruction, and cruelty in the created world at large. Human life, ethics, culture in its essence, is a revolt against death and destruction, both in society and nature. This revolt is inscribed in our very being. We are born to revolt.[28] There is no final reconciliation with Mother Earth in this life, according to Løgstrup. The revolt against death and destruction is not a return to a lost harmony, but it is always progressive. Life is neither "dwelling" nor longing for a paradise lost.

Sustained by the creative forces of life we are engaged in a lifelong struggle against evil, destruction and death. From one point of view, this revolt seems to be in vain. Death always wins in the end. We all have to die. However, Christianity proclaims that in the resurrection of Jesus Christ, God has anticipated a kingdom to come where death and destruction exist no more. It is in this eschatological perspective Christians revolt against all kinds of destructive forces. We have a home in the world to come, but this does not make life in this world less valuable. On the contrary. Eschatological hope makes life in this world even more meaningful.

NOTES

1. Jas Elsner and Ian Rutherford (eds.), *Pilgrimage in Graeco-Roman and Early Christian Antiquity: Seeing the Gods* (Oxford, UK: Oxford University Press, 2007), 2.

2. Elsner, *Pilgrimage*, 2.

3. Marco Galli, "Pilgrimage as Elite Habitus: Educated Pilgrims in Sacred Landscape During the Second Sophistic." In Elsner, Pilgrimage, 275. Cf. Gerhart B. Ladner, "Homo Viator: Medieval Ideas on Alienation and Order," *Speculum* 42 (1967), 233–59.

4. Pierre Hadot, "The Genius of Place in Ancient Greece." In *The Selected Writings of Pierre Hadot. Philosophy as Practice* (London: Bloomsbury Academic, 2020), 177.

5. Eyvind Johnson, *Strändernas svall. En roman om det närvarande* (Bonniers, 2004/1946). Cf. Eyvind Johnson, *Return to Ithaca* (London: Thames and Hudson, 1952).

6. Knut Hamsun, *Under Høststjærnen* (Gyldendal, 2011/1907). *En Vandrer spiller med Sordin* (Gyldendal, 2011/1909). *Den sidste Glæde* (Gyldendal, 2011/1912). Cf. Knut Hamsun, *Wanderers* (White Fish, MT: Kessinger Publishers, 2004).

7. Knut Hamsun, *Markens Grøde* (Gyldendal, 2009/2017). Cf. Knut Hamsun, *Growth of the Soil* (New York: Penguin Classics, 2007).

8. Hannah Arendt and Martin Heidegger, *Briefe 1925 bis 1975 und andere Zeugnisse* (Frankfurt am Main: Klostermann RotheReihe, 2013), 62.

9. Svein Aage Christoffersen, "The Beginning: K.E. Løgstrup's Metaphysics of Existence in the 1930s." In Marius Timman Mjaaland, *The Reformation of Philosophy* (Tubingen, Mermany: Mohr Siebeck 2020), 184.

10. Martin Heidegger, *Wegmarken* (Frankfurt am Main: Vittorio Klostermann, 1967), 189.

11. Diana Aurenque, "Heidegger on Thinking about Ethos and Man's Dwelling," *Architecture Philosophy*, Vol. 2, No. 1 (2016), 42.

12. Aurenque, "Heidegger," 47.

13. Aurenque, "Heidegger," 42.

14. Aurenque, "Heidegger," 48.

15. *Encyclical letter Laudato Si' of the Holy Father Francis on Care for our Common Home:* https://www.vatican.va/content/francesco/en/encyclicals/documents/papa-francesco_20150524_enciclica-laudato-si.html.

16. Laudato Si,' 10.

17. Laudato Si,' 4; 45.

18. Laudato Si,' 4.

19. Paul Lynch, "On Care for Our Common Discourse: Pope Francis's Nonmodern Epideictic," *Rhetoric Society Quarterly*, Vol. 47, November 5 (2017) 463–82.

20. Laudato Si,' 68.

21. Laudati Si,' 67.

22. Laudato Si,' 67.

23. Laudato Si, e.g., 11, 57, 157.

24. Christoffersen, "The Beginning."

25. K. E. Løgstrup, *The Ethical Demand*, translation and Introduction by Robert Stern and Bjørn Rabjerg (Oxford, UK: Oxford University Press, 2020). K. E. Løgstrup, *Beyond the Ethical Demand*, Introduction by Kees van Kooten Niekerk (Notre Dame, IN: University of Notre Dame, Press, 2007). Robert Fink, *The Radical Demand in Løgstrup's Ethics* (Oxford, UK: Oxford University Press, 2019). Svein Aage Christoffersen, "The Ethical Demand and Its Ontological Presuppositions." In Hans Fink and Robert Stern (eds), *What Is Ethically Demanded? K.E. Løgstrups Philosophy of Moral Life* (Notre Dame, IN: University of Notre Dame Press, 2017).

26. K. E. Løgstrup, *Ophav og Omgivelse. Metafysik III. Betragtninger over Historie og Natur* (Denmark: Klim Forlag, 2013), 11–20.

27. K. E. Løgstrup, *Skabelse og Tilintegørelse. Metafysik IV. Religionsfilosofiske Betragtninger* (Denmark: Klim Forlag, 2015), 295–96.

28. Løgstrup, *Skabelse*, 57.

PART II

Homes, Bodies, and Society

Chapter 5

The Body as Home and Horizon

Allen G. Jorgenson

In the midst of this volume with its focus on the phenomenon of the home, I want to insert the question of the body. How are we to relate these two words? On the one hand, in English, a homebody is someone who doesn't want to leave home, a place of comfort and solace. On the other hand, we hear Paul proclaim that "even though we know that while we are at home in the body we are away from the Lord." (2 Cor. 5:6) He seems to draw on a Hellenistic discontent with the body—to be endured until we finally receive the post- resurrection house to which the pre-resurrection tent pales in comparison. Home is off in the distance, at the horizon of our existence. In what follows, I want to propose that the body can serve as both home and horizon, and as such might inform other iterations of the phenomenon of home.

TURNING TO THE BODY

The loosely associated work of those theologians identified with Scandinavian Creation Theology (SCT) seem to be natural location for considering the phenomenon of the body as informative for a theology of home in that creation remains the "universal horizon for the articulation of the gospel."[1] The body, of course, is of a piece with this creation in which we live, and is, in fact, that bit of creation with which we are most intimate. Further, insofar as salvation is about becoming human again, and being human is about being embodied, the body is an inescapable theme of creation and soteriological discourse both. The body is both in the world and an instantiation of the world—a microcosm.

The theme of the world, as addressed in SCT can be understood as informative for an apprehension of the body. The created world is identified as our home,[2] but as more than a home.[3] The world locates us, and meets our needs, and yet insofar as we confess it as created, it bespeaks a Creator. This body, then, cannot be seen as simply a problematic Cartesian accoutrement and something to be shed in service of the soul. Rather, insofar as creation is a peer of redemption, an accounting of the body is *de rigueur*. Prenter's affirmation that everyday experience is critical data for theological reflection most surely draws us more deeply into the body.[4] Feminists have, of course, pressed for understanding the body and its sensuality as theological data in its own right and more than an afterthought for the "real work" of doctrine.[5] Of course, this turn to the body presumes that there has been a turn from the body.

ANTIPATHY TO THE BODY IN THE BODY OF CHRIST

The tale of Western alienation can be variously told. We might start with the platonic propensity of certain interpreters of the Christian faith. We might begin in the modern era with the arrival of the ghost in the machine anthropology via Descartes. We might begin with the institutionalization of Christianity that lost the "transcorporeal and intercorporeal" view of the body of Christ.[6] But I will begin with a story. This story comes out of a series of interviews associated with a project I am working on with Dr. Laura MacGregor and funded by the Louisville Institute under the title "Beyond Saints and Superheroes: A Phenomenological Study of the Spiritual Care Needs of Parents Raising Children with Disabilities." The study aims to determine how the church might better respond to the needs of such parents and their families. One might ask how can we better make the church home to those at home in bodies unlike ours? I relate here a story told by a mother I interviewed (whose identity has been altered) concerning the first time Joanna (not her real name) brought her child—born with severe disabilities because of medical malpractice—to her church home. I share Joanna's description of her church, chosen by her and her husband:

> Joanna: And so when we ended up going to a new church I think around the time we were 18 or so. And, you know, we did our marriage counselling there and we got married there and knew a lot of people. And it was kind of like just a family place to be—
>
> Interviewer: Right, a family—like the community was quite helpful and strong.
>
> Joanna: It was, it was nice just to have a support and to have other people who believed the same things. Or when I had questions or was struggling with

something, you had somebody to go to. First years of marriage aren't always easy so it was nice to have somebody to talk to and they could tell you you're being stupid. Everybody needs somebody who can be honest yeah, so it was a very friendly—I felt welcome, like part of the community. And then I had Noah and I had gone with the hopes that that community would rally around and help me.

Because I was struggling, I had postpartum depression, I was struggling with the guilt of, you know, I thought maybe I had done something during his delivery. I had asked them to do a C-Section because things just didn't feel right and they refused. So there was all—like I had so much guilt around his delivery and I just wanted somebody to help me work through all of that and support me. And we were running back and forth to hospitals and I sat all day by myself in the hospital with Noah. Joab had to go to work and it wasn't his fault; I was alone.

And I had hoped that somebody would see that we needed some help but nobody did, nobody did. . . . The church does not help, they're not there to help you with this. We went to church regularly; we went to a nondenominational Christian church, active participants. Married in the church, I was happy to be there, we took Noah for his first time to church when he got out of the hospital. So he was maybe five, six months old and he was so happy to be there. And the music was playing and he was, you know, carrying on and he just got so excited by it.

And then the pastor came to me after and said he was too noisy and he was disturbing everybody. And they said "Next time if you come with him you need to sit at the back of the church because sitting where you were disturbed everybody." So that like—and they told me that his disability was the result of my sin, that I'm paying the consequences for it because of that. So I was—never went back.

Just to be clear: the pastor shared this with Joanna immediately after the service ended with the congregation within earshot. And no-one intervened, nor comforted her. Of course, this is one story, but unfortunately our 20 interviews included multiple iterations of parents of children with disabilities being reproved, or corrected, or informed concerning their children. As I read and reread these interviews it strikes me that the body of Christ is uncomfortable with bodies that do not fit purported norms.

Of course, it is not only the body of Christ with this problem, the body politic also imagines normal bodies and seeks to normalize those that do not fit.[7] This idealization of the body, however, is not an affirmation but a denial of the body. An inability to accept bodies in diversity is finally a rejection of the body. Within the context of the church, this rejection of the body bespeaks a discomfort with the message that the body is. The body speaks finitude, failure, and passion when institutions are more interested in control, propriety, and predictability. Nothing more unsettles the desire for certainty than a broken body, and that is why people with disabilities rarely feel at home in the church. And yet all bodies are the bodies of God, and what they say needs to be heard. What might we hear if we begin to attend to the body—to that bit of creation most intimate to us, and so described as a home?

STARTING WITH SENSATION

Knut Løgstrup provided a phenomenology of the body against the backdrop of a philosophical preoccupation with the phenomenon of language. A history of phenomenology in the twentieth- century charts a movement toward language, with the body seen as an epiphenomenon. Merleau-Ponty was an outlier, as was Ricouer in certain works, but philosophically, priority was placed upon the importance of language.[8] To this Løgstrup asserted that to choose one over the other was a false choice.[9] How, then, does the body look for Løgstrup?

Løgstrup's anthropological explorations attend the two simultaneous and inter-related themes of sensation and understanding. These two interplay in integrity without ever merging.[10] Sensation is informed by our senses but not in the sense that in using our seeing we *receive* information about what we see; rather we *merge* with what we see.[11] The parity of this with Aristotle is noted.[12] Sensation places us in the world in a way whereby we identify with it as source rather imagine it as our environs.[13] He notes that the sensing and the sensed are together as we become one with the universe sensing us in turn.[14] There is a lack of distance in sensation.[15] We experience a kind omnipresence, then, in sensing.[16] But what is the relationship between sensation and the body?

The activity of sensation is limited by the body.[17] We cannot become one with a world we cannot see, for instance. And yet he notes, "the independence of our sensation from our corporeality and the conditionality of our sensation by our corporeality."[18] Sensation really does set us free as I am at unity with the bird my eyes affix to. There is no distance in sensation, possible by grace of the senses, of which sight is given a kind of priority:

> Space belongs to sensation, given with sight, motion, touch, smell and taste— but first and foremost with sight. If space is a condition for our understanding, sensation is as well and is, to anticipate what follows, already actual space, thanks to its infinity. . . . A human being can only be free to be and become if he can be without any relationship to [everything that exists in space] and this can only occur with the help of infinity. Yet how can infinity come into our existence and make it into understanding when our existence is, in the end, finite? The

answer is that there is this infinity in the middle of our existence in all its finiteness: that limitless space gives our sight the chance not to dwell on anything.[19]

Two points emerge from this in addition to the emphasis Løgstrup gives to sight. First, space is a condition for both understanding, as is sensation. But foremost, space belongs to sensation in that our senses, especially as evidenced by sight, have the freedom to wander from this to that. Second, the capacity of the senses to be free is the infinity of sensation that funds understanding. But what is this relationship between understanding and sensation?

It might be best to first note that the human capacity for sensation is our instinctual capacity, shared with animals. Understanding happens as we withdraw from the distanceless relationship with the cosmos via our intellectual capacity to note distance, causality, etc. This withdrawal from the world is condition for the possibility of inventing tools, apprehending history, and creating culture.[20] Tools, he notes, compensate our instinct but paradoxically also enable outstripping our instinctual capacities, sometimes to our detriment.[21] This withdrawal from the world is not a resignation from the world and so calls to mind Aristotle's assertion that all knowing takes place by the *conversio ad phantasmata*,[22] even understanding its most abstract level is funded by the senses.[23] Understanding, then, might draw us to the edge of the universe but we cannot absent ourselves from it by understanding.[24] And yet understanding approximates a kind of transcendence for us.[25] Understanding takes place against a horizon informed by the freedom of sensation and allows thought the space for difference, which make it possible to know; in understanding the lack of distance of sensation is forfeited: we need to stop seeing in order to understand.[26] And yet sensation and understanding remain engaged and engaging.

Løgstrup also addresses the phenomenon of need alongside that of sensation. When need's demands are restrained, culture and history accrue in a fashion akin to the way that tools emerge with the attenuation of sensation as we make space for understanding.[27] There is the possibility of danger in the production of culture and history, as there is in the creation of tools.[28]

In sum, Løgstrup images the human as a sensing, understanding being whose identity as such is embodied but free to be, in limited ways, beyond the body paradoxically by attending to the data the body presents. This withdrawal from the body is both our glory and our shame. The human, for Løgstrup, is especially drawn to sight, which he names a "sovereign sense"[29] even while he affirms that hearing and seeing are both needed for understanding.[30] At this point, I want to return in a cursory fashion to the story told above, and lesson from it that might inform this.

A TOUCHING SENSATION

As I review the interviews of Joanna, and others in our study, I become increasingly aware of the way that ableism shapes and informs our way in the world. It is regularly presumed that there is a normal body, and we can reference that in discussing human experience. The lens of disability challenges this propensity to imagine a normal that can emerge as hegemonic.[31] I am guilty of imaging this normal, which I see in my body and yet I am struggling to unlearn some of these prejudices, mindful that people that are differently abled engage in and contribute to our life together. As I think about the people we interviewed, I am now more sensitive to the fact that Løgstrup's language leans heavily on the role of sight and hearing in sensation, which is the condition for the possibility of understanding. And yet, blind and deaf people understand. Of course, I could suppose Løgstrup imagining these as master metaphors that bespeak the unity of the senses in sensation. But still, privileging two senses not only could possibly alienate those without these, but it might also fail to apprehend nuances possible if we were to imagine how other senses could inform sensation. And so I here propose a little *essai*: what might happen if we explore sensation via touch?

My interest in this turn is informed by both the research I have participated in with people with disabilities, and in the work of carnal hermeneutics advanced by Richard Kearny. In *Carnal Hermeneutics* he speaks to the interdependence of what Løgstrup identifies as sensation and understanding, but yet in a slightly different way. He advances that the very word "sense" betrays three meanings: sense as in physical sensation, sense as in meaning ("What is the sense of that?") and sense as in orientation, as evidenced in Romance language.[32] The import of this is evidence in his assertion that

> Before words, we are flesh, flesh becoming words for the rest of our lives. Matter no less than form, is about what matters—to us, to others and to the world in which we breathe and have our being. The old dichotomies between "empirical" and "transcendental," "materialism" and "idealism" are ultimately ruinous. Life is hermeneutic through and through. It goes all the way up and all the way down.[33]

Kearney's assertion that there is no hermeneutically free zone might first seem to stand in contradiction to Løgstrup's distinction between sensation and understanding, but in the latter's conviction that these cannot be divorced, there might be some possibility for an *rapprochement* as evidenced in Kearney's assertion that "all our sensations involve *interpretation* (albeit in the primal sense of orientation prior to theoretical understanding)."[34] But this is not really my concern at this point. Rather, I am more intrigued by

Kearney's attention to flesh and touch, wondering what might happen when this is used to "flesh out" sensation. What, then, of touch?

First, Kearney asserts that touch crosses all senses.[35] It is a basic part of being human that is spread across our bodies, ever at work, sensing changes in temperature, the presence of objects soft and hard, wet and try. Touch is foundational to negotiating our way in the world and its indispensability is evidenced in the English word tact, which notes that those whose touch is acute are better able to negotiate the vicissitudes of life.[36] Indeed, to touch others is to be touched by them and so touch immerses us in an intimacy that presumes vulnerability.[37] Kearney notes that Aristotle imagined flesh as the medium of touch in the same way that air is the medium of smell and sound and light the medium of sight.[38] Skin, then, is the between that reminds us that all modalities of knowing are relational. Skin is always sensing difference, the condition for the possibility of knowing the self via the other, and the other via the self. Skin is the touching self that poses the possibility of being reflexive.

Kearney reminds us of Husserl's insight that touch is unlike other senses in that we can touch ourselves so that we can be agent and patient in the same moment. I can't hear my hearing, or see my seeing, or taste my tasting, but I can feel my touching.[39] This might have some utility for thinking about the body as home. The body is both familiar and strange—both touching and touched, and as such is the first and most intimate experience of the world. The world is the horizon of our experiences, always providing us with more possibilities and contributing the backdrop against which we evolve. And yet that world is already written into the text of our body. The body is world, composed of carbon hydrogen, iron, etc. So, this bit of the world I am means that the home that my body is, is also world, the horizon against which I live my life. And so, the body bears both the phenomena of being home and horizon. This home that is also horizon provides us with doors that allow ingress and exit via the skin. The porosity of our flesh speaks to its medium-like characteristic that instantiates the body as the home of our *coeur* and the horizon identified with the liminality of the flesh. The flesh is always negotiating in and out, letting sweat out and vitamin D via sunshine in. The flesh is always meeting the other as it plays with an apple, caresses the cat, digs in the dirt, and when it feels the unusual lump where there did not use to be one. The phenomenon of home that is the subject of this volume, insofar as it is informed by the primordial home that is the body, is both familiar and strange: both the locus of identity and the disruption of the same as death becomes us, and overcomes us. To be at home, then, is to be at the precipice of leaving home. Home is always a place of landing and launching. But what might be said theologically about the home?

Luther famously described God's creations as words of God, and that most assuredly accrues to the home which our bodies are. Kearny notes that we both are and have bodies.[40] We both are and have homes. We both are and have God's words such that our bodies can be our home as well as the horizon that speaks to possibility of another home, which is the resurrection body—our home away from home. Home intimates both our dying—that most intimate of all experiences—and the death of our dying as the horizon for our living even now. We can be at home in death precisely because the intimacy of flesh touching flesh preaches to me that I am both patient and agent. Death is the experience par excellence of the body as patient, but what is body as agent?

Moore tells us that bodies speak, emote, and remember.[41] The body that knows itself in touching speaks of capacity to transcend itself. The body that emotes expresses itself: that is, it presses itself out in service of relationality. The body that remembers announces that incursion of time into our experience such that we know that we are not only related to those whom we touch, but also those whom we have touched and by extension those whom we will touch. The agential body takes leave of itself to know others (including the other that is the self) both in and across time. The body that is home, is also horizon. But what might this mean for the body that is Christ's? How is that body both home and horizon?

RE-TURNING THE BODY

SCT is well positioned to understand the power of the body for revisiting the theme of home. Wingren, for instance, counters the common antipathy to the body found in modernity and certain iterations of Christianity when he asserts that the gospel is a yes to the body.[42] Of course, this affirmation is nested in an understanding of *creatio continua* as per Luther, and which allows him to affirm a notion of continuing goodness in created reality, including that of the human.[43] Wingren also affirms that the Irenaean motif of recapitulation comes with the healing power to restore the body in its possibility.[44] Wingren, of course, isn't thinking about correcting the abilities of those living with disabilities, nor the reversal of illness and death in the experience of humans. Rather, he is imagining the reversal of the erasure of the body by Cartesian imaginaries. The body can be experienced as informative, and so Wingren can observe eternity in the joyful play of children[45] and is also able to assert that the loss of play and spontaneity is the condition for the possibility of sin.[46] This is all very body-friendly language and accords with the thesis that the body is both home and horizon: the place of play, discovery, and *extasis*. The church, insofar as it is a body, is to be such a place. But often, the body which is the church is informed by an image of the body as a vehicle rather than home and horizon. The church receives a utilitarian identification in such an imaginary, and the ministrations of the church becomes very serious—without place for play, and very neat and tidy. Vehicles, unlike homes, need to be safe and so frivolity is discouraged. Propriety is preferred.

I experienced a different vision for the church among the informants of our study, who were very much at home in their bodies—so much at home, in fact, that they expanded my horizon about how ministry might look. Chloe (not her real name) is a mother of a young man who has Down's syndrome. She is also the wife of a pastor who has been in the position where he was able to ensure that their son Mark was not kept at the margins of the body, but brought to the centre, where he could show what a holy heart might be like. Chloe spoke of how people were touched by Mark's reading of scripture, or doing prayers in the Sunday morning services. At one point in the conversation, she shared:

> Chloe: I want the church to embrace Mark as Mark and talk to him, not talk to me. So what can happen is, we come into church, he's always with me and people talk to me, "Oh, how's Mark" but he's standing right next to me. So my goal is to get them to engage him and understand that he's quite capable of explaining how he's doing. . . . . But I don't know that they always understand what he's capable of or how they can engage him. And that's not only church people, that's people in general. That's society in general. You know, when you go to the store, the [store name], we're in line, they look to me to order for him. Well he's perfectly capable of ordering. But people look right at me instead of at him.

> So that's one of the challenges in church is to get him to be known as to who he is and not just who I am or who his dad is. I think his dad being a pastor has helped us in that he's visible right away.

> They don't realize that, you know, these are multifaceted human beings just like we are, and that, you know, despite—I always say Mark has a much purer, different kind of faith than I do, because he doesn't have the piece that worries about what's God up to. He just doesn't have that piece, you know. I'm trying to figure out what is God up to and how is this going to work out. And he doesn't have those things. He just believes it's going to work out. Whenever Mark's been a part of the worship service, when he's praying or reading scripture, it has a real impact on the entire community. I never get more emails about how wonderful a service is than a week when Mark prays or Mark reads.

> First of all, people are shocked he can read the Bible. Like he's a good reader. So, when he gets up and reads, people are quite shocked that he can do that. Like that just for me is education right from the get-go, that you're educating this

community that there's a lot more to this guy than you think, that he's capable of reading. And that these words are very meaningful to him.

And watching how he interacts with faith has been very encouraging to our church community because he prays with great faith. He just is very simple and it's very straightforward. And he asks God for what he needs and he thanks him all the time for . . . Every day is a gorgeous day. If he says grace at our table, he'll say, "Thank you for this beautiful day, Lord." And he doesn't mean that, it doesn't have to be a sunny day. It's a beautiful day because it's a beautiful day. It's been a great, you know, he's enjoyed it is what he means.

Interviewer: Wow.

Chloe: So there's education. And so watching him be involved, I think to myself how come this isn't something that happens as much as it should, right, letting him lead.

Interviewer: Letting him lead, yeah, wow. He sounds like an amazing young man.

Chloe: Yeah, he is. He really is. He could be a pastor. I tell him that all the time. Like he really could. He has a real intuition for people who are hurting. He knows who to hug in the room. You know, if there's a room full of people and he doesn't know them, he knows which person needs him to be friends with them. He's got a real sense of, a real intuition about people's hearts and what their needs are.

The two true stories bookending this *essai* stand in such stark contrast. In the first, a person with disabilities was pushed to the edge, and, in the second, a person with a disability was drawn to the *coeur* of the congregation. And interestingly, the perspectives of the parents of these two were both so informative because the center and the edge are both vantage points from whence revelation happens. The heart and the skin, the home and the horizon of the body bespeak how other bodies can be both a home and a horizon—including the body that is the church. Prenter claimed that the church is called to leave the world, receive the world, and serve the world.[47] This is because the church is the world, in the three senses of "sense" that Kearney proposes: sensation, meaning, and orientation.[48] The church *feels* the world because the edge of the church is the skin of the church that interacts with world. The church *understands* the world because the members of the church are participants in the world. And finally, the church is *oriented* to the world because the world is everywhere. There is no place where the world is not, and so the body of Christ that is home is also the body of Christ that is horizon.

CONCLUSION

In this chapter, I have explored the notion of home via the interpretive lens of the body. In so doing, I have used Løgstrup's phenomenology of the body to explore the significance of sensation for the experience of being human, and then augmented that exploration with a carnal hermeneutic reading sensation from the location of the skin. In so doing, I imagined that the body is both home and horizon; both familiar and strange; both a landing and launching pad. In part, this exploration has been informed by the experiences of persons with disabilities. They invite us to think more intentionally about our body, and to live more fully in our body—embracing both death and life, and between these two, they call us to attend to those mystical and everyday moments where doors and pores both open to the divine on either side to the end that God is encountered in the skin that is both our home and horizon.

NOTES

1. Niels Henrik Gregersen, Bengt Kristennson Uggla, and Trygve Wyller, eds., *Reformation Theology for a Post-Secular Age: Løgstrup, Prenter, Wingren and the Future of Scandinavian Creation Theology* (Göttingen: Vandenhoeck & Ruprecht, n.d.), 130.

2. Gregersen, Uggla, and Wyller, 11.

3. R. Prenter, "Worship and Creation," *Studia Liturgica* 2, no. 2 (June 1, 1963): 158, https://doi.org/10.1177/003932076300200202.

4. Regin Prenter, *Creation and Redemption.* (Philadelphia: Fortress Press, 1967), 249.

5. Jennifer Lewis, "Theological Leadership for Sense-Ational Leadership: Cognitive Science, Christian Agility, and the Case for Sensory Theological Education," *The Wabash Center Journal on Teaching* 2, no. 2 (2021), 220.

6. Ola Sigurdson, "How to Speak of the Body: Embodiment Between Phenomenology and the Body," *Studia Theologica* 62 (2008), 27.

7. Aarne Siirala, *The Voice of Illness: A Study in Therapy and Prophecy* (Philadelphia: Fortress Press, 1964), 91.

8. Richard Kearney, "The Wager of Carnal Hermeneutics," in *Carnal Hermeneutics*, ed. Richard Kearney and Brian Treanor (New York: Fordham University Press, 2015), 17.

9. Knut E. Løgstrup, *Metaphysics, Volume I* (Milwauukee, WI: Marquette University Press, 1995), 121.

10. Løgstrup, 121.

11. Løgstrup, 121.

12. Aristotle, *On the Soul, Parva Naturalia, On Breath* (Cambridge, MA: Harvard University Press, 1995), 171.

13. Knut E. Løgstrup, *Metaphysics, Volume II* (Milwaukee, WI: Marquette University Press, 1995), 1.

14. Løgstrup, 20.

15. Løgstrup, *Metaphysics, Volume I*, 22.

16. Løgstrup, *Metaphysics, Volume II*, 38.

17. Løgstrup, 11.

18. Løgstrup, 11.

19. Løgstrup, *Metaphysics, Volume I*, 124.

20. Løgstrup, *Metaphysics, Volume II*, 42.

21. Løgstrup, 42.

22. Aristotle, *On the Soul, Parva Naturalia, On Breath*, 177.

23. Løgstrup, *Metaphysics, Volume II*, 33.

24. Løgstrup, 23.

25. Løgstrup, *Metaphysics, Volume I*, 122.

26. Løgstrup, 125.

27. Løgstrup, *Metaphysics, Volume II*, 45.

28. Løgstrup, 53.

29. Løgstrup, *Metaphysics, Volume I*, 129.

30. Løgstrup, 130.

31. Deborah Beth Creamer, "Embracing Limits, Queering Embodiment: Creating/Creative Possiblities for Disability Theology," *Journal of Feminist Studies in Religion* 26, no. 2 (Fall 2010), 124–25.

32. Kearney, "The Wager of Carnal Hermeneutics," 15–16.

33. Kearney, 15.

34. Kearney, 20.

35. Kearney, 20.

36. Kearney, 20.

37. Kearney, 21.

38. Kearney, 25.

39. Kearney, 27.

40. Kearney, 30.

41. Darnell L. Moore, "Theorizing the 'Black Body' as a Site of Trauma: Implications for Theologies of Embodiment," *Theology and Sexuality* 15, no. 2 (2009), 175.

42. Gustaf Wingren, *Creation and Gospel: The New Situation in European Theology*, Toronto Studies in Theology (New York: E. Mellen Press, 1979), 106.

43. Gustaf Wingren, *Creation and Law*, [American ed.]. (Philadelphia: Muhlenberg Press, 1961), 48.

44. Wingren, *Creation and Gospel*, 28.

45. Gustaf Wingren, *Credo, The Christian View of Faith and Life* (Minneapolis, MN: Augsburg Publishing House, 1981), 172.

46. Wingren, 57.

47. Regin Prenter, *Spiritus Creator* (Philadelphia: Muhlenberg Press, 1953), 545.

48. Kearney, "The Wager of Carnal Hermeneutics," 15–16.

Chapter 6

Who Does Not Want
to Have a Family?

Home and Family, Reality and Ideal

Elisabeth Gerle

"Today, the first mate was drunk" the captain wrote in his log. Of course, the first mate was upset about this and the next time he took charge of the ship when the captain was asleep, he wrote in the log that "Today, the captain was sober." We usually do not mention the normal, only the exceptions. Hence, we do not often talk about our homes. We think of them as given, which is good. For many people in the world today, homes are, however, not a given. It is therefore so important to reflect on what it is to have a home. I will do so from a perspective that holds that ethical reflection starts with reality, namely, how life is lived in practice. Drawing on a few specific observations, or experiences, I will make some more general conclusions of what it is to have a family and a home after wrestling with experiences as well as visions, for instance, practice and ideal. Here, I will also discuss our cultural heritage of Biblical narratives and some interpretations that for centuries have formed family ideals. I will argue that a fluidity between our private homes and a wider society is valuable both for the small home and for the world, as also homes are part of the vocation to serve the world, *coram mundo*. In this latter part, I will open for the unexpected, breaking into our now, with prospects and new openings as Messianic Moments or an Eschatological Future/Now.

WHO DOESN'T WANT TO HAVE A FAMILY?

Who does not want a family? This is something I heard a lesbian feminist say during one of the UN special conferences on women in New York, and I have never forgotten her words. It is less of a rhetorical question, more of a counter argument against people claiming that lesbian, homosexual relationships would undermine the traditional family. She expressed a conviction that we all want a family, independently of sexual orientation. So what is undermining the family? Maybe not her desire for a family but those family experiences many try to escape, during Christmas or other holiday seasons, due to lack of sensitivity or too much alcohol. The question Who does not want a family refers to a family that we long for, that is a family that cares, supports, and gives nurture, strength and freedom to your body and soul, to your whole being, helping you to cope with public life.

This is a reality for many, as well as an ideal. Without ideals life would be poor, but reality is after all part of our material existence and hence maybe what matters most. Theologically, a family as a community flows out of an understanding of life given as a gift and that we all are created to live in relationship. It is also an understanding of materiality as God's blessing.

As Niels Gregersen, Bengt Kristensson Uggla and Trygve Wyller wrote in *Reformation Theology for a Post-Secular Age*, "The gospel has something to say about what it means to live together in everyday life. . . . Our relationship to God is not something that starts when we enter the church or a presumed religious territory, but a reality always already given in and with life itself."[1] My first conclusion is thus that we all have some concrete experiences of having a family. A good family is, for many, a given in life. Lack of, or abuse, does not remove a deep sense of what a good family is. It seems to be given with life. And just as we all want a family, we also desire good fathers.

Who Does Not Want a Good Father?

Feminist theologians in the early days started to talk about God as a mother rather than as a father due to painful experiences of violent, aggressive, negligent, or absent fathers. The image of God as mother, or friend, did not have such negative associations as God the father. Once again, a woman's voice gave me another perspective. She grew up with a quite destructive father as a child but told me that when she heard about God the father, she always thought that he was a real father, that is, a caring, good father with wisdom and love. These two anecdotes from two individual female voices reinforce my first conclusion, emerging out of a phenomenological analysis. Deep within ourselves we know what a good family is. We know what a good father, or mother means, even if we have had bad experiences.

The desire to have a good father can, however, easily be exploited. Peter Pomerantsev is a British journalist of Russian heritage. In his book *Nothing Is True and Everything Is Possible,* he describes meeting young Russian women who all are fatherless, dreaming fairytales about being chosen by the tsar taking her in his private jet plane home to his castle. They are searching as much for a father as for a wealthy admirer, lover. Today, president Putin represents this profile, Pomarantsev claims. My second conclusion is therefore that our desires and dreams can be exploited as material and existential experiences vary. Relations between human beings are still inflicted by the rupture. Seen through the lens of Scandinavian Creation Theology human beings are all created and thus sharing humanity and vulnerability and life in relation. However, context and values vary tremendously. K. E. Løgstrup, is best known for his emphasis on *interdependence* and how every human being is carrying the life of the other in her/his hands as an ethical demand.[2] Interdependence is for Løgstrup "prior to the possibility of setting ourselves apart from the social nexuses of which we are part."[3] Niels Henrik Gregersen points out

> the inescapable fact of life is that human interactions neither take place in a value-free nor in a power-free vacuum. As human persons, we live in differently structured positions, in which wealth and opportunity no less than power and dependence are unevenly distributed, and so the ethical demand arises from the prior fact that we always "have something of the other's life in our hand," as Løgstrup argued in "The Ethical Demand from 1956.[4]

Ambiguity and inequality are always part of our shared lives as human beings. Today, we hear many stories also about difficult relations between mother and child, some even abusive, something that leads to my third question:

Who Does Not Want a Good Mother?

A mother is so deeply connected to the idea of having a home and a family that we hardly think or talk about her. Many children in single parent households direct their desire toward an absent father. Also, in families with two parents, the father is often more absent due to work, sport, or other activities outside home. Hence he becomes a person to desire, to long for. A mother, as well as her unconditional love, is, on the other hand, often taken for granted. As we all know this anticipation has occasionally transformed some women into not so good mothers, too tired to be mature grown-ups, or reacting against the expectations by demanding the right to pursue their own interests, sometimes at the expense of her children. Hence, mothers are often persons who are blamed by other people, in a different key than men, often also by themselves. Woman as mother is namely part of an essential ideal where she is supposed to create a spirit of harmony and care for the entire family.

An idealized mother figure as Mary, mother of Christ, is in the Catholic world and in Orthodox faith traditions an ideal that seems completely impossible. Being both virgin and mother makes this ideal difficult to combine with reality. Seeing her as an exception does not really helps. Her described character as unselfish, obedient, and good has often been oppressive for women, sometimes in ways that have been destructive for their children. Mary is, however, an ambivalent ideal.[5] She is stronger than most, according to St Luke 1–2, revolutionary with a gift for real friendship and thus inspiring women throughout history.

Throughout long periods in history, she has been portrayed as the heavenly queen, with power to balance male dominance in heaven and on earth, not without associations to strong female goddesses in the Orient. Hence, many suffering mothers have found consolation in identifying with and praying to the Virgin. She has also gained more appreciation in Evangelical Lutheran Contexts due to her insights, mysterious knowledge, closely related both to materiality, body and divinity. In Uppsala Cathedral, Sweden, she is portrayed by the artist Anders Widoff as a contemporary, ordinary, not too tall woman dressed in blue with a headscarf, like a woman you could meet in any street. In the cathedral you meet her behind the altar, and it takes a few moments for you to discover that she is not just passing or walking away. Mary meets you there, eye to eye.

The early narratives in the Bible are in the tradition of Scandinavian Creation Theology not read as historical descriptions but as myths saying something about our lives. In relation to motherhood, it is interesting to note that this is something mentioned after the rupture in Genesis 4. As part of the punishment for Eve, gender hierarchy and pain while giving birth, is listed in Gen. 3:16 and for Adam the ordeal of work. Now Adam is naming Eve Mother of Life in Genesis 3:20 as all life came through her.

To name someone, to give someone a name, is a sign of power. However, it is also intimate. When the first human being in Genesis 2 feels alone, God creates animals and birds as company, and they are all given names by the first earth creature. However, first when another human being is made, created from one side of the first creature, similar yet different from the first, the introduction is well received with the exclamation "this is bone from my bone, flesh from my flesh" (Gen. 2:23). I consciously avoid using the name Adam, as this became a male name, and these words have therefore been used to reinforce male superiority.[6]

Nothing is here being said of children or procreation as in Genesis 1. What counts is the intimate recognition of somebody similar but different. This can be read as a blessing partnership between human beings that may be sensual, sexual, and intimate but not necessarily with the purpose of conceiving children. Even the naming can thus be read as a narrative to highlight and be inclusive both to homosexual relations and to women and men without children.[7]

I do not see the early myths as prescriptions for how life ought to be lived. However, I see the value of making new interpretations of these ancient texts as the cultural presuppositions repeated during centuries often form our unconscious ideals and assumptions without reflection. Based on human experiences we have, however, more and more come to broaden the modern Western concept of a family as father, mother, and child. In many cultures, a family includes many more and, in a growing number of contexts, we also acknowledge that a family can exist without children. The Church of Sweden, consequently, performs marriage ceremonies for men marrying women beyond menopause, as well as same-sex marriages. Inspired by Genesis 2 one can say that the most important relationship is between two similar but different grown-up persons. The argument that God in creation made women and men complementary, purely directed toward procreation is only one exegesis, one that has been used to diminish the variety of how people live their lives. Starting with lived experiences rather than with the ideals, allows for more flexibility and inspiration to restore a paradise lost, or as Scandinavian Creation Theology claims, to restore and fulfill creation inspired by the readings of Irenaeus and Grundtvig.

Children are, however, gifts connected to our personal lives, a joy shared by male and female persons, independently of sexual orientation. To give birth is a crucial experience for many women, but to care for children is shared by many, some of whom nurture not only biological children. Nurture, sustenance and care are important for all. There are many who perform motherhood activities without being biological mothers.

A third conclusion is therefore that life and interpretations are ambiguous but also more open than we may think at first. This is also visible in relation to my next and fourth rhetorical question, which reveals a gender hierarchy that has been with us throughout history. The question is:

Who Does Not Want to Have a Wife?

This question has a more ironic undertone as a wife seems to indicate somebody who takes care of you, serves you and gives nurture, but in an asymmetrical way. Here we get close to why so many are afraid of the traditional family. The family is namely filled with asymmetry, not only a "natural" asymmetry of heterogeneity where a person may be a child in one relation and a parent in another.

As already said, the creation narratives are not seen as prescriptions for Scandinavian Creation Theology, nor as historical or scientific reports about an origin. The narratives of creation are, however, always being re-interpreted also within this tradition. Niels Henrik Gregersen contends that the blessing of sexual intercourse lived on after the Fall. It would, therefore, be more sensible to speak of original godliness than original sin.[8] In my reading, this original blessing and godliness include equality and mutual respect, to see each other as persons. Contemporary Biblical scholars have guided me by casting new light over these early narratives, showing that the traditional interpretation of seeing woman as a helper is not the only possible understanding.

The two creation stories introducing the Bible have completely different contexts for their narratives of the creation of man and woman. One is situated in a coastal area, the other in a desert. While the younger version in chapter 1 concludes with the creation of the human being as male and female, the second and older narrative in chapter 2 starts with the creation of the first human being. Adam, which simply means earth creature, however, became a male name. Eve was then described as a helper of Adam, a word with associations to maid. However, the Hebrew word in Genesis 2 is *ezer*, a word that Phyllis Trible long time ago taught us is used when God acts to save and help.[9] Tamara Cohn Eskenazi points out the rabbinic perspective that many different interpretations may be correct, not only one.[10] One word for help in Hebrew is *ezer*, the other is *neged*. The latter can mean both resistance from someone standing up to you and standing in front of you. Hence, it could also be translated as "counterpart" or "complement." Both interpretations can be found within Judaism.[11] Norwegian Kari Elisabeth Börrsen, who made her main work in Patristics, has shown that the debate on how to understand male and female has been a discussion within Christianity since the first century.[12] The Church father St Augustine (354–430), for instance, claimed an original equality that was destroyed with the encouragement to reproduce in Gen 1:28. For Augustine this made woman more flesh and partly destroyed her rationality, which for him was the essence of being like God. Amusingly enough, according to his exegesis, reproduction did not destroy the male rationality.

Luther's important break with Augustine was to abandon his connection between sensuality and sexuality to sin. As all good gifts sexuality as well as sensuality can be exploited by selfishness, but it is not in itself bad or sinful.[13] Further, the body is no longer seen as a path to the divine, to union with God, neither through libertinism nor by asceticism and control of the body as a way to get closer to God. The body is regarded as something good, but it is there for humanity and its wellbeing. As a means of salvation—for saving the body and the soul from death—it is of no interest.[14] A reading of male and female and HBTQ persons more as companions, lovers, and deep friends that I have highlighted in this section may be an important contribution to what it is to have a home, introducing more of material mutuality and democracy also in the household.

Woman or Home as a Nest

Emmanuel Levinas writes beautifully about being at home with oneself. He describes a home as a nest to rest. It is ours as we understand it, we may even control and own this our life.[15] I have in some earlier writings been critical to his imagery, especially of the woman as a nest where the man can rest, claiming in line with what I have argued above that a nest is something we all desire or need, independent of gender or sexual orientation. A nest, a home, is not only for hard working men, but for most people.[16]

However, having said that, Levinas' image of a home is important for being able to meet *the other*. Windows open for the other to be seen. The others meet us face to face with a claim, to acknowledge the other as other. We encounter a choice, either to be content with ourselves as selves and believe that we understand everything, also about the other, or to open the door for the other whom we do not know much about and thus cannot control or own. Such a meeting can never take place in abstraction, it is always concrete.

The other, therefore, breaks into our world, our understanding, and our context. Ethics problematizes my world as Peter Kemp writes in his introduction to Levinas. The other disturbs the peace of home as (s)he represents the foreign. We have no shared homeland. However, this also brings another freedom, a reality that I cannot control or exercise power over. I thus need to meet the other and allow him/her the right to break my egotism that I otherwise do not want to give up.[17] The other drags me out of my home Ulrica Fritzson writes in her book on Reconciliation. He makes me realize what I cannot understand within my own reality, my own totality, my own horizon. Hence, the other can help us take responsibility for what I have not seen. The other helps us to be subjects in our lives.[18]

Many of the Levinasian thoughts are related to Løgstrup's interdependence and his description of the ethical demand, to understand ethics as prior to ontology. Ethics is especially important as we live in a tension between an imagined paradise lost and a future kin-dom, queen-dom to break into every moment.[19]

Visions of life before the fall, as well as those of a future to long for, are always breaking into our present. It is namely, as Robert Musil reminds us, all too easy to be trapped in the present as a prison that makes us silly and diminish our fantasy and power of political transformation.[20] In the tradition of Grundtvig, however, the fall is not understood as destroying everything. The blessedness of creation lasts. Hence, we encounter a choice, either to be content with ourselves as selves and believe that we understand everything, also about the other, or to open the door for the other that we do not know much about and thus cannot control or own.

HOUSE AND STREET: DISTINCTION AND CONNECTIVITY

How the distinction between private and public is drawn is never innocent and has been interpreted differently by for instance the Early Christians, Augustine, Luther and contemporary scholars and political thinkers. The American-Brazilian Luther scholar Vitor Westhelle holds that the distinction between "house" and "street" in Brazil is comparable to *oeconomia* and *politia*.[21] The house is the "space of intimacy, sexuality, and also of production for the sustenance of life," a realm that is "protected from the public sphere, even architecturally so." A sharp distinction has, however, often reinforced, or created a gender divide where women have been relegated to the private and thus left outside of the public. In Greek antiquity there was a hierarchy between the household and the public, *Res Publica*. While the household was run by women and slaves, free male citizens gathered in *Res Publica*, to make public democratic decisions. The household was not democratic but hierarchically organized.[22] This was a given for Aristotle, and a tradition Hannah Arendt pursues in her political reflections where she in the *Human Condition* seems to repeat the Aristotelian hierarchy between the household and the public.[23] As a political theorist she focused on the political, *Res Publica*, and some feminists have therefore accused her of being genderblind.[24]

A free man who only had concerns for the private and the household was in ancient Greece seen as an "idiot." Today we all need to care about public affairs, the private, and the world. So how can we think about this? In a recent book, I claim that not to care about societal issues transform us into "idiots" in the way the ancient Greek philosophers used the word. It undermines democracy. Yet, I do not want to repeat the ancient dichotomy with contempt for the household, as we live in a time when the public need to learn from the household and from the pre-political.[25]

Hannah Arendt was, however, a complex thinker. She also points to the miracle of birth, a third kind of human activity, or "action." Here, she undermines the dichotomy between private and political, between pre-political and political. Feminist scholars, such as Julia Kristeva and Grace Jantzen, have highlighted Arendt's notion of natality as "the principle of freedom," as "every human being can be seen as unique and therefore as capable of newness." Arendt writes: "In this sense of initiative, an element of action, and therefore of natality, is inherent in all human activities. Moreover, since action is the political activity par excellence, natality and not mortality, may be the central category of political, as distinguished from metaphysical thought."[26]

Kristeva describes this concept of natality as "a modern version of the Judeo-Christian affection for the love of life through her constant drumbeat of the 'miracle of birth.' "[27] Further, Grace Jantzen holds that making natality central rather than the concept of death, as Arendt criticized Heidegger for doing, would make the world another place. She asks about how the world would have been if the symbolic and the social order had been influenced as much by "an imagery of natality as of mortality. What if we were to begin with birth?"[28] Sigríður Guðmarsdóttir claims that Arendt's political philosophy is grounded in the ethics of Augustine and his concept of natality. She holds that "the principle of newness and forgiveness is for Arendt the capacity for initiative and freedom."[29]

Natality and initiative are a given in homes, but they also point to the essence of what makes political life possible. To be an idiot in our times may be not to see that we need to learn from the private spaces, from the house or household, transforming some of the decisions that take place in the street, in public, *politia*.[30] Natality and new lives, children, are intimately connected to having a home as well as to care for the future.

The distinction between the pre-political and the political was not as sharp in the days of Luther. *Familia*, the sphere of *oeconomia*, was not particularly private but a space for big communities. And the political task of the ruler in *politia* was to uphold justice, and increasingly also to care for the people, as Luther saw the king as a father figure who loves and cares for his people, in line with the Song of Song. He also read the Song of Songs together with Magnificat were Mary gives praise to the one that "put down the mighty from their seats and exalted them of low degree."[31] In Martin Luther's own case *familia/oeconomia* was organized by Katharina von Bora, who through her brewery and lodging house for students, was the main breadwinner in the household. For the early Christians, as well as for Martin Luther, ordinary life was reclaimed as holy and given new dignity.[32]

Martin Luther did, therefore, not see home and household as unimportant or less important. Quite the opposite. The work of a maid is something he values higher than the work of monks.

a servant-girl would leap and praise and thank God; and with her tidy work for which she receives support and wages she would acquire such a treasure as all that are esteemed the greatest saints have not obtained. Is it not an excellent boast to know and say that, if you perform your daily domestic task, this is better than all the sanctity and ascetic life of monks? And you have the promise, in addition, that you shall prosper in all good and fare well. How can you lead a more blessed or holier life as far as your works are concerned?[33]

I have elsewhere argued that Luther uplifted the household arena as valuable and as a gift of God.[34] However, he did not create another dichotomy or hierarchy seeing the public as irrelevant. Instead, he saw society as deeply related to the family and the home. It would be anachronistic to describe him as a feminist or insisting on democracy in the household where he rather confirmed traditional hierarchies, yet he did express his indebtedness to Katarina who was the breadwinner for the household. He was also very clear about valuing the home and to compare God's love for us as human beings with the love of a mother or father in relation to a baby that needs new diapers. Sin makes us smell bad, but God's love is still able to embrace us.[35]

For Martin Luther everyday life is not merely subject to laws and constraints but can also be interpreted as desire and play. In his Large Catechism, he describes this as if the heart could dance and overflow: "Should a heart not dance and overflow with joy as it goes about its work, doing what it has been enjoined, such that it might be said: Look, this is better than all holiness of the Carthusian monks, even if they fast until death and pray uninterruptedly on their knees."[36]

Concrete examples of everyday work and how even intimate family experiences are being used to describe God are some of the early sources of Creation Theology, later developed by Scandinavian theologians N. F. S. Grundtvig (1783–1872), K. E. Løgstrup (1905–1981), and Gustaf Wingren (1910–2000).

This approach has also had consequences for politics both in national and global arenas. In the Nordic region it has been influential in creating democratic welfare states, thus blurring the distinction between the traditional *oeconomia* and *politia*, house and street. Nevertheless, throughout history women have often, also in Lutheran contexts, been seen as being part only of the pre-political, something that for many years has been criticized by feminists, who argue that the personal is political and that women need to be visible. heard, and also in the public.

Also, stateless people who work hard to make life easy and good for those with citizenship in developed states are often seen as pre-political, in this context without a democratic voice. They are not always referred to as slaves but sometimes treated as such

I therefore argue that a fluidity between home and society, personal and political, house and street is crucial. This is valuable both for our homes and for the world. Our homes that we want to see as our nests namely can also be the most dangerous places, especially for women and children. More porous borders to the street may thus be somewhat of a protection. Further, homes are also included in the universal vocation to serve the world, *coram mundo*. We need both private spaces and the broader belongings to the world and to cosmos, living in interdependence.

THE TREE OF EDEN

The tree in the Garden of Eden was, according to Luther the church before the fall. Now church is part of the public arena as well as caring for families and individuals, a community where existential, spiritual, and sometimes material needs are met

According to Westhelle, Luther saw church as a third space, when he used the metaphor of the tree, or many trees in paradise. Now it is growing in the front yard, standing between house and street. However, as an "instituted reality" the church is "dependent both on *oeconomia* and *politia*," Hence, it has a "hybride character and can be said to exist only as an event; it happens. It is not of our doing."[37]

It is, however, our doing to invite the other under our tree providing shadow and shelter, together with other people of good will, maybe people under other trees as a metaphor for many faith traditions. This is also to restore and nurture a not completely lost paradise. In line with Irenaeus' thoughts of restoration, *recapitulatio*, this is something more than original creation—it is growth into fulfillment and maturity. Many trees can be seen as a metaphor for many ways of seeing life in the third space, where "religion, to use a more generic word for *ecclesia*, is a space in-between."[38] Westhelle draws on Walter Benjamin and his discussion of "Parisian galleries, arcades or *passages*. These are the architectural expressions of the mingling of house and street, of economy and politics."[39] They are both entrance and exits.

Many are today inspired by Jewish, German philosophers from the early parts of last century. Göran Rosenberg, a prize-winning Jewish author living in Lund, writes about the Messianic moment in his most recent book. He draws on Franz Rosenzweig and his interpretation of the Messianic time as something that can break into history at any moment and transform what *is* to what *ought* to be. It is not a time beyond or after the end of our time but a spark of hope, present in every moment, about the possibility of another world, here and now.[40]

For Scandinavian Creation Theology, which does not understand creation as something belonging to the past as a historical event, I think that this way of thinking about the Messianic time is helpful. Just as Scandinavian Creation Theology does not see creation as a historical past but as an ongoing activity in life, it is "not interested in establishing an ethnic theology for Scandinavians.

To the contrary, Scandinavian creation theology is not centered on identity politics, and is sharply critical of self-profiling attitudes within churches or other religious communities wanting to bolster themselves over and against their surrounding cultures."[41] Hence, the hospitality they offer as churches, communities, and homes, are often organized in broad coalitions with society. Christians and others work side by side, sometimes separate, but often together. This is a way of materializing a Messianic moment, or the Kin-dom here and now. One can see this as Restoration including resisting some of the curses after the fall, such as work being difficult and hard, exercised without joy, pain during childbirth and gender hierarchy. Restoration thus means appreciating and supporting equality and good working conditions where man and women again are seen as partners, in family life, in Church and society. Just as homes have windows open for the other, so our communities have porous borders. They are passages or galleries, not for consumerism but for something more. A porous character between our private homes, churches, and the wider society is valuable both for the small home, congregation, and for the world. The pre-political arenas are drawn into the vocation to serve the world, *coram mundo*. It is also the place to nurture care, mutuality and, thus, core values of democracy that includes a sense of belonging and sharing the future with others. The dichotomy between the private and public, or between the pre-political and political, house and street, is being blurred in contemporary society by a global neo-liberal economy that cuts through our private and political lives, but also due to the homelessness and statelessness emerging out of forced migration and war.

To focus on the pre-political and its porous borders to the world may therefore be crucial to the renewal of an effectual Lutheran/theological ethos, both national and global. A shared vulnerability as emphasized by Scandinavian Creation Theology is related to the social and a shared responsibility for the world, a calling *coram mundo*. This could possibly cut across the standard progressive opposition of social justice politics to the pre-political local/tribal/communal/national. Such an opposition is easily combined with the distorted slamming together of the pre-political and the political by the current right wing, something that also frees them to remain silent about the supervening powers of neoliberalism, or authoritarianism, dividing societies locally and worldwide. A rediscovered sense of interdependency may help us focus on structures of solidarity and democracy, within homes, churches, homelands, and the world.[42] We need both, private homes and a belonging to the world in a planetary existence.

CONCLUSION

In this chapter I have argued that our deep desires about home and family reveals a sense of what is given in life, sometimes interpreted as a memory of paradise, but experienced in an ambivalent world where desires sometimes are unfulfilled, even exploited. Our vocation at home, in Church and society is to be servants of *recapitulatio*, restoration, to facilitate for human beings to be human again.[43] This indicate for fathers to be able to be good fathers, for mothers to be good enough mothers and for both to give nurture and care for each other in a joyous dance celebrating life together with others who may have other vocations but still desire to have a family and a home. Given that natality, new life, and new beginnings are central, children representing the future are here to be cared for now and to respect their future not to be destroyed.

In this vocation we may experience openings that occur as Messianic moments where the restoration of paradise, and the fulfillment associated with the Kin-dom breaks into our present now to make us fully human. Church as a tree growing in the courtyard between house and street may have a special vocation to facilitate this becoming.

NOTES

1. Niels Henrik Gregersen, Bengt Kristensson Uggla, and Tryggve Wyller, *Reformation Theology for a Post-Secular Age: Logstrup, Prenter, Wingren, and the Future of Scandinavian Creation Theology,* eds. (Göttingen: Vandenhoeck and Ruprecht, 2017), 23.

2. K. E. Løgstrup, *The Ethical Demand.* Introduction by Hans Fink and Alasdair MacIntyre (Notre Dame, IN: Notre Dame University Press, 1997), 14.

3. Niels Henrik Gregersen, "Towards a More Generous Creation Theology: On Mutuality and the Circulation of Gifts," in *American Perspectives Meet Scandinavian Creation Theology,* eds. Gerle, et al. (Church of Sweden Research Department, Aarhus University: The Grundtvig Study Center, 2019), 65–66.

4. Gregersen, "Towards," 65–66.

5. Else Marie Wiberg Pedersen, "The Holy Spirit," in *Cracks in the Walls: Essays on Spirituality, Ecumenicity and Ethics* ed. Else Mare Wiberg Pedersen (New York: Peter Lang, 2003), 23–41.

6. Augustine, *On Continence*, 1.19, 2.13. In chapter 11 woman is described as a helper. The man is supposed to rule, she to obey. "Augustine argued that a gender hierarchy formed part of the original creation. Man should rule over woman and the rest of creation." in Elisabeth Gerle, *Passionate Embrace: Luther on Love, Body, and Sensual Presence* (Eugene, OR: Wipf and Stock, 2017), 265.

7. My interpretation is partly inspired by Gerald West, senior professor in Old Testament at University of KwaZulu-Natal, and a lecture he gave at Stellenbosch University a few years ago.

8. Niels Henrik Gregersen, "Skabelse og forsyn." in *Fragmenter af et speil: Bidrag til Dogmatikken*, ed. Niels Henrik Gregersen (Frederiksberg: Anis, 1997/1978), 59–130.

9. Phyllis Trible, *God and the Rhetoric of Sexuality* (Philadelphia: Fortress Press 1998), 90.

10. Tamara Cohn Eskenazi, "Att läsa Bibeln i vår egen tid, ett judiskt perspektiv." in *Att tolka Bibeln och Koranen: Konflikt och förhandling* ed. Hanna Stenström (Lund: Studentlitteratur, 2009), 219, 221; cf. Eskenazi and Andrea L. Weiss, *The Torah: A Women's Commentary* (New York: URJ Press, 2008).

11. Eskenazi, "Att läsa Bibeln," 220.

12. Kari Elisabeth Börressen, *From Patristics to Matristics. Selected Articles on Christian Gender Models* (Rom: Herder, 2002), 292.

13. I have developed this further in Gerle, *Passionate Embrace*, 125–26.

14. Elisabeth Gerle, *Passionate*, 229.

15. Emmanuel Levinas, *Etik och oändlighet* (Stockholm/Stehag, Symposium, 1990), 89, 117.

16. Elisabeth Gerle, "Sig själv nog eller ömsesidig längtan? Levinas läst av den andre 50 år senare" in *Rit* nr 14, 2012, (Lund's Center for Theology and Religion's online publication from a symposium on Levinas in December 2011) .

17. Peter Kemp, *Levinas—An Introduction* (Göteborg: Daidalos, 1992), 40.

18. Ulrica Fritzson and Ebba Älvebrandt, *Försoningens väg. Teologiska och diakonala perspektiv på försoning, upprättelse och liv* (Stockholm: Verbum, 2022), 117.

19. I have written more on this more gender-neutral term for the Kingdom to come in Elisabeth Gerle, "Eschata, the Kin-dom of God, in a Time of Presentism, Patriarchy, and Neo-Nationalism: Writing Back to Luther through Hannah Arendt and Judith Butler in *The Alternative Luther. Lutheran Theology from the Subaltern,* ed. Else Marie Wiberg Pedersen (Lanham, MD: Lexington Books/ Fortress Academic, 2019). Kin-dom is a notion that is not gendered as kingdom.

20. Robert Musil, *Über die Dummheit* (Berlin; Edition Holzinger. Taschenbuch, 2016/1937).

21. Vitor Westhelle, "Planet Luther," in *Lutheran Identity and Political Theology*, eds Carl Henric Grenholm and Göran Gunner (Eugene, OR: Wipf & Stock, 2014), 25.

22. See Jone Salomonsen, "The Ritual Powers of the Weak: Democracy and Public Responses to the 22 July 2011 Terrorist Attacks on Norway," in *Reassembling Democracy: Ritual as Cultural Resource*, Jone Salomonsen et al., eds (London: Bloomsbury Academic, 2021), 158.

23. Hannah Arendt, *The Human Condition* (London: Routledge, 2008).

24. Mary G. Dietz, "Hannah Arendt and Feminist Politics," in *Hannah Arendt and Critical Essays*, eds. Lewis P. Hinchman and Sandra K. Hinchman (Albany: State University of New York, 1994), 243.

25. Elisabeth Gerle, *Vi är inte idioter: Klimat, ekonomi och demokrati* (Göteborg: Korpen. 2021).

26. Arendt, *The Human Condition*, 128.

27. Julia Kristeva, *Hannah Arendt* (New York: Columbia University Press, 2001), 46.

28. Grace Jantzen, *Towards a Feminist Philosophy of Religion* (Bloomington: Indiana University Press, 1999), 127; cf Sigríður Guðmarsdóttir "The Natal Abyss of Freedom: Arendt, Augustine and Feminist Christian Ethics," in *Gendering Christian Ethics,* Jenny Daggers, ed. (Newcastle upon Tyne, UK: Cambridge Scholars Publications, 2012), 97–117.

29. Sigríður Guðmarsdóttir, 101.

30. Elisabeth Gerle, *Vi är inte idioter,*

31. Elisabeth Gerle, *Passionate*, 296–97, 305.

32. I have developed this in Elisabeth Gerle, ed., "Var dags pcj varke människas upprättelse," in *Luther som utmaning. Om frihet och ansvar* (Stockholm: Verbum, 2008).

33. "Martin Luther's Large Catechism, Comments on the Fourth Commandment," translated by Benter and Dau, Project Gutenberg Etext of The Large Catechism, by Martin Luther, 1722.txt (1999) https://www.gutenberg.org/cache/epub/1722/pg1722.html.

34. Elisabeth Gerle, "Var dags." *Passionate Embrace.*

35. "Vom ehelichen Leben " in WA 10 II, 295:16–296:11; cf. LW 45:39–49, 1522. For full quote see Elisabeth Gerle, *Passionate embrace*, 102.

36. WA 30 I, 149, "Deutsch Cathechismus." 1529. See also Gerle, *Passionate Embrace,* 177.

37. Westhelle," Planet Luther," 27.

38. Westhelle, " Planet Luther," 26.

39. Westhelle, " Planet Luther," 26.

40. Göran Rosenberg, *Rabbi Marcus Ehrenpreis obesvarade kärlek* (Stockholm, Bonniers, 2021), 21.

41. Niels Henrik Gregersen, Bengt Kristensson Uggla, and Trygve Wyller, eds., *Reformation Theology for a Post-Secular Age*, 8.

42. I have developed this more in Elisabeth Gerle, 2021, "Becoming Society Again: Reimagining New Social Contracts through Scandinavian Creation Theology" in Dialog, A Journal of Theology, vol. 60, no. 2, 2021, 9.

43. This expression was therefore used as title for a biography on Gustaf Wingren, Bengt Kristensson Uggla, *Becoming Human Again* (Eugene, OR: Cascade, 2016).

Chapter 7

Home Is Where Trust Is

Exilic Existence and Theological Trust Culture in Luther and Løgstrup

Sasja Emilie Mathiasen Stopa

What does it mean to have a home? To a real estate agent, it means owning a house or a place of residence. "Get home safe" is the slogan of Home, a Danish real estate agency. In general, having a home often means being part of a social unit comprising a number of family members; a domestic sphere ideally characterized by feelings of trust and love. Home is where the heart is. Having a home can also just mean inhabiting a familiar or usual setting. My balcony is unfortunately home to a number of doves. A person who develops special needs no longer has a home, but lives in a home in the sense of an establishment providing residence and care. However, the term 'home' refers not only to a dwelling or a building, but also to larger social units of one's native town or land.[1] Moreover, with the globalization of information, trade, and politics, individuals regard themselves as at home in a global, international society. This is perhaps especially the case among the well-educated elite, where belonging to the global community is a status marker.

Recently, though, the thrill of belonging to an increasingly globalized world has been challenged. During the corona virus pandemic, nation states turned against each other in the fight for vaccines, and month-long lockdowns made home seem more like a prison cell than a castle. Moreover, the ongoing war in Ukraine has reinforced the boundaries around the nation state and strengthened international alliances, which cut through the international community and turn the world into a broken home.

Biologically speaking, the human species has a home on earth. Yet, several religious traditions proclaim that this home is defective, temporary, or even illusory. Indeed, they argue for the need to *exit* this world in favor of another truer reality. Such world-renunciation is a defining trait of what several scholars have termed "axial religion"; a philosophical and religious strand of thought developing across the world from around 800 BC onwards.[2] It responds to basic human experiences with the world as unreliable and even destructive and copes with how fraught with suffering existence can be by introducing a notion of transcendence; a "vision of a true world beyond the phenomenal world of experience and history."[3] Through a conception of relating to another, truer reality, religious social imaginaries and practices function as an antidote to these common experiences and aim to reduce existential anxiety and establish well-functioning and trustful communities.[4]

The axial moment of world-renunciation with reference to a transcendent reality is central to Christianity. Hence, the Old Testament describes how God spoke the world into existence and gifted his creation to humans, and the New Testament narrates a divine incarnation and Jesus' promise of an eschatological homecoming to make the earth more reliable as a home away from home. With these ideas, transmitted throughout the history of Christianity, believers learned to interpret their earthly existence as *exilic* and dependent upon divine intervention, both in the present and eschatologically. By transmitting certain social imaginaries, theologians and religious practitioners nourished a culture of trust, which enabled them to face the harsh realities of earthly life and feel at home in the world against all odds.[5]

In the present essay, I examine this axial line of thought in the works of the German reformer Martin Luther (1483–1546) and the Danish Lutheran theologian K. E. Løgstrup (1905–1981). I argue that despite their locations on different sides of Lessing's ugly, broad ditch separating the premodern world of metaphysical truth-telling from the contingent historical truths of the modern world, they both transmit a Christian tradition defined by axial notions of world renunciation and transcendence and deal with common human experiences of suffering by proclaiming a conception of creation as penetrated by divine transcendence through the omnipresence of Christ.

I begin the essay by briefly defining the concept of axial religion as it has been theorized by Karl Jaspers and Robert Bellah. Moreover, I argue for an intimate connection between this kind of religion and the development of a religious culture, in which individual faith in the sense of trust and loyal obligation towards the religious community takes center stage. Then, I analyze Luther's understanding of postlapsarian existence as exilic and of religious practices of prayer and worship as ways to nurture trust culture amidst suffering and death. Finally, I examine how Løgstrup reinvigorates metaphysics and reinterprets the conception of divine transcendence through phenomenological analysis of the so-called sovereign life utterances.[6] I focus the analysis on part six of *Creation and Annihilation* on the relationship between the experienced world, which is "lavish with wonders, cruel with sufferings, unjust with coincidence,"[7] and the proclaimed kingdom of God.

AXIAL ANXIETY AND RELIGIOUS TRUST CULTURE

The notion of an axial period in the history of religion was introduced by philosopher Karl Jaspers in *Vom Ursprung und Ziel der Geschichte* from 1949.[8] Jaspers argues that in the period from around 800 to 200 BC, with a zenith around 500 BC, important cultural patterns developed concurrently in China, India, and in the Western World, meaning Greece, Palestine, and Iran, which continue to influence modern society.[9] Recently, sociologist Robert Bellah has developed Jaspers' notion as part of his influential theory on the cultural evolution of religion.[10] Bellah distinguishes among four evolutionary ages within the history of religions: the tribal age, which concerns religion in pre-state societies, the archaic age of early state religion, the axial, and the post-axial age. According to Bellah, the axial age is a period in the middle of the 1st millennium BC in which radical and intellectual ideas and practices that were skeptical and world renouncing appeared in China, India, Greece and among the ancient Israelites promoted by figures such as Confucius, Lao-Tse, Buddha, Zoroaster, Plato, and other Greek philosophers as well as the Hebrew prophets.[11]

Whereas tribal and archaic religions are cosmological in the sense that "supernature, nature, and society were all fused in a single cosmos,"[12] the axial breakthrough includes a division between this-wordly and otherworldly and introduces a notion of transcendence. The comprehensive perspective from above personified by a transcendent God serves as precondition for the critical reflexion of metaphysics: "A God who is finally outside society and the world provides the point of reference from which all existing presuppositions can be questioned, a basic criterion for the axial transition."[13] Jaspers describes the influence of this transition for human self-understanding:

> What is new about this age, in all three areas of the world, is that man becomes conscious of Being as a whole, of himself and his limitations. He experiences the terror of the world and his own powerlessness. He asks radical questions. Face to face with the void he strives for liberation and redemption. By consciously recognising his limits he sets himself the highest goals. He experiences absoluteness in the depths of selfhood and in the lucidity of transcendence.[14]

Jaspers' definition of the axial breakthrough seems to mirror his contemporary situation when the devastating realities of the first and the second world war had destroyed all illusions. He describes the postwar situation as one of spiritual chaos defined by a lack of trust in science, humanism, and in the church and argues for a need to reestablish trust culture based on a transcendent source[15]:

> Today the situation demands: We must return to a deeper origin, to a fountain-head from which all faith once welled forth in its particular historical shapes, to this wellspring which can flow at any time man is ready for it. When trust in that which is manifest and given in the world no longer supports life, then trust in the origin of all things must lay the foundations.[16]

According to Jaspers, human beings need certain ideas such as that of perpetual peace in order to form sound and meaningful communities, even if they are impossible to realize and remain "an infinite task beyond the possibility of being fashioned into a reality."[17] These ideas depend on faith or trust in a metaphysical source of meaning: "Its basis, however, is an inexplicable confidence, namely, the certitude of faith that everything is not null and void, not merely a senseless chaos, a passing from nothing into nothing. The ideas that guide our passage through the world are revealed to this confidence."[18] For Jaspers, this quest for or directedness towards transcendence becomes a humanizing force that defines true human beings: "It is impossible for man to lose transcendence, without ceasing to be man."[19] Jaspers understands faith as an immanent mode of existence that is aware of and directed towards transcendence, which includes a longing for unity and is captured in the symbol of God, which is one among other symbols central for human existence: "Always we live with symbols. In them we experience and apprehend transcendence, authentic reality. Loss of this reality occurs both in making this symbol a real existence in the world, and in aestheticising the symbol into an optional guide for emotions."[20]

Hence, in Jasper's view, the axial breakthrough answers to a situation of spiritual—as well as emotional and material chaos—by introducing an idea of transcendence, which individuals apprehend through faith. This metaphysical idea serves as the basis for other ideas, such as that of eternal peace, which are necessary for establishing sound communities. I understand this as an example of religious trust culture and in the following, I examine how such a culture develops in Lutheran theology based on a notion of immanent transcendence.

CREATION AS A HOME AWAY FROM HOME

The New Testament transmits a world-renouncing tendency and points towards a better world to come. "My kingdom is not of this world" (John 18:36), is Jesus' cryptic statement spoken to his interrogator, Pilate, in the Gospel of John's depiction of the Roman trial. It relies on the Johannine distinction between the kingdom of the world and the kingdom of God. Accordingly, Paul maintains that existence on earth is exilic, since the followers of Christ have their citizenship in heaven (Phil. 3:20): "We know that if the earthly tent we live in is destroyed, we have a building from God, an eternal house in heaven, not built by human hands" (2 Cor. 5:1). This knowledge leads to a life characterized by trust in God and his promise of an eternal homecoming: "For we live by faith, not by sight. We are confident, I say, and would prefer to be away from the body and at home with the Lord" (2 Cor. 5:7–8).

In the synoptic Gospels, the striving towards eternal life involves a radical taking leave of one's family home: "Whoever comes to me and does not hate father and mother, wife and children, brothers and sisters, yes, and even life itself, cannot be my disciple" (Luke 14:26). However, breaking with the earthly home will be richly rewarded: "And everyone who has left houses or brothers or sisters or father or mother or wife or children or fields for my sake will receive a hundred times as much and will inherit eternal life" (Matt. 19:29).

These statements among others inspired a decisively axial tendency in the history of Christianity defined by a longing for another, truer world and a denouncing of this-worldly existence. At the same time, though, a new horizon opened when the expectation of Christ's imminent return faded and theologians began cultivating the idea of immanent transcendence based on the New Testament notion of divine incarnation, which inspired the doctrine of Christ's two natures, decided by the Council of Chalcedon in 451. This then fueled the development of ideas on Christ's divine presence in the eucharistic meal, in the human being through a mystical union, or in creation as such. These doctrines inspired normative notions or imaginaries of divine presence, which served the purpose of turning the world into a reliable home away from home, counterfeiting basic human experiences of suffering and death through trust in God's loving presence.

MARTIN LUTHER: TRUST IN GOD AS AN
ANTIDOTE TO EXILIC EXISTENCE

Falling into Mistrust

The New Testament notions of earthly existence as exilic and of God's immanent presence in Christ play a crucial role in Luther's theology. In *Lectures on Genesis* from 1535, Luther interprets the fall narrative as a story of how human beings became estranged from their heavenly father and were expelled from the paradisiacal home and thrown into a life in exile.[21] After the fall, humans have lost their part in God's image and glory and live like strangers on earth with limited knowledge of God and his creation: "By citizenship we belong to that homeland which we now look at, admire, and understand, yet like strangers and exiles; but after this life we shall look at these things more closely and understand them perfectly."[22] Luther describes this post-lapsarian situation as defined by mistrust in God's words and misplaced trust in humans and contrasts it with Adam and Eve's exemplary relationship with God prior to the Fall, characterized by absolute trust and obedience toward God's words:[23] "In this way Adam and Eve, resplendent with innocence and original righteousness, and abounding in peace of mind because of their trust in him, who was so kind, walked about naked while they discoursed on the Word and command of God and praised God, just as should be done on the Sabbath."[24] With the commandment not to eat from the tree of knowledge of good and evil, God provides Adam and Eve with an incomprehensible word in order for them to have something to believe in, since without it they would have no opportunity to confess their trust in him and acknowledge him as God. Hence, according to Luther, the commandment gives them a directive for worship, for giving thanks, and for instructing their children.[25] Created in the divine image, Adam and Eve know, trust, fear, and love God and confirm their trust in him by keeping his commandment.[26]

In the fall, however, first Eve and then Adam question God's words and distrust his commandment. According to Luther, exactly such distrust in God is the epitome of sin and the source of every other sin.[27] From Luther's perspective, the fall narrative does not tell of a specific offense against God's law but explains how Adam and Eve lost their trust in him: "[. . .] confidence towards God has been lost and the heart is full of distrust, fear, and shame."[28] In this state of exile, human beings try to cover their naked shame with worldly honor or by doing good works with the aim of forcing God to glorify them. In doing so, they reveal their devastating lack of trust in God and thus fail to honor him as God and steal his honor.[29]

In this way, Luther maintains that even prelapsarian humans were separated from God and obliged to sustain their trusting relationship with him through worship and depended on an eschatological hope of unity with him.[30] What is lost in the fall is first and foremost the loving and trusting relationship between God the father and his loyal and obedient children. Therefore, the central task of theology in exile is to facilitate a reestablishment of this trusting relationship and, thus, recreate the safe home-environment known to Adam and Eve in Paradise.

Reading Creation as a Divine Book

As I noted above, Luther claims that the fall not only destroys the human ability to trust and worship God, but also limits human knowledge about God and his creation. Consequently, knowledge of the world is only accessible through a variety of sciences, which speak different languages. Thus, in Genesis, the Holy Spirit interprets the world by means of a theological language different from the language of philosophers or astronomers, who speak of spheres or epicycles: "Thus we see that the Holy Spirit also has His own language and way of expression, namely, that God, by speaking, created all things and worked through the Word, and that all His works are some words of God, created by the uncreated Word."[31] Luther maintains that "every science should make use of its own terminology"[32] and, thus, confirms how knowledge belongs within a certain linguistic framework of interpretation and depends on a mediating principle, which theology names the Holy Spirit.

In the language of the Holy Spirit, God creates through speech and nature consists of divine words that relate to his uncreated Word. Building on Gen 1, the notion of creation as infused with God's words is reoccurring in Luther's works. Hence, in a 1521 writing against Hieronymus Emser, Luther claims that "every work and creature of God are sheer living signs and words of God."[33] However, Luther refuses the attempt to describe God being based on observations about nature and maintains that, because of sin, the book of nature is not first and foremost a book of wonders, but rather a manifold and ambiguous book testifying to the world's fundamental wretchedness. Thus, in an exposition of the Book of Jonah from 1526, Luther explains that from nature and natural law, humans can tell *that* there is a God, but not *who* this God is, that is, whether his intentions towards them are good or bad.[34] Reason and nature do not know where to seek refuge when confronted with divine wrath in the form of suffering and death.[35] They are unable to conceive God as God *pro nobis*, who reveals himself in Christ to justify the human being. This unequivocal promise of salvation is revealed solely in the New Testament (*sola scriptura*) and can only be acknowledged through faith (*sola fide*) in Christ (*solus Christus*). Rather than a human work, Luther stresses that such faith is a gift of divine grace (*sola gratia*).

With the incarnation of God's uncreated Word in the flesh and blood of Christ, creation—including the human being—is respoken by means of a new theological language. Luther maintains that when divine presence incarnates in the world, reality is created anew.[36] When believers join together to proclaim their trust in God—and in the social imaginaries of Lutheran theology—the world no longer appears merely as a place of suffering, but also as a testimony to God's saving grace.

Prayer and Ritual Induce Trust

The exilic character of human existence on earth is at the heart of Luther's exposition of the Lord's Prayer from 1519, *An Exposition of the Lord's Prayer for Simple Laymen*, one of his first writings aiming to educate the laity in their daily religious practice.[37] According to Luther, the initial address "Our Father" comforts the believer, since it describes the relationship to God as a loving relationship between a father and a child and shows that God prefers to be honored as a parent rather than as a judge, as Lord or simply as God. Thus, when believers confess that they are his children, they are able to placate and move God.

However, the statement "who is in heaven" breaks the domestic bliss and reminds the children of their distance to God, who has left them suffering and abandoned on earth and subject to sin: "He knows himself to be wretched and all alone on earth. From this must result a fervent yearning, like that of a child who lives far from his father's country among strangers, desolate and miserable."[38] At the end of his book, Luther recaptures the prayer in a dialogue between God and the soul, which begins with the soul lamenting because of this estrangement: "O our Father, who art in heaven, we your children dwell here on earth in misery, far removed from you. Such a great gulf lies between you and us. How are we to find our way home to you in our fatherland?"[39] Distanced from God, humans lead miserable and sinful lives, while they long to return to their paradisiacal home in heaven.

To reconnect with their absent father, they have to acknowledge their sin, but they are unable to do so naturally and spontaneously, since it requires fundamental trust in God's forgiveness. Luther describes this trust as a divine gift of faith that emerges when humans have the spirit of Christ in their hearts and realize their dependence on him. The practice of prayer, though, holds the potential for reestablishing this trust relationship, since it incites faith in God's gospel of forgiveness. Luther's understanding of the practice of prayer resembles his description of the sacraments as crutches for the weak of faith, that is, every human being confronted with the ambiguous experience of life in exile. Humans need faith, that is, trust in God, to mediate between the terrifying experience of exilic existence and Jesus' counterintuitive proclamation of God's promise of forgiveness and eternal salvation and this faith is nurtured and embodied through religious practices of prayer and rituals.

With its genuinely pastoral aim, Luther's theology aims to foster trust and reinterprets these religious practices as central for nourishing a culture of trust among believers. This culture is instigated when they kneel at the altar to confess their sin and receive forgiveness mediated through divine presence in the flesh and blood of Christ. Luther transmits the conceptions central to axial religion that the world is a foreign and potentially hostile dwelling and that humans depend on trust in a transcendent reality in the midst of existential anxiety and suffering. In the twentieth century, this theological framework for understanding human existence was developed further by Løgstrup.

K. E. LØGSTRUP: TRACING GOD'S KINGDOM IN CREATED LIFE

Phenomenology Pries Open the Iron Cage of Modernity

"The age of religion is over."[40] Løgstrup writes this provocative statement on the very first page of *Creation and Annihilation*. The book was published in 1978 as part of his Metaphysics: an ambitious four-volume attempt to reintroduce the metaphysical question and provide a foundation for a religious interpretation of the modern age based on phenomenological analysis of basic human experiences.[41] In the preface, Løgstrup admits that his contemporaries will probably regard this attempt as futile: "Seen through the eyes of the epoch, when its gaze is softest, this book will appear as a retreating army fighting a rear-guard action before the army and the rearguard disappear into the darkness of anachronism."[42]

The epoch follows Max Weber in understanding the modern secular world as the result of an ongoing process of rationalization characterized by increasing knowledge about and mastery over nature and the social sphere. This results in elaborate systems of teleological efficiency, rational calculation and control, which according to Weber incarcerate the individual in an iron cage.[43] The process was initially driven by religion, which interprets the world and regulates behavior through myths, cult, rituals, ceremonies, and magic. With increasing rationalization, though, religion ends up obliterating itself as the natural sciences, politics, economics, and technology take over when it comes to explaining and mastering the world.

However, according to Løgstrup, the process of rationalization has led to a blind spot with regard to phenomena that present themselves to the individual's immediate experience and are too fundamental to become objects of human knowledge and mastery.[44] These are for instance meaning, color, language, sensation, immediate understanding, unconditional life utterances such as mercy, trust, love, and the openness of speech as well as death and its premonitions suffering and illness.[45]

The modern sciences agree on promoting an irreligious ontology, which theology has responded to in two ways. First, in a Kierkegaardian manner, by focusing on ethics and retreating from philosophy, leaving the ontological question to neopositivist descriptions of an objective reality based on empirical observations. Second, by emphasizing the faith relation to God through Christ and dismissing creation theology, as in dialectical theology.[46] However, Løgstrup claims that neither the prevailing irreligious ontology nor existentialist and dialectical theology are able to grasp the basic phenomena of human existence. He attacks on both fronts by propounding a religious ontology that rehabilitates creation theology and reinvigorates philosophy of religion through phenomenological analyses of phenomena that invite a religious interpretation.[47] Theology should engage with philosophy and propound an ontology of faith that focuses on these phenomena as they are interpreted through language.[48] This analysis functions as a crowbar breaking the iron cage of rationalism and contributes to what Løgstrup terms a "religious total interpretation" of existence and creation, that is, a metaphysics for the contemporary world.[49]

Divine Presence in "Pre-Cultural" Phenomena

Løgstrup describes the basic phenomena including the sovereign life utterances as pre-cultural and an inherent part of the universe. In this way, he argues for a pre-human shaping of the world in terms of meaning; a force of good that pushes through the harsh reality of life in exile: "The meaning that the universe in its unfamiliarity gives human existence consists of pre-cultural phenomena, which we are not source of and which carry our existence. What is alien appear in life utterances that are so familiar to us as trust, openness, sincerity, compassion."[50]

Løgstrup's description of these phenomena as pre-cultural relies on his specific and rather narrow definition of culture, which is influenced by neo-Kantianism: "Culture endows man with a distance to his surroundings and to his own actions, in which knowledge and dominance, administration and planning can unfold."[51] Phenomena such as language and the sovereign life utterances are "pre-cultural" since they are beyond human control.

Relying on a Lutheran understanding of the human being as utterly determined by self-interest, Løgstrup emphasizes how these phenomena occur spontaneously behind the back of the individual, who finds him- or herself utterly consumed by their fulfilment. Only when the utterance fails, when for instance trust is deceived, does the individual become aware of it and its inherent, the unconditional demand of neighborly love, which prohibits any ulterior motive.[52] This demand, then, serves as the basis for formulating ethical norms and in that sense, the phenomena "generate ethics."[53] For instance, the misused frankness of speech results in the norm not to lie.

When interpreted religiously, the phenomena belong to a shaping of the universe by its creator and testify to his immanent presence in the everyday: "From within our life and from within our surroundings, the religious interpretation emerges from phenomena which are not extraordinary but, on the contrary, familiar."[54] Løgstrup explains this religious ontology by referring to Luther's distinction between God's omnipresence in the world and his presence toward the individual in his saving Word and sacraments. Against the focus on the latter in dialectical theology, Løgstrup insists that according to Luther, God is present not only in his word and sacraments, but also in creation through Christ's omnipresence. Following Luther, Løgstrup insists on speaking of God in a twofold manner: indirectly, God can be spoken about as a determination of reality; directly, God is spoken about in the historical proclamation of Jesus. Løgstrup argues that there is an analogy between the two: The proclaimed Jesus is equivalent to God's presence in reality. In this way, creation—and more specifically the basic phenomena of human experience—becomes a universal interpretive frame for the Christian proclamation. In this decisively religious ontology, the sovereign life utterances testify to God's presence in interpersonal relationships.[55]

Thus, refusing a return to traditional pre-Kantian metaphysics, Løgstrup advocates a metaphysics that emanates from problems and phenomena of existence itself that "lie near to a religious interpretation."[56] With this often repeated phrasing, Løgstrup plays on the meaning of the Danish word *nærliggende*, near-lying, which does not merely mean adjacent or approximate, but *suggests* that a religious interpretation of these phenomena seems obvious. The truth of this religious interpretation can never be proven, but according to Løgstrup it is more adequate, plausible, and close to experience than the interpretation emerging from an irreligious ontology.[57]

Metaphysics as a Social Ontology of Faith

The phenomenological analysis constitutes the backbone of Løgstrup's religious ontology. Løgstrup defines ontology as "an understanding of and talk about the universe's being."[58] As Ole Jensen points out, Løgstrup uses the terms metaphysics and ontology almost analogously.[59] This concurs with the original meaning of ontology as a theory of being, which was first employed in the late sixteenth century. In *Philosophisches Lexicon* (1733), Johann Georg Walch defines this relatively new notion: "Ontology means the doctrine of being (*Ente*) and is understood as a name whereby a new philosophy of metaphysics is established, for instance, that discipline that treats being in general and its properties."[60]

However, Løgstrup also explains ontology in a more modern way as a certain "understanding of life" or a "world view" and criticizes dialectical and existentialist theology for denying that a certain world view is part of Christianity, since that means cherishing "the illusion of a standpoint outside of the time and the space we live in."[61] This does not necessarily mean that Christianity is merely a world view, but its proclaimed truth claims lose their credibility without a connecting point in people's lived experience. On the one hand, the contemporary world view is able to function as a criterium for eliminating outdated Christian ideas such as "detailed apocalyptic conceptions."[62] On the other hand, the Christian proclamation holds the power to overthrow contemporary delusions.

On this basis, Løgstrup underlines how the life utterances receive their content from history and tradition, in which children are reared, and are then shaped by the individual. This suggests an understanding of ontology as a social category that has little to do with a naturalistic ontology or with traditional metaphysics. At the same time, though, he warns against a strict separation between nature, history, and individuality and claims that "culture, history and language do not exist without nature cropping up in all their phenomena as their foundation."[63] Hereby, he seems to overlook that even this notion of nature is culturally shaped and probably differs vastly from the perception of nature among the natural sciences. While Luther seems almost modern when claiming that the Holy Spirit speaks a certain kind of language that differs from the equally valid languages of other sciences, Løgstrup risks slipping back into premodern metaphysics with his notion of pre-cultural, natural phenomena. Peter Widmann is to the point when asking if he relies on "a pre-critical pre-supposition, namely that we have access to reality as such?"[64]

Even though biology might play a part in basic phenomena such as trust and love, they appear to individuals as social phenomena that define interpersonal relationships. Løgstrup seems to admit this cultural shaping when arguing for Christianity's need to develop or nurture culture: "If nothing but monstrosity ['*unatur*,' literally 'un-nature'] and lack of freedom prevail humanly and among people, Christianity has to create nature and freedom, for they are necessary conditions for receiving the Christian proclamation."[65]

Charles Taylor's notion of the social imaginary implies a broader concept of culture than Løgstrup's neo-Kantian emphasis on culture as the result of a human control-gaining effort. Taylor developed the notion as an alternative to social theory, focusing on how ordinary people imagine their social existence in pre-theoretical images, stories and legends. Social imaginaries constitute a "common understanding that makes possible common practices and a widely shared sense of legitimacy."[66] They capture "the ways in which [people] imagine their social existence, how they fit together with others, how things go on between them and their fellows, the expectations which are normally met, and the deeper normative notions and images which underlie these expectations."[67] From this perspective, Løgstrup's phenomenological analysis deals with phenomena that are cultural in the sense that they present themselves within a specific cultural framework and are interpreted by means of a language as well as certain conceptions and social imaginaries that belong to a Christian world view.[68]

Løgstrup distinguishes metaphysics from religion and argues for a division between the phenomenological analysis that invites a religious interpretation and this interpretation itself: "In metaphysics we reflect on the circumstances with which the universe endows our lives and which we experience immediately. Moving from the effects which the universe has on our lives to the question whether the universe is concerned with us, we are moving from metaphysics to religion."[69] In this way, Løgstrup distinguishes between the experience that the universe endows individuals with wonders and terrors and the claim that this universe shows consideration with them. He reveals himself as a genuine Lutheran theologian in emphasizing the *pro nobis*-aspect as central to the notion of religion: Natural phenomena might reveal *that* there is a God or a universe with agency, but not *who* this God is to us. Based on the broader concept of culture presented above, though, Løgstrup's distinction between a metaphysics of "pre-cultural" phenomena and the Christian proclamation of divine care seems to evaporate. The gap between them arises from the cultural distinction between the language of phenomenology or metaphysics and the language of theology. However, both belong within a specific social ontology and transmit a certain world view that relies on Christian social imaginaries. In Løgstrup's analysis of the relation between creation and the kingdom of God in part six of *Creation and Annihilation*, it becomes clear how this world view depends on an axial conception of immanent transcendence.

Suffering at the Hand of the Amoral God

The starting point of Løgstrup's reflections on the relationship between creation and the kingdom of God is the basic phenomena of human suffering and death. In the premodern world, suffering was interpreted metaphysically and religiously as caused or, at least, allowed by God.[70] From this follows the question of why God, who is good, righteous, and almighty, has created a world with suffering and death? As a response, G.W. Leibniz presents his theodicy: a defense of God's righteousness in the face of evil and suffering.[71]

Whereas Leibniz answers with a defense of God, the problem of suffering invites an irreligious, nihilistic answer in the modern world. Confronted with the brutal facts of life, the nihilist claims that everything is pointless, empty, or even absurd. Løgstrup responds to the widespread nihilism—not least propounded by trendsetting existentialist philosophers such as Jean Paul Sartre—by almost teasingly demanding a "nihilodicy" that would "defend meaninglessness and nothingness against the attack on them from happiness."[72] Løgstrup takes the fact that only suffering and not happiness and joy demand an explanation to suggest that even the irreligious, nihilistic attitude is rooted in a religious notion of creation. The passion with which the nihilist protests against suffering is fueled by an understanding of created life as given. Thus, even modern humans believe that the cosmic order is good and wise and are deeply affected and shocked when accidents and disasters break it down.

Whereas the Jews of the Bible—most strikingly Job's friends—explain disasters as morally righteous and caused by the individual's wrongdoings, today this individual guilt has become collective: "The individual has been replaced by humanity as regards the causal relation between evil and physical suffering."[73] However, Løgstrup claims that both explanations ignore how disaster and misery are often utterly coincidental and, hence, a part of the world's make-up: "It is true that we inflict indescribable suffering as well as sudden and early death upon each other, in war, in competition, in carelessness, but there is also a kind of suffering that would exist, just as illness and natural disasters would exist, even though everyone was a saint."[74] With reference to Darwin, Løgstrup maintains that cruelty is built into creation, since every species lives at the expense of other species.[75] He interprets this annihilation religiously and claims that the eternal and divine force of creation has built not only the wonders of life utterances such as love, mercy, and trust, but also annihilation with its suffering and contingency into creation.[76] According to Løgstrup, both Judaism and Christianity interpret annihilation in relation to a notion of immanent transcendence: "In contrast to many other religions and cultures, in which the thought of annihilation does not play a decisive part, the Jewish religion and Christianity accept the consequence of annihilation with the realization that as long as something exists, an eternal and divine power is keeping annihilation away from it for every moment of its existence."[77]

In this way, Løgstrup's religious metaphysics rests on the claim that suffering and pain stem from the creator God: "Seen from a human perspective, God in his creation is lavish with wonders, cruel with sufferings, unjust with coincidence." The God of creation is "the ubiquitous power to be in everything there is."[78] This power is pre-ethical, eternal, and imperishable and allows for everything that exists to vanish, connecting creation with annihilation, glory with cruelty.

Referring to Martin Buber, Løgstrup distinguishes between the personal and the impersonal God: "In the actions and words of the meeting, God becomes person for the human being, but as the power to be in everything there is, God is beyond any personality."[79] Behind the distinction is Luther's claim that humans experience God as both *deus absconditus*, the unreliable and wrathful hidden God, and *deus revelatus*, Christ, who is trustworthy and loving.[80] From a human point of view, the impersonal God is an amoral, heathen god and individuals respond by blasphemously judging him on the basis of their own morality, " . . . for we want God, the universe, the worldly order, fate on our moral conditions, not on God's."[81]

Based on Luther, Løgstrup states that the experience with the impersonal God and his ambiguous alien work is contradicted by the personal God, Jesus, who proclaims God's own work of grace and forgiveness. However, even this seems amoral, since he forgives everyone regardless of their moral ability to fulfill the law. In this way, God becomes personal "on his own God-human conditions, not on our morally-human conditions [. . .] If we stick to our morality, we are left to blasphemy. Christianity is not about our morality, but about an offer of faith and a hope."[82]

Something New Happens!

This offer of faith and hope is the content of Jesus' proclamation of God's kingdom: "The coming of God's kingdom means that the work of creation and annihilation, its wonders, sufferings and contingencies, is not the last word and work of God. Something new happens."[83] Without any warning, Løgstrup oscillates from a phenomenological analysis of existence that aims at providing a connecting point for the Christian proclamation in human experience to actually proclaiming the end of suffering and universal forgiveness; that is, he moves from indirect to direct talk about God. Widmann rightfully criticizes Løgstrup for failing to explain the connection between the two kinds of God-talk and argues that Løgstrup jumps from ontological considerations concerning basic phenomena that testify about something unknown in the known to metaphysical statements on the universe, being, annihilation, power and God as if they were known and without placing them in a historical textual tradition, that is, a specific cultural setting.[84] Turning to the proclamation of the kingdom of God something new happens, not only in God's encounter with the human being, but also in Løgstrup's analysis.

At the same time, though, Løgstrup seems to have anticipated this proclamation throughout the book, since the basic phenomena of his metaphysics transmit a Christian worldview by relying on conceptions of immanent transcendence and of unconditional phenomena emerging from a force of creation. The difficulty of distinguishing the phenomenological analysis from the Christian proclamation is evident in Løgstrup's description of Jesus. From a phenomenological perspective, his life was without a basic illusion[85]—Løgstrup's term for sin—and therefore life utterances were able to flow freely. Løgstrup states that a religious interpretation would understand this as a sign of the fact that "God was present in Jesus' life in another way than he has been present in any other human life."[86] However, Løgstrup fails to acknowledge that his claim concerning the lack of a basic illusion is itself of a religious interpretation that belongs to a Lutheran world view.

Similarly, his distinction between creation and the kingdom of God is theological. With these notions, Løgstrup reinterprets Luther's conceptions of exilic existence and immanent transcendence.

Bridging the Gap between Creation and the Kingdom of God

Løgstrup stresses the indispensable tension between creation and the kingdom of God and maintains that Jesus provides no theodicy, since he fails to explain why glory and annihilation belong together in creation. Løgstrup expands the unilateral focus on the ethical-existential consequences of this kingdom in existentialist theology and argues that God acts unconditionally in a twofold manner: in his grace and absolute demand, described in *The Ethical Demand*, and in creation as the unconditional power to be in everything there is.[87] Løgstrup proclaims the kingdom of God as a metaphysical eschatological kingdom, where suffering will end and the oppressed will be free, in contrast with existentialist theology, where eternity merely concerns the unconditional demand and forgiveness. Without the hope of eschatological satisfaction for wrongdoings, absolute forgiveness is ethically untenable.[88] With this statement, Løgstrup seems close to agreeing with Kant's understanding of God as a moral absolute. Whereas forgiveness is part of an ethical-existential battle between the kingdom of God and the basic delusion of sin, the sovereign life utterances express a pre-ethical discrepancy between the kingdom of God, defined by carefreeness, and the fact that life is subject to annihilation and requires self-preservation.

At the same time, though, Løgstrup maintains an intimate connection between the two realms and argues that the kingdom of God includes both forgiveness and the spontaneous flow of sovereign life utterances such as trust, mercy, and love. Moreover, he claims that humans know of the goodness and eternity that define God's kingdom on the basis of creation. Sovereign life utterances that break through sin's basic illusion reveal goodness, and the human rebellion against time hints at eternity. Furthermore, humans experience the carefreeness characteristic of God's kingdom when they engage in sound relationships with family, friends, and colleagues: "Carefree we are carried by our living and being together."[89]

However, faith understood as trust in God remains the middle term necessary for countering the human tendency toward self-preservation, thus bridging the gap between creation and the kingdom of God: "Accomplishing carefreeness, which belongs to the kingdom of God, can only occur by anticipating its eternity in faith."[90] Løgstrup situates this trust in the church, that is, in the Christian community. As opposed to Jesus, who forgives spontaneously and has immediate faith in the coming kingdom as part of his nature, human beings only know faith through ritual. In an almost Kierkegaardian way, Løgstrup claims that each individual must decide whether to believe, but reveals himself as anything but a pietist when stating that this decision "will never amount to much else than a ritual confession to a ritual."[91]

Proclaiming God's Immanent Transcendence

When Jesus proclaims the kingdom of God, something new happens both ethically and cosmically. As opposed to many other religious and philosophical traditions, his proclamation does not point beyond this world to another ideal divine world of order to be emulated. Hence, according to Løgstrup, Christianity is not about a diffuse transcendent reality, but about divine immanent transcendence realized in "the personal and eventful relationship between God and the human being."[92] Based on Luther's thoughts on Christ's omnipresence in his later writings on the Lord's Supper, Løgstrup defines God as the power to be in everything there is: "The power is at the same time present in all that exists—and is also eternal and divine, distinct from all that exists."[93]

Løgstrup argues for a realised eschatology when interpreting the life of Jesus. In this life the cosmic and the ethical coincide, since the expectation of the coming kingdom shapes his actions to such an extent that it is already emerging.[94] Modernity, though, has rendered the notion of a cosmic turn of events untenable. Consequently, existentialist theology argues that the kingdom of God only concerns unconditional forgiveness and the radical demand and maintains that speculating on God's presence elsewhere is shameless curiosity. Behind this lies Luther's refusal to speculate on God's metaphysical being *per se* and his emphasis on God in his relationship with humans, *pro nobis*. Løgstrup argues for a rehabilitation of metaphysics, but remains within the limits to human cognition set by Luther's *pro nobis*, that is the human relationship to God, which plays out in interpersonal relationships. Against existentialist theology, he points to God's immanent presence beyond the

ethical horizon of forgiveness and demand by drawing attention to unconditional phenomena that reveal themselves in human existence.

Hope Against Hope

One such phenomenon is the life utterance of absolute hope "that transcends
death."[95] It offers itself even in apparently hopeless situations and has its
source in existence as a rebellion against annihilation. Hope does not rely on
any human ability to conquer death and suffering, but is directed toward "that
which reaches beyond our power. In everything that we have in our power, we
live in a deeper dependency towards that which escapes our power."[96]

Upon presenting itself, this hope leaves the individual with two options: To
disavow it, because there is no experiential foundation for its fulfilment, or
to believe the Christian message. The former option entails a way of life pre-
conditioned by death in which life is postponed death and being is postponed
annihilation. The latter relies on Jesus' statement that humans have to become
like children in order to enter the kingdom of God, that is, appropriating a
childish attitude of hope and trust, not in what one can accomplish, but in
what one is to receive.[97]

Løgstrup describes this experience of a sovereign hope as a precondition
for understanding the Christian notion of eternity.[98] At the same time, though,
experiencing the sovereign hope depends on a certain way of relating to the
future, which has already been shaped by a Christian notion of eternity; a
social imaginary breastfed to children, who are brought up in a Christian
cultural setting. Thus, Løgstrup's distinction between the basic human experience of hope and the Christian notion of eternity seems less a question
of pre-cultural vs. Christian than a question of the common pre-theoretical
social imaginary vs. religious doctrine.

COPING WITH EXILE BY NOURISHING TRUST

Luther defines human existence on earth as exilic. After breaking the rules
of the divine household, humans are kicked out of their ancestral home and
left to lead estranged lives defined by constant longing for their paradisiacal homeland. The process of justification centers on the restoration of trust
between sinners and their loving heavenly father, who promises them a glo-
rious return to their heavenly home. Trust in this eschatological promise is
at the heart of the Christian community. When Christians come together to
acknowledge their trust in God's recreation of the world, they manage their
experiences of suffering and become aware of his good creation. Religious

practices of prayer and worship aim to establish homey communities and foster a culture of trust in a world defined by mistrust.

From the eighteenth century onward, the gradual demythologization of the modern world caused by increasing knowledge of science and history devalued the eschatological remedy for domestic disturbances. Løgstrup is among the leading scholars to take up the daunting task of reinterpreting the meaning of the eschatological kingdom of God in a secular world. Through phenomenological analysis, Løgstrup points to aspects of existence that seem other-worldly in that they counter human self-centeredness and provide reassuring glimpses of trust, love, and mercy amidst our exilic existence. With his analysis of these allegedly pre-cultural phenomena, Løgstrup formulates a distinct social ontology that includes culturally transmitted social imaginaries defining of axial religion. Moreover, he contributes to the ongoing nurturing of this culture, not in the Løgstrupian sense of a human control-gaining effort, but as a cultural framework within which individuals express and interpret their experiences. Interpersonal phenomena such as trust, mercy, and the openness of speech are never immediate, but appear to us through the interpretive lens of the social imaginary. This does not belong to the autonomous, individual consciousness, but to human communities that speak a certain language and extend through time and space.

Ingolf Dalferth concurs with the prevailing irreligious ontology when stating that in today's world "the idea of an ontological transcendence has lost its point."[99] Within this ontology, reality is perceived as one. As Løgstrup states: "The antimetaphysical and irreligious conception is monistic (. . .) Reality consists only of what can be determined in one and only one context, namely space-time continuum."[100] Løgstrup counters this ontology and rehabilitates the idea of ontological transcendence through phenomenological analysis. Løgstrup relies on the axial distinction between transcendence and immanence while arguing for experiences of immanent transcendence rooted in Luther's statements on Christ's omnipresence and expressed in Løgstrup's definition of God as a power to be in everything there is: "Being immanent, the power is omnipresent, but being omnipresent it is still hidden and as being hidden it is transcendent."[101] This power is known to individuals from their experience with sovereign life utterances that testify to a universe of meaning in an apparently meaningless world.

In this way, Luther and Løgstrup proclaim that humans are no longer home alone. God has descended from above and taken up residence among us. To both theologians, this is a statement of faith, which depends on religious learning and practice— ritual in Løgstrup's terminology—to sustain itself.

NOTES

1. According to the Merriam-Webster Dictionary, the English notion stems from the Middle English "hom, hoome" and goes back to the Old English term "hām," meaning landed property, estate, dwelling, house, inhabited place, or native land. This is derived from the Germanic 'haima' meaning dwelling, cf. Old Saxon & Old Frisian 'hēm,' meaning home or dwelling, Middle Dutch 'heem, heim,' meaning dwelling, Old high German 'heima,' meaning dwelling, homeland, Old Norse 'heimr,' meaning abode, land or this world, and the Gothic 'haims,' meaning village, countryside, or home.

2. Cf. Robert Bellah, *Religion in Human Evolution. From the Paleolithic to the Axial Age* (Cambridge, MA: The Belknap Press of Harvard University Press, 2011).

3. Ingolf U. Dalferth, "The Idea of Transcendence," in *The Axial Age and Its Consequences*, Robert Bellah and Hans Joas (eds.) (Cambridge, MA: Harvard University Press, 2012), 146–88 (147).

4. According to Clifford Geertz's influential—and at least to religious practitioners rather controversial—definition "Religion is (1) a system of symbols which acts to (2) establish powerful, pervasive, and long-lasting moods and motivations in men by (3) formulating conceptions of a general order of existence and (4) clothing these conceptions with such an aura of factuality that (5) the moods and motivations seem uniquely realistic" ("Religion as a Cultural System," in *The Interpretation of Cultures,* New York: Basic Books, 1973 [1966], 90.) While adhering to Geertz' definition, Bellah adds a Durkheimian accent that includes a notion of the sacred and emphasis on morals: "Religion is a system of beliefs and practices relative to the sacred that unite those who adhere to them in a moral community" (Bellah 2011, 1). In this essay, I analyze the conceptions of a general order of existence characteristic of axial religion such as worldly existence as exilic and awaiting God's eternal judgement and an eschatological homecoming. Using a term coined by Charles Taylor, I argue that these conceptions, formulated by religious experts and expressed in doctrine, inspire the development of certain social imaginaries that define how people imagine their social existence and deal with common experiences such as suffering and death (Charles Taylor, *Modern Social Imaginaries,* Durham, NC: Duke University Press, 2004).

5. As an exemplary case of how religions create cultures of trust, I have analyzed the influence of Lutheran theology on the development of Danish trust culture specifically in the article "Trusting in God and his Earthly Masks: Exploring the Lutheran Roots of Scandinavian High-trust Culture," *Journal of Historical Sociology*, 33:4, 2020, 456–72.

6. Løgstrup translates these utterances "the unconditional manifestations of living" in the article "The Metaphysical or Religious Triad," *Religious Studies* 15:2, 1979, 227–37 (230), but "utterance" seems a more accurate translation of the Danish "ytring," since it refers to an understanding of creation as a manifestation of God's speech central to the Jewish-Christian tradition (cf. Sasja E. M. Stopa, "'Ich werdend spreche Ich Du': Creative Dialogue in the Relational Anthropologies of Martin Luther and Martin Buber," *Religions* 14:5, 2023, 1–19).

7. K. E. Løgstrup, *Skabelse og tilintetgørelse. Metafysik IV. Religionsfilosofiske betragtninger* (Aarhus: Klim, 2015 [1978], 296). I have translated the quoteations from *Creation and Annihilation* myself, while consulting with the excerpts published in K.E. Løgstrup, *Metaphysics vol. 1 & 2;* trans. and with an introduction by Russell L. Dees (Milwaukee, WI: Marquette University Press, 1995).

8. I refer to the English version *The Origin and Goal of History*, trans. by Michael Bullock (New York: Routledge, 2021). Jaspers' term "Achsenzeit" was most likely inspired by Hegel's understanding of Christ as "die Achse der Weltgeschichte" (Kurt Salamun, "Einleitung des Herausgebers," in *Vom Ursprung und Ziel der Geschichte*. Karl Jaspers Gesamtausgabe. I. Werke, Bd. 10, Kurt Salamun, ed., Basel: Schwabe Verlag, 2020 [VII–XXII]).

9. Jaspers, *The Origin and Goal of History*, 9. Plato's Allegory of the Cave from book VII of *The Republic* is an outstanding example of this world-renouncing tendency, which leaves human beings homeless on earth. Imprisoned in a cave, humans inhabit a reality consisting of mere shadows of artificial objects projected onto a wall by people behind their back, who hold various objects in front of fires. Plato calls the cave the first home (VII., 516 c) and a prison home (VII., 517b). Upon seeing the reality of the beautiful, the just and the good outside of the cave, the philosopher is to ascend to the old home and govern with a waking mind (519c-d). At the intermediate stage, however, the philosopher finds himself in a confused state of *aporia*, profound uncertainty, unable to recognize the old familiar shadows and unable to see anything in the blinding light above. According to Andrea Nightingale, this state is "(among other things) a state of homelessness," which leads to a permanent state of *atopia*: "For the person who has detached himself from society and gone on the journey of philosophic *theoria*, will never be fully 'at home' in the world" (*Spectacles of Truth in Classical Greek Philosophy. Theoria in Its Cultural Context,* Cambridge, UK: Cambridge University Press, 2004, 106).

10. Bellah, *Religion in Human Evolution.*

11. Bellah, *Religion in Human Evolution*, 265ff.

12. Bellah, *Religion in Human Evolution*, 266.

13. Bellah, *Religion in Human Evolution*, 322.

14. Karl Jaspers, *The Origin and Goal of History*, 9.

15. In the lecture *Vom europäischen Geist* (München: R. Piper & Co. Verlag, 1947), held at the Rencontres Internationales de Genève in September 1946, he likewise emphasizes the lack of trust in humanism, in modern civilization, science and technology, and in the society of Germanic-Romance nations.

16. Jaspers, *The Origin and Goal of History*, 235, cf. 199–200.

17. Jaspers, *The Origin and Goal of History*, 234.

18. Jaspers, *The Origin and Goal of History*, 234–35.

19. Jaspers, *The Origin and Goal of History*, 241. As Dalferth underlines, Jaspers' view of transcendence is rooted in the mystic traditions of both the East (Buddhism) and the West (e.g., Meister Eckhart, Nicholas of Cusa) and transmits the neo-Platonic contrast between a changing temporal world of immanence and an unchanging eternal world of transcendence (Dalferth, "The Idea of Transcendence," 147).

20. Jaspers, *The Origin and Goal of History*, 241.

21. Martin Luther, *Lectures on Genesis. Chapters 1–5. Luther's Works*, vol. 1 (LW 1), Jaroslav Pelikan (ed.) (Saint Louis, MO: Concordia, 1958); cf. Martin Luther, "Genesisvorlesung (cap. 1–17)," in *D. Martin Luthers Werke. Kritische Gesamtausgabe. Schriften* (WA), (Weimar: Böhlau, 1883–1993), WA 42: 1–176. Luther lectured on Genesis from 1535 to 1545. Because his own notes have not been handed down, the Weimar Edition bases its text on Georg Rörer and Caspar Cruciger's notes, which were published in four volumes by Viet Dietrich (1544–1554). Luther authorized the first volume on Gen. 1–11 by writing its preface and postscript.

22. LW 1:46; cf. WA 42: 35b.13–14.

23. Luther understands obedience as intimately connected with trust. This is evident, for instance, for his understanding of hierarchic social relationships as characterized not by blind obedience, but by obedient trust (cf. Sasja E. M. Stopa, "'Honor your father and mother'—the influence of honor on Martin Luther's conception of society," in *Lutheran Theology and the Formation of Society: The Danish Kingdom as Example*, Bo Kristian Holm & Nina Javette Koefoed (ed.), Göttingen: Vandenhoeck & Ruprecht, 2018, 107–27 [123–24]).

24. LW 1:144; WA 42: 108.28–31.

25. LW 1:154; WA 42: 116.12–16.

26. LW 1:165; WA 42: 124b.6.

27. LW 1:149; WA 42: 112.20–21.

28. LW 1:167; WA 42: 125.28–29.

29. Cf. Sasja E. M. Stopa, *Soli Deo Honor et Gloria. Honour and Glory in the Theology of Martin Luther (Berlin:* LIT *Verlag, 2021), 85–90. Luther abandons the scholastic distinction between forgivable and mortal sins and maintains that whether an act is sinful is determined not by its content but by the intention or emotion behind the work, i.e., whether the person performing the act trusts God or creatures. Since human beings are unable to fully trust God, Luther maintains that every act is sinful.*

30. Luther underlines how both men and women partake in the glory of the future life (LW 1:68; WA 42: 51b.34–35. With the statement in Gen. 1:27 ("male and female he created them"), Moses wants to refute the false assertion that women have limited access to salvation because of their weaker nature, according to Luther (cf. Sasja E. M. Stopa, "Women as Wives and Rulers in Martin Luther's Theology," *Dialog. A Journal of Theology* 62:1, 2023, 104–117 [109]).

31. LW 1:47; cf. WA 42: 35b.37–40.

32. LW 1:48; cf. WA 42: 36b.12–13.

33. Martin Luther, "Auff das ubirchristlich, ubirgeystlich und ubirkunstlich Buch Bocks Emszers zu Leypczick Antwortt D. M. L." in *D. Martin Luthers Werke. Kritische Gesamtausgabe,* (Weimar: Böhlau, 1883–1993), WA 7: 614–88 (650.27–28). I have translated this and other quotations that are not in *Luther's Works*.

34. Martin Luther, "Der Prophet Jona ausgelegt," in: *D. Martin Luthers Werke. Kritische Gesamtausgabe. Schriften* (WA) (Weimar: Böhlau, 1883–1993, WA 19: 169–251 (206.32–33).

35. WA 19: 223.13–16.

36. Cf. Stopa "Creative Dialogue," 7–8.

37. Martin Luther, "An Exposition of the Lord's Prayer for Simple Laymen," trans. Martin H. Bertram, in *Luther's Works*, vol. 42, Martin O. Dietrich (ed.) (Philadelphia: Fortress Press, 1969), 15–81; cf. Martin Luther, "Deutsche Auslegung des Vaterunsers für die einfältigen Laien," in *D. Martin Luthers Werke. Kritische Gesamtausgabe. Schriften* (WA). Weimar: Böhlau, 1883–1993, WA 2: 80–130. After its publication, the book became widely read and was translated into Italian, Latin, and Bohemian within a year (WA 2:75). Its catechetical and pastoral purpose is evident in Luther's focus on the questions of *how* to pray, *to whom* to pray, and *what* to pray for.

38. LW 42:23; cf. WA 2: 83.27–28

39. LW 42:78; cf. WA 2: 128.4–6.

40. Løgstrup, *Creation and Annihilation*, 11.

41. The volumes center on four central issues: Language, art, nature (the universe), and religion. Although *Creation and Annihilation* is the fourth volume, it was published as the second due to "practical reasons" (Løgstrup, *Creation and Annihilation*, 13). The first volume *Breath and Fullness* (*Vidde og prægnans: Sprogfilosofiske betragtninger*, 2nd ed., København: Gyldendal, 1995) had been published in 1976, while the two remaining volumes, *Art and Knowledge* (*Kunst og erkendelse: Kunstfilosofiske betragtninger*, 3rd ed., Aarhus: Klim, 2018) and *Source and Surrounding* (*Ophav og omgivelse: Betragtninger over historie og natur*, 3rd ed., Aarhus: Klim, 2013) was published posthumously in 1983 and 1984.

42. Løgstrup, *Creation and Annihilation*, 11.

43. In the influential 1930-translation of Webers "Die Protestantische Ethik und der 'Geist' des Kapitalismus" (*Archiv für Sozialwissenschaft und Sozial Politik*, 1905, vol. 20, 1-54; vol. 21, 1-110), Talcott Parsons translated Webers description of capitalist reality as "ein stahlhartes Gehäuse" (vol. 2, 108) into an iron rather than a steel cage.

44. Løgstrup, *Creation and Annihilation*, 11. In 1933. Løgstrup studied with Hans Lipps and Martin Heidegger, who were both students of Edmund Husserl. In an "Autobiographical Sketch," published posthumously as part of *Solidarity and Love, and Other Essays* (*Solidaritet og kærlighed og andre essays*, København: Gyldendal, 1987). Løgstrup states that "there is no one from whom I have learned more than Hans Lipps" (cf. Russel L. Dees, "Translator's Introduction," in K. E. Løgstrup, *Metaphysics; translated and with an introduction by Russell L. Dees,* Milwaukee: Marquette University Press, 1995 [iii]).

45. Løgstrup, *Creation and Annihilation*, 12.

46. Løgstrup, *Creation and Annihilation*, 354.

47. According to Løgstrup, the process of rationalization itself "depends on phenomena which cannot be rationalized nor subdued to our dominance. As to their empirical contents they are unconditional and in so far open to a religious interpretation" (Løgstrup "The Metaphysical or Religious Triad," 227).

48. Løgstrup, *Creation and Annihilation*, 354–55.

49. Løgstrup, *Creation and Annihilation*, 289, 296.

50. Løgstrup, *Creation and Annihilation*, 112; cf. Løgstrup, "Triad," 234). Behind the determination of the universe as alien is Luther's understanding of the world as God's unfamiliar or alien work.

51. Løgstrup, "The Metaphysical or Religious Triad," 233.

52. Løgstrup gives charity as an example: "Charity consists of an impulse to free another person from suffering. If it serves another purpose, say to stabilize society, it is replaced by indifference to the sufferings of the other person. The ulterior motive converts the charity to its opposite" (Løgstrup, "The Metaphysical or Religious Triad," 231).

53. Løgstrup, "The Metaphysical or Religious Triad," 232.

54. Løgstrup, "The Metaphysical or Religious Triad," 230. Løgstrup unfolds this understanding of the universe as a speaking and acting agent in *Source and Surroundings*. In Peter Widmann's wording: "The universe is the all-procuring source, which unfolds in natural processes, in the analogic force of language, in the distanceless-ness of sensation etc." ("Metafysikeren Løgstrup. Om 'Ophav og Omgivelse' samt et tilbageblik på Metafysik I-IV," *Religionsvidenskabeligt Tidsskrift* 7, 1985, 65–90 [71], my translation).

55. For example, Løgstrup, *Creation and Annihilation*, 290, 357.

56. Løgstrup, *Creation and Annihilation*, 290.

57. Løgstrup, *Creation and Annihilation*, 282, 356.

58. Løgstrup, *Creation and Annihilation*, 77. The Danish word is not "univers" (universe), but "altet" (lit. "the all").

59. Ole Jensen, "Efterskrift," in *Skabelse og tilintetgørelse. Metafysik IV* (Aarhus: Klim, 2015), 373–433 (376).

60. Quoted in Dennis Bielfeldt, "Ontology," in *The Oxford Encyclopedia of Martin Luther*, Derek R. Nelson and Paul R. Hinlicky (eds.) (New York: Oxford University Press, vol. 3, 2017), 1–21 (3).

61. Løgstrup, *Creation and Annihilation*, 355, 357.

62. Løgstrup, *Creation and Annihilation*, 357. In this way, Løgstrup supports Bultmann's incentive to demythologize Christianity.

63. Løgstrup, *Creation and Annihilation*, 113.

64. Widmann, "Metafysikeren Løgstrup," 90. Widmann detects a development in Løgstrup's understanding of this religious interpretation and argues that in his late Metaphysics, Løgstrup no longer restricts himself to mere phenomenological analyses, as in *The Ethical Demand*, , but propounds universal assertions with inherent truth claims, even though they are not called true, but defined as most likely. ("Den dialektiske teologis sene metafysiske vending hos Løgstrup," *Tidsskriftet Fønix*, 2023, 92–109 [102]). According to Widmann, this metaphysics is theistic: "The ultimate authority is neither being nor nothingness, whether this opposition is interpreted monistic or dualistic, but a sovereign third, elevated above being and nothingness. The divine third can also be interpreted differently: Either God is identified with being, or else God is elevated above being and nothingness." p. 104, my translation).
(*Den etiske fordring*, København: Gyldendal, 1956),

65. Løgstrup, *Creation and Annihilation*, 323.

66. Taylor, *Modern Social Imaginaries*, 23.

67. Charles Taylor, *A Secular Age* (Cambridge, MA: The Belknap Press of Harvard University Press, 2007), 171.

68. In their introductory chapter on Scandinavian creation theology, Niels Henrik Gregersen, Bengt K. Uggla and Trygve Wyller overlook that the conception of the world as God's creation is part of the Christian social imaginary and, hence, a result of Christianization when stating: "There is no need for theology to 'Christianize' the world. The world is already God's creation" ("Reconfiguring Reformation Theology: The Program of Scandinavian Creation Theology," in *Reformation Theology for a Post-Secular Age: Løgstrup, Prenter, Wingren, and the Future of Scandinavian Creation Theology*, Gregersen, Uggla & Wyller, eds., Göttingen: Vandenhoeck & Ruprecht, 2017, 11–34 [11]).

69. Løgstrup, "The Methphysical or Religious Triad," 234.

70. For more on Løgstrup's analysis of the phenomena of human suffering and death in response to Darwin and Leibniz, see Jakob Wolf's essay in this volume.

71. In *Versuch in der Theodicée über die Güte Gottes, die Freiheit des Menschen und den Ursprung des Übels* from 1710, Leibniz explains his theodicy as a trial concerning God with reason as judge and defends God by maintaining that because of the difference between the creator and his creature, this world is finite and imperfect, but still the best of all worlds.

72. Løgstrup, *Creation and Annihilation*, 291.

73. Løgstrup, *Creation and Annihilation*, 293.

74. Løgstrup, *Creation and Annihilation*, 295.

75. Gregersen argues that this problem was unknown to Luther because he lived prior to Darwin (Niels Henrik Gregerson, "K.E. Løgstrup and Scandinavian Creation Theology," in *Reformation Theology for a Post-Secular Age: Løgstrup, Prenter, Wingren, and the Future of Scandinavian Creation Theology*, 2017, , 37–66 [63]). However, even though Luther did not know of natural selection, he anticipates Løgstrup's point when stating that the world is fallen and therefore becomes increasingly hostile towards humans, as it heads towards judgment day. Luther claims that this is evident from the increasing amount of weeds in the wheat.

Gregersen, Uggla, and Wyller, eds., Göttingen: Vandenhoeck & Ruprecht,

76. Løgstrup, *Creation and Annihilation*, 295–96.

77. Løgstrup, "The Methaphysical or Religious Triad," 227.

78. Løgstrup, *Creation and Annihilation*, 296, 302.

79. Løgstrup, *Creation and Annihilation*, 296.

80. Løgstrup refers to *De servo arbitrio (152)*, where Luther unfolds this distinction.

81. Løgstrup, *Creation and Annihilation*, 297.

82. Løgstrup, *Creation and Annihilation*, 297.

83. Løgstrup, *Creation and Annihilation*, 297.

84. Widmann "Den dialektiske teologis sene metfysiske vending," 106. Hence, according to both According to both Jensen and Widmann, Løgstrup makes dogmatic statements.

86. Løgstrup, *Creation and Annihilation*, 301.

87. Løgstrup, *Creation and Annihilation*, 303, 307. In the concrete case, Løgstrup discusses the theology of Herbert Braun, a Bultmann disciple. In a handwritten

fragment on the theologian Carl Heinz Ratschow's *Gott existiert* from 1966, Løgstrup criticizes Bultmann's narrow ethical definition of existence as determined by a decision and argues for its aesthetic corporeality, playing on Kierkegaard's dichotomy of the ethical and the aesthetical: "[Human existence] is in its corporeality a material existence; being itself nature it is incorporated in nature, which is why it is also an aesthetic existence" (quoted in Svend Andersen, "Welche Metaphysik braucht die Theologie? Mit einem Deutsch-Skandinavischen Rückblick," *Neue Zeitschrift für Systematische Theologie und Religionsphilosophie* 64:4, 2022, 320–37 [324], my translation).

88. Løgstrup, *Creation and Annihilation*, 313.

89. Løgstrup, *Creation and Annihilation*, 303. The Danish words "samliv" and "samvær" literally mean "together-living" and "together-being."

90. Løgstrup, *Creation and Annihilation*, 303.

91. Løgstrup, *Creation and Annihilation*, 315. Moreover, Løgstrup counters a pious understanding of eternity, a "pilgrim's myth," which serves as an ulterior motive ("bagtanke") that he claims enables people to keep a distance to the experiences of life (Løgstrup, *Creation and Annihilation*, 330).

92. Løgstrup, *Creation and Annihilation*, 317. Here, Løgstrup once again refers to Martin Buber, this time to *Gottesfinsternis*. In his philosophy of dialogue, most famously propounded in *Ich und Du* (1923), Buber states that the human relationship to God is lived out in interpersonal relationships; an understanding that Løgstrup agrees with (cf. Stopa, "Creative Dialogue."

93. Løgstrup, "The Metaphysical or Religious Triad," 229.

94. Løgstrup, *Creation and Annihilation*, 317.

95. Løgstrup, *Creation and Annihilation*, 319.

96. Løgstrup, *Creation and Annihilation*, 320.

97. Løgstrup, *Creation and Annihilation*, 329.

98. Løgstrup, *Creation and Annihilation*, 324.

99. Dalferth, "The Idea of Transcendence," 148.

100. Løgstrup, "The Metaphysical or Religious Triad," 229.

101. Løgstrup, "The Metaphysical or Religious Triad," 228.

Chapter 8

Expectations of a Second-Skin Dwelling

Theo-political Reflections on the Significance of Homes

Trygve Wyller

A THEOLOGICAL CHALLENGE OF NO-HOME

Imagine there is a refugee family living in a garage in a backyard of a medium-sized South African city. They invite a white pastor to come and bless their home. And imagine there is a traditional xenophobia against blacks of non-Zulu origin in this area. Due to this xenophobia, the living conditions for the refugee family are seriously lacking. And they are even worsened because the refugees need cash in a very short time to make their regular payment for a prolonged-stay permit. Migration policies in South Africa require regular cycles of payment for new periods of residency. If they are not paid, you cannot stay and must leave the country.

Imagine further that the pastor, upon entering the house, was actually not asked to offer a blessing. The immediate claim, instead, was how much cash he could contribute to prolong the duration of their permit. Only when the cash was on the table could the blessing take place . . .

IS THERE AN SCT POLITICAL THEOLOGY?

One fundamental focus in Scandinavian Creation Theology (SCT) is to build and facilitate just and generous life worlds and life forms for all, Christians and non-Christians. It is a well-established SCT position that Christian faith cannot escape from critically discussing the content of all life forms and life worlds. In the following I shall discuss the kind of universality, which must be reflected if the SCT can continue to contribute to contemporary political theology. Having a home might be a fruitful approach to elaborate this perspective.

The content and significance of the so-called "universal" has been part of the SCT discussions since the early days of the first SCT generation. Løgstrup wrote that there is no specifically Christian ethics.[1] And Wingren insisted that the core of the Reformation was that God's call is available for all because it comes from the everyday neighbor, not necessarily from the pious saint or from pastoral power.[2] Løgstrup's spontaneous expressions of life and philosophy of sensations were explicitly presented as universal and philosophical, even if they might "suggest a religious interpretation." Due to this position, Løgstrup (and Wingren in his way) claimed that there is a responsibility for theology to analyze and discover life forms that expand beyond the specifically Christian. This has been, and is, one of the fundamental characteristics of Scandinavian Creation Theology. Løgstrup called it the universal in Christendom.

One basic challenge in contemporary SCT discussions is, therefore, how we today, with new knowledge of the colonial aspect of the pretentions to universality still can stick to the elements of the universal in the tradition of Løgstrup. This chapter's intention is to point to some significant aspects of what a universal might mean within the context of SCT today.

To make it short: the pretention of universality in the SCT tradition is not a pretention that all people, no matter context and no matter gender, race and class, can be presented on an equal ground. Post-colonial thinking is, of course, right in pointing to all kinds of oppressive powers and discourse concealed in naïve universality pretentions. The universality of SCT, however, is based on the distinction between the specific Christian and the universal. When Løgstrup claims there is a universality in Christianity, he means that Christianity addresses all life forms, not only the life forms that express themselves with a specific Christian discourse. The universality pretention, on this background, is a theological pretention, not a political one. The fundamental challenge today is, therefore, whether the SCT tradition can contribute to contemporary issues of otherness, justice, and transformation and still claim that there is a universality in Christianity. In my view, the task is to argue how issues of otherness, justice and transformation can be interpreted as part of the theological universality in the SCT.

The simple narrative introducing this chapter presents this challenge as a narration. It is about a migrant and his struggle to keep a place to live for himself and his family. It is, however, also about the role of the specific Christian in the struggle for justice and it is about whether theologians should take roles as activists or not. The narrative is, first of all, a constructed perspective that illustrates how one might approach the universality issue in current SCT discussions. As stated above, the SCT universality perspective implies that Christianity cannot be about the specifically Christian only. The universality in Christianity is the horizon, which can be interpreted philosophically, that is open for all. The narrative, however, challenges what the content of this universality is about. Discussing what it means to have a home is also a discussion on how we today should give meaning to the universality in Christianity.

PHENOMENOLOGY AND THE
SPECIFICALLY CHRISTIAN

The relation between the specific Christian faith and the universal is a complex and entangled aspect of Løgstrup's thinking. A superficial interpretation often presented is that Løgstrup distinguishes so strongly between the two that they never meet. It is, however, much more complex. It seems to be more adequate to say that the universal is the kind of reality, which corresponds to the specifically Christian, even if the universal does not require the specifically Christian to manifest itself. Early in *The Ethical Demand* Løgstrup writes:

> The one thing in our existence which the proclamation of Jesus of Nazareth touches upon more than any other is the individual's relation to the neighbor. The question therefore arises with the respect to this proclamation: What does it conceive to be the essential thing in our life with and against and how can that be stated in strictly human terms? The question this introduces is a distinction between the content of Jesus' proclamation—which in a very general and vague sense is religious—and the attitude to the neighbor which, although it is included in the religious content of the proclamation, should be susceptible of formulation in strictly human terms.[3]

The focus in *The Ethical Demand* is, accordingly, to discover and analyze the life-realities that correspond to the proclamation of the Kingdom of God. The Løgstrup project is, again and again, to spell out this reality. Sometimes it is called ontology, sometimes spontaneity, sometimes other concepts are used. The main argument, however, is that theology needs to analyze and reconstruct this reality, for the sake of what life is about and for the sake of being able to proclaim the gospel at all. This is a decisive theme in the SCT tradition. The issue of "what life is about" is a highly contested issue, both the content of it and the way we approach it and interpret it. It is important to be aware that what Løgstrup calls the universal is not identical with the current societal context. Løgstrup comes from German phenomenology in the tradition of Husserl and Heidegger. In this tradition, the so-called *epoche* is a basic, fundamental premise. *Epoche* means that all everyday details and current social features are set into "brackets." What then remains is what is phenomenologically significant. Phenomenology focuses on the phenomena which remain when everything else is bracketed out. These are the phenomena which are the formatting aspects of life. One of those phenomena is intersubjectivity, and another is sensibilities.

Life is given as intersubjectivity. This is the phenomenological position, also shared by Løgstrup. For the future discussions on how the SCT tradition can contribute to political theology, I think there is a need to distinguish between how life is, ontologically and phenomenologically given, and how it sometimes actualizes in concrete historical contexts. From a concrete, historical point of view, intersubjectivity is not always a dominant force. There is a distance between the phenomena as given and life as it takes place in the everyday. The current historical situation might not realize the given intersubjectivity at all. In my view, it is exactly from this point that a future SCT political theology can unfold. This implies that we need to involve additional phenomenological analyses than the one given by Løgstrup and his tradition. To pursue an SCT approach presupposes (1) to stick to the claim that there needs to be correspondence between the specific Christian proclamation and concrete life-condition and (2) that the analysis of the life-conditions is based on phenomenological reflections. Apart from these two conditions, other phenomenologists and thinkers might be both significant and important.

SPONTANEITY AND HISTORICITY

Løgstrup's most important contribution to a political theological position is his insistence that spontaneity is before historicity.[4] Behind this abstract claim lies the same basic thoughts as were presented in the introduction to this chapter. Something fundamental precedes our empirical, historical acts. The basic insights from The Ethical Demand that we always keep something of the other in our hands, is one famous case of what spontaneity means. Løgstrup's intention is not to claim that all humans keep someone in their hands everywhere and always. The intention is to say that living in this kind of interdependence is what life means—ontologically—as given before our reflections and actions. Other fundamentals of the kind are sensible spaces, compassion, trust, and a hopeful future, among others.

These fundamentals belong to what Løgstrup calls spontaneity. The intersubjectivities, sensible spaces and trust worlds are not invented by us. They are there, spontaneous, in the sense of just happening—"spontaneously"—before we intentionally act. They are Løgstrupian modes of what Husserl and his followers called "being-in-the-world." We do not invent intersubjectivity. It is there as a fundamental of life. What is expected from us is to format our historical life in accordance with this spontaneity. This, in my view, is the important starting point for a future SCT political theology.

Because of that, Løgstrup claims that spontaneity is before historicity. This position, accordingly, is fundamental to how a SCT political theology can be developed. One central position in the following, however, is that there are more options for how to elaborate on spontaneity than the one presented by Løgstrup. Spontaneity in itself is a common denominator in all serious phenomenology, and so it might be fruitful to look into some other traditions than by Løgstrup himself. What needs to remain, however, is that the analysis of spontaneities is a philosophical one and that all theology needs to insist on a correspondence between the specific Christian and the analysis of spontaneity. This is also why traditional empirical sociology cannot be the only dominant methodological approach in SCT political theology. Spontaneity is the fundamental theme of what humanity is about. A SCT political theology must strive for practices, where what is actual develops to become more and more like the spontaneous. Sociology starts with historicity, which is only second in line in a SCT analysis of the social.[5]

As stated above, the distinction between the historical and the spontaneous was presented by Løgstrup in his 1972 book *Norm and Spontaneity*. This book was an effort to translate the radical demand of the spontaneous expressions of life to possible political contexts ("norms") in his own time. In other words, the book was an effort to present and analyze life-realities that correspond to the proclamation of Christ. The central point in the analysis, is that the spontaneity (the spontaneous or sovereign expressions of life) cannot construct a society. The reason is, again, that the spontaneous expressions are not identical with actual social norms. It is the spontaneity, which corresponds with the proclamation of Christ. The spontaneity is how life is in its origin. The social norm of current history is a different thing.

In my view, this position should be more developed towards a critical political theology than Løgstrup (and many of his followers) did. The distinction between spontaneity and the historical is decisive, but this distinction should be further pursued in order to develop critical perspectives on societal practices and institutions. It should be the task of political theology to work out creative reflections and analysis on current kinds of spontaneity and how societies should critically format practices, institutions, and rules to realize as much spontaneity as possible.

This is why the concrete suggestions of *Norm and Spontaneity* are sometimes disappointing and boring. What they do lack is the critical approach that comes from the distinction between the historical and the spontaneous. The spontaneous, this is what we know from the *Ethical Demand,* is what corresponds to the proclamation of Christ. In my view, the political theology of SCT initiates here. How to analyze history from the point of view of spontaneity in order to improve and make society correspond more and better? This critical approach will look for possibilities to bring concrete contexts closer to the spontaneous. Accordingly, this analysis will also be an analysis of how the specifically Christian (the proclamation) can have a stronger (phenomenological) correspondence in the world of humans. Reconnected to the introductory narrative in this chapter, one might ask: What role does spontaneity have in having a home have when you are about to lose it? Fundamentally, spontaneity is not something people lose, but life experiences, which are in accordance with spontaneity can be more or less present. What does it mean to have a home, when you are about to lose it?

BAUEN, WOHNEN, DENKEN AND THE CHALLENGES OF UNJUST CONTEXTS

This is the complex situation: Life as spatial practices of living-together might work as an important correspondence between the proclamation of the Kingdom and human life conditions. The challenge for a SCT political theology is to contribute to actual life forms where life as concrete living-together happen. A responsible faith position is to narrow the difference between spontaneity and historicity. Translated into the imagined narrative, the refugee, who is about to lose his home, is a person, who is about to get a radical reduction of his concrete experiences of the spontaneity of spatial living-together.

It is, however, just at this point, that there is a need to expand the content of the spontaneity of the spatial (homely) living-together from the Løgstrup-Heidegger tradition, which has dominated the home trajectory in this tradition. There is much to learn about this expansion if we compare the Heidegger/Løgstrup tradition with more recent proposals, especially the one from Sara Ahmed. What Ahmed adds to this tradition is the significance of otherness as part of the spatial living-together. This means that there are aspects of the refugee life that belong to the spontaneity. Being a refugee in itself is not necessarily something that completely disconnects the refugee life from the lives of nonrefugees humans. Otherness belongs to the spontaneity; it is not something that disrupts what spontaneity is about. We see that through a simple comparison with how the Heidegger tradition interpreted home as spontaneity.

Martin Heidegger's famous essay "Bauen, Wohnen, Denken" from 1951 has impacted at least two academic generations on what it is to have a home.[6] The basic argument from Heidegger is that you do not simply live somewhere, you dwell (Wohnen). "Dwellen" is the German word that one cannot easily translate into English. However, it refers to the basics of existential phenomenology. When humans dwell, they are deeply interwoven in the world, in nature and in death as horizon. "Dwellen" is to live with the consciousness of what being as being-in-the world in the context of living means.

On one level, there are significant similarities between the *Dwellen* analysis by Heidegger and the Løgstrup analysis of the spontaneous expressions of life. As a student with Heidegger in Freiburg, the focus on being-in-the-world and intentionality as the mood to study humans were among the most basic elements of philosophical study. In the years to come, Løgstrup developed his ethical demand, which was not the focus of Heidegger. In this sense, the normativity inherent in intersubjectivities is a significant difference between Heidegger and Løgstrup. Yet the notion of intentionality, the conviction that one cannot explore humans outside their being with the world or with others, dominated the thinking of both scholars.

Accordingly, when Løgstrup claims in *The Ethical Demand* that one must search for life conditions that correspond to the proclamation of the Kingdom of God, it is the life conditions following from being-in-the-world that are omitted. The specifically Christian must relate to the intentionality of the beings-in-the-world. In this way, to dwell could also be part of an intentionality approved by Løgstrup. In *Norm and Spontaneity* Løgstrup writes that it is spontaneity that should analyze history, not the other way around. The point is that intentionality comes first; humans are humans-in-the-world, and therefore *Dwellen* is one of the basic life conditions related to all humans. The basic human should be the point of departure for interpreting culture and society.

To seriously build (*bauen*), you need to build to dwell, that is to build in ways where nature is not only a context but interwoven in the architectural design itself. Parallel, to build requires building in ways where death is also what is interwoven in the design. Nature and death are two fundamental moods of being in the world. Therefore, houses and homes have to reflect these modes. To dwell is to build houses and establish homes where the non-human nature and threatening death are sensed aspects of the house and the home. There is no dwelling in homes if these kinds of otherness do not participate in the sensible of the home and the house.

The Norwegian theologian Margunn Sandal has given an interesting analysis of how the Heideggerian approach has had a lasting impact on the church architecture of the influential architect Christian Norberg-Schultz.[7] Norberg-Schultz took a lot of inspiration from both Heidegger and Merleau-Ponty and was explicitly interested in the consequences of the dwelling concept for church architecture. The Norwegian architect's interest in "sacred" buildings seemed to have brought him to the same position as Løgstrup with regard to the connections between, on the one hand, the specifically Christian proclamation of the Kingdom and on the other the universality of the dwelling as a being-in-the-world, where nature and death cannot but be organic parts of buildings and houses. According to Sandal, Norberg-Schulz opposed the idea that a church building should be an architectural proclamation of the Kingdom. Church buildings should not be designed as instruments for the proclamation of Christ. To translate into Heideggerian vocabulary, church architecture is about the implications of dwelling, not about the proclamation of anything specifically Christian.

The architect Norberg-Schultz has had, and still has, significant impact on contemporary theories of architectural aesthetics, even though his theories have drawn strong criticism in the last generation.[8] In our context, however, the interesting perspective is that Norberg-Schultz, following Heidegger, claimed that modern church architecture failed to reflect on how church buildings had their *own* message. They should relate to the surrounding nature, the sensibilities, colors, sounds, smells and, of course people. This totality is the church dwelling and what Sandal, drawing from Norberg-Schultz, calls the "spatial aspect" of the church building. This spatial message has a significance and should be an organic part of what churches communicate.[9]

In the context of this chapter what is interesting in the Norberg-Schultz approach is how he, following Heidegger, insists that church architecture must establish experiences of a dwelling, a being-in-the-world, where all otherness of life is included. This is the message of church buildings. This totality of life must be communicated through the ecclesial space structure. In the SCT tradition we might add: The totality of life included in the ecclesial space means that this totality is what the specific Christian aims at and relates to.

What does it mean, theologically, to have a home in this context? Following the Heidegger interpretation of Norberg-Schultz, one might claim that the theological meaning of having a home must reflect how otherness is part of homes. And it must also imply that this kind of dwelling might be what corresponds to the proclamation of the Kingdom, to use Løgstrup's vocabulary one more time.

SARA AHMED AND HOME AS SECOND SKIN

Among current contemporary phenomenologists, the British-Australian phenomenologist Sara Ahmed is among current scholars, who has continued to reflect all creatively within this Heideggerian phenomenology of home. Otherness is a basic category in Ahmed's thinking. She does, however, follow a different path than the radical philosophy of Levinas. Ahmed rejects

Levinas' claim that we can never reach the real other. Ahmed opposes this and calls it a fetishizing of otherness. Phenomenologically, Ahmed claims, we are always connected. Humans cannot be aliens. We can be strangers. Strangers, however, are connected in less tight modes than neighbors.

The same approach is given when Ahmed analyzes homes. Strangeness must be a part of what home is:

> There is already strangeness and movement within the home itself. It is not simply a question then of those who stay at home, and those who leave, as if these two different trajectories simply lead people to different places. Rather, 'homes' always involve encounters between those who stay, those who arrive and those who leave. We can use Avtar Brah's notion of diasporic space here: there is always an intimate encounter at stake between natives and strangers.[10] Given the inevitability of such encounters, homes do not stay the same as the space which is simply the familiar. There is movement and dislocation within the very forming of homes as complex and contingent spaces of inhabitance.[11]

In this way, Ahmed deepens and expands Heidegger and Norberg-Schultz. To stay with Heidegger's famous concept; dwelling implies also an otherness inside. Otherness is not only what homes relate to. Dislocation and location, strangeness and belonging: together this is the meaning of what it is to have a home.

On this background, Ahmed claims that home is "a second skin": "The immersion of a self in a locality is hence not simply about inhabiting an already constituted space (from which one can simply depart and remain the same). Rather, the locality intrudes into the senses: it defines what one smells, hears, touches, feels, remembers. The lived experience of being-at-home hence involves the enveloping of subjects in a space which is not simply outside them: being-at-home suggests that the subject and space leak into each other, inhabit each other. To some extent we can think of the lived experience of being at home in terms of inhabiting a second skin, a skin which does not simply contain the homely subject, but which allows the subject to be touched and touch the world that is neither simply in the home or away from the home."[12]

The home analysis from Heidegger, Norberg-Schultz, and Ahmed are all developed from a perspective of phenomenology. They share the basic insight that the potentiality of death meaning what it is to have a home cannot be decided by sociology, or anthropology, and especially not by specific Christian interpretations. Heidegger coined the concept of dwelling, insisting on a home as something inserted into relations and connectivities that link houses, nature and the potentialities of death. Homes necessarily intersect with all these perspectives simultaneously, and without them one does not really communicate what home is about.

Norberg-Schultz takes this position further into the classical discussion of the relation between the specifically Christian and the universalities of phenomenology. Norberg-Schultz emphasizes that even churches (as spiritual "homes") must be constructed as spaces that communicate the universal, namely humanity as "dwelling." This means that their spatial relations should reflect and intersect with surroundings of nature, culture, and memories in the best ways possible. In an astonishing parallel to Løgstrup, Norberg-Schultz claims that churches are spaces for communicating Christ, yet only when the church building reflects and communicates what dwelling is. It comes very close to Løgstrup, for whom the proclamation of the Kingdom presupposes a communication of the conditions of life in a relevant and appropriate way.

In my view, the contribution from Ahmed is to expand on the content of the home as space. Otherness needs to be reflected in order to grasp what it is to have a home. Homes are spaces where some stay, some leave and some relate. There are perspectives of strangeness and otherness in the "dwelling." as presented by Ahmed. Her approach is not about home as a religious space. Nevertheless, Ahmed's analysis is, in my view, more than relevant, when it comes to develop what it is to (almost) have a home in the context of Scandinavian Creation Theology.

CONCLUSION

One basic SCT presupposition is that the proclamation of the Kingdom must correspond to how people live their lives. For Løgstrup, phenomena like trust, compassion, etc. were among the fundamental ways of being human. In my view, the act of dwelling (in the sense of including otherness in what it means to have a home) might be one other basic correspondence. It seems evident to interpret homes as "second skin" as good candidates for relevant life worlds as well. The second skin home can be one of the life worlds, which the specific Christian need to relate to.

The imagined narrative presented in the beginning of this article, however, is about a refugee family on the edge of losing their second skin. Their home was definitely not a romantic Heideggerian cabin in the deep woods in the Black Forest of Germany. Nevertheless, dwelling in the spatial, second-skin sense of Ahmed is about relating to and being touched by particular others and even strangers. And it is about the hybridity, which comes about due to permanent departure and arrival. This is a form of being-in-the-world, which, to use Løgstrup's words, "suggests a religious interpretation."

Løsgtrup's distinction between spontaneity and historicity also becomes central to the interpretation of this narrative. Following Ahmed's home as second skin, one might say that this interpretation is about the spontaneous. Being touched from all the senses of mobile people and the coming and leaving is a basic human "pre-ethical" presentation of what homes are, seen from phenomenology. Homes as second skin belong to the basic human. In empirical history, not all humans live in spaces and contexts that can be called a second skin. The narrated refugee family risked losing it all.

Following Løgstrup and the SCT tradition, one could, therefore, conclude, that the task of a SCT formatted political theology is to contribute, practically as well as theoretically, to the restoration of the spontaneous level of what it is to be human. Once it has been restored, it can finally be blessed.

NOTES

1. K. E. Løgstrup, *The Ethical Demand* (Notre Dame, IN: University of Notre Dame Press, 1997), 105 ff.

2. Gustaf Wingren, *Luther on Vocation* (Eugene, OR: Wipf and Stock, 2004), 171–84.

3. Løgstrup, *Ethical Demand*, 105.

4. K. E. Løgstrup, *Norm og spontanitet* (Århus: Forlaget Klim, 2019 (1972).

5. A very interesting and promising tradition is the phenomenological sociology, initiated by Alfred Schütz in the 1940s and 1950s. Schütz's contribution is to analyze and discover different kinds of social givenness, before our empirical (ontic) practices. A future SCT political theology might also gain from implementing Schützian perspectives.

6. Martin Heidegger, *Bauen, Wohnen, Denken: Vorträge und Aufsätze*. (Pfullingen: Verlag Günther Neske, 1954).

7. Margunn Sandal, Overskridande arkitektur: ei undersøking av det sakrale i nyare kyrkjebygg, doctoral thesis, University of Oslo, 2019.

8. Christian Norberg-Schultz, *Existence, Space and Architecture* (London: Præger Publications, 1974) and *Genius Loci: Towards a Phenomenology of Architecture* (Milano: Rizzoli, 1979).

9. Sandal, 294.

10. Avtar Brah, *Cartographies of Diaspora: Contesting Identities* (Abingdon, UK: Routledge, 1996), 181.

11. Sara Ahmed, "Home and Away: Narratives of Migration and Estrangement," in *International Journal of Cultural Studies*, vol. 2:3, pp. 329–47, here at 340.

12. Ibid., 341.

Chapter 9

Ordinary Lives and the Home as a Safe Place

Else Marie Wiberg Pedersen

BEING AT HOME IN THIS TEXT

I propose that a home, a place where one carries out domestic or everyday life, is a safe place for any individual in the here and now. A home is a place where being an individual human being of whatever kind is safe. To me, a home, and to be at home, imply that it is not merely about a place, for example in a family setting, where an individual survives abuse like violence and other atrocities. In other words, I define a home as a safe place where a human being can live a life in its own right without being threatened or abused.

Taking my point of departure in this ideal understanding of a home, of being at home, as a place or space where a person can feel safe, I in this (con-)text will focus on homing those women who became homeless in their home. I will do that by way of different strategies for homing women who through history have been exiled from their place in humanity, be it homing women displaced in biblical texts, homing women displaced in tradition and life, and homing women in the politics of a shared humanity. My approach is inspired by feminist philosopher Karen Barad's theory of entanglement, that we live in a world of everything's ultimate interconnectedness, and agential realism, the connectedness of material-discursive practices[1] – that the displacement of women in Bible texts and tradition is deeply interconnected with women's displacement in history and humanity. Vice versa, homing women in Bible texts and tradition has great significance for women being homed and feeling at home in history and humanity as fully honored individuals. Furthermore, women's displacement or homing has a bearing on how they are perceived and treated, whether that be as dehumanized creatures or as fully honored individuals. The agents to "prove" my claim are the German reformer, Martin Luther (1483–1546), and the two Danish creation theologians N. F. S. Grundtvig (1783–1872) and K. E. Løgstrup (1905–1981). My reason for choosing those three agents is this: I find that Luther laid the foundation of a sustainable creation theology by reconfiguring theology as an inclusive matter of a shared humanity living an ordinary life (in opposition to the lofty and exclusive scholastic theology with its accentuation of divine maleness over against devilish femaleness), and by recognizing the interrelatedness of science and religion.[2] In my view, Scandinavian creation theology—here represented by the nineteenth-century theologian and hymn writer, Grundtvig, and the twentieth-century theologian and philosopher of religion, Løgstrup, each in their way continued and developed Luther's view of everyday life as a God-given and God-created life where every person can find his or her place and be at home.

Before doing so, however, I will first reflect on the opposite of being at home, namely, being homeless or exiled, misplaced or displaced, and second lift up a few feminist insights about biblical texts and the lost sense of safety in texts that terrify and make us tremble.

BEING HOMELESS OR EXILED

When reflecting on what it is to be at home or to have a home, the question of what it means to not be at home, to be homeless or exiled, immediately comes to mind. When one searches the definition of homelessness in a contemporary Danish context, homelessness is simply defined sociologically in two ways. Either one is homeless when living in the streets or when living with friends and family without a place of one's own, and the main reason given is mental disease of various kinds, and in about 66 percent of the cases it is related to abuse of drugs or/and alcohol. Around 22 percent of the homeless in Denmark never had a family home but spent their childhood and adolescence in institutions; and about 25 percent have no form of education beyond basic school.[3] This is only one side of being homeless, however. There are so many ways that people can feel homeless or not at home—even if they on the surface have a home.

In fact, "homelessness" is a term we utilize in many ways: psychologically, socially, culturally, bodily, or otherwise. People can feel homeless in their family, in their school, at work, in their own body or soul, and in their own life as such. They just do not feel at home, and this can be for a multitude of reasons, whether living in a dysfunctional family or feeling *mis*placed somehow.

Homelessness indeed is also about being *dis*placed, physically and geographically. This happens when—due to war, cataclysms, poverty, and different kinds of atrocities around the world—millions of people are homeless, refugees in our time and day. In the endeavor to survive and in the search for livelihood and an ordinary life, they leave their house (if they have one), their family (if they have one), and eventually their country (if they are not stateless). They leave the country whose culture and language they know. Some succeed in building a home in another place (area, country) where they want to stay and live. Most end up in refugee camps where they try to make an everyday life, but they are homeless—typically stripped of privacy, safety, and dignity. Particularly women and children are vulnerable in such camps, and many of them are victims of violence and rape; some already have been victims of rape and violence when they fled, some becoming victims of rape and violence in the camps or during their flight.

In an article on heterotopic creation, Trygve Wyller relates the story of a young, black woman, Nisha, who as a nine-year-old girl fled from the Democratic Republic of Congo after the killing of her parents, and who spent many years in a refugee camp in Tanzania where she entered an arranged marriage with a Tanzanian man. Nisha, a displaced woman now living in a South African township, tells Wyller, in an interview taking place in 2016, why she and her husband were no longer in the refugee camp in Tanzania: because of the life-threatening situation, the couple and their children had to flee and ended in South Africa, where she then lived with her husband and five children, herself being only thirty-one years old. But her life was dominated by South-African xenophobia. Her brother had been killed a year before, her friend . . . raped by a neighbor.[4]

Nisha has been through the whole register of a woman losing her home as a child and as an adolescent to now struggling to make a home for her five children despite the dire circumstances. As I write these lines, women struggle to be at home in their home country, Ukraine, in Russia's war on Ukraine where multiple rapes of women are reported. These women cannot feel safe anywhere; they have become homeless in their home, mentally and physically.

However, women need not be victims of war or refugees to be exiled and homeless. They may be exiled and homeless in their own family, not least due to child or adult abuse. This is what will be the theme of the latter part of this text.

STRATEGIES OF FAITH FOR CONSOLING AND
HOMING WOMEN EXILED FROM THEIR HOME

In her seminal book *Texts of Terror*, the feminist Old Testament scholar
Phyllis Trible offered literary-feminist readings of four biblical narratives of
women who were victims of terror in or around their home in order to give
strength to women with exactly those experiences. Trible picked the stories
of (1) Hagar—the slave used, abused, and rejected (Genesis 16:1–21), (2)
Tamar—the princess raped and discarded by her brother, prince Amnon
(2 Samuel 13:1–22), (3) an unnamed woman—the concubine raped, mur-
dered, and dismembered (Judges 19:1–30), and finally of (4) the daughter
of Jephthah—a virgin slain and sacrificed (Judges 11:29–40). Trible read the
stories of these female figures as texts that raised disturbing questions about
women's lives. As we shall later see Luther operate when interpreting texts
that silence and/or terrorize women, Trible lifted up these specific texts of terror to employ them as texts that could be reconfigured as texts consoling and
homing women in similar situations. In Trible's words, "Women, not men,
are suffering servants and Christ figures. Their stories govern the use of the
leitmotifs, Scripture thus interpreting scripture undercuts triumphalism and
raises disturbing questions for faith."[5]

Trible, who had witnessed the four female figures employed in the streets
of New York by abused women, perceives the telling of the stories as
wrestling demons and at the same time as a seeking a blessing parallel to
what Jacob did in the Genesis narrative on his wrestling with God (Genesis
32:22–32). She explains how this happens in spite of the terror taking place:

> To tell and hear tales of terror is to wrestle demons in the night; without a
> compassionate God to save us. In combat we wonder about the names of the
> demons. Our own names, however, we all too frightfully recognize. The fight
> itself is solitary and intense. We struggle mightily, only to be wounded. But yet
> we hold on, seeking a blessing; the healing of wounds and the restoration of
> health. If the blessing comes—and we dare not claim assurance—it does not
> come on our terms. Indeed, as we leave the land of terror, we limp.[6]

Trible does not write about texts of terror for the sake of terror; she writes
about texts of terror for the sake of seeking a blessing from God, "the healing
of wounds and the restoration of health," and her book has become a classic
as such, helpful as it is for women wounded and needing healing.

While Trible employs Bible texts to rebuild women's self-esteem and home
them in their lives, Beverly Wallace narrates contemporary black women's
stories for the sake of constructing an American Lutheran black womanist ethics. Wallace, herself a womanist theologian, quotes several Black American

women who experienced the good side of family life based on a strong maternal line and the church, on the one hand. However, they certainly also experienced the darker side of family life—a life that went astray and did not exactly create a safe place for the women who nevertheless found their way to being at home, for example by cutting loose some family members.[7] Icelandic theologian Arnfríður Guðmundsdóttir in her article on sexual violence and abuse of power writes explicitly about a bishop of Iceland who, after having been accused of sexual assault by three individual women, finally resigned. After his death, his daughter finally broke her story as sexually abused by her powerful father since she was a little girl.[8] Guðmundsdóttir recounts several other stories of sexual violence and abuse of children and women with the purpose of showing how widely common this is. Not least, though, she aims at calling for churches to be prophetic by listening to and seeing the victims of abuse in such a way that they are honored as co-humans and God's creatures. Hence, she quotes the Lutheran World Federation's Gender Justice Policy from 2013: "Each act of gender-based violence injures the creation in God's image and violates the community of believers who are called to live in just relationships. Therefore, silence needs to be broken. The church's prophetic role is to provide processes for healing and safe places for victims and survivors in mutual collaboration with multiple partners in healing ministries."[9]

Note that the LWF does not simply place the problem of abuse within an anthropological or cultural framework. As Guðmundsdóttir emphasizes, the strength of the message from the LWF is that it places the problem of abuse in a theological framework: Gender-based violence is not simply wrong because it infringes the rights of the victim but because it "injures" God's creation, and "violates" the community of believers. Silence must be broken, and the victims provided safe places—mentally, culturally, and physically.

MARTIN LUTHER: HOMING WOMEN
IN LIFE AND TRADITION

To Luther, people's livelihood in an ordinary societal life is central. Thus, he saw the Ten Commandments as the best prescription of how to live a socially sound and well-ordered ordinary life in order to create a home for everyone. Having rendered their meaning, his conclusion to the commandments is emblematic, "when a priest stands in a golden chasuble, or a layperson spends a whole day in church on his or her knees, that is considered a precious work that cannot be sufficiently extolled. But when a poor servant girl takes care of a little child or faithfully does what she is told, this is regarded as nothing."[10]

In this brief quotation, Luther problematizes how ordinary life is often isolated from what is regarded as sacred and God-created life. Reversing the priorities, Luther repeatedly stresses that the ordinary, everyday-life is not only God-created but is, indeed, God-given and should be celebrated as such. Every citizen is regarded a civilian and a spiritual person obligated to act in a socially and ethically acceptable way to his or her neighbor, regardless of age, ethnicity or sex.[11] Therefore, when Luther interprets the fourth commandment (that children should honor their parents), he also emphasizes the duty of parents (and of authorities of all sorts) to pay honor to their children and tend to their education. Luther envisions a strong, social framework of a people, and hence he stresses,

> For if we want capable and qualified people for both the civil and the spiritual realms, we really must spare no effort, time, and expense in teaching and educating our children to serve God and the world. We must not think only of amassing money and property for them. God can provide for them and make them rich without our help, as indeed he does daily. But he has given us children and entrusted them to us precisely so that we may raise and govern them according to his will; otherwise, God would have no need of fathers and mothers.[12]

Note that Luther does not speak of boys or fathers only. He writes inclusively of *children*, girls and boys, as he writes inclusively of *parents*, mothers and fathers. The family, consisting of female and male elements alike, is concerned about presenting the family in a most inclusive way. This understanding for Luther constitutes a social basis for building a sustainable society where every citizen has a place, not least founded on solid education.[13]

At other times, like in his *Enarrationes in Genesin*, Luther finds stories of suffering that he asserts he can "hardly read with dry eyes." Thus, Luther does not simply focus on Sarah and Abraham in his exegesis, but he extends a most caring empathy with Hagar, the harshly treated woman slave and her slave son, Ishmael, who rouse Sarah's jealousy (Genesis 21: 8–21). Luther disagrees with Paul in the interpretation of the narration and Hagar's role. In Luther's perception, Hagar is nothing but righteous while male power goes wrong of God's will and justification.

Hagar is not the only female Bible figure that Luther reconfigures as righteous contrary to main tradition's writing them out of the narrations as important characters. Like Hagar, Luther in his exegesis chose to give many other female figures of the Bible a home and a future contrary to the role as insignificant women, whores, or "women on the loose" that the tradition before him attributed them. In the following, I'll lift up two of them: Dinah and Mary Magdalene. The tradition about both women as loose has been so thick, and still is, that even feminist biblical scholars of today buy into it; and that despite the exact wording, or lack of it, in the Bible text as such.[14] These women have become homeless in the original text as well as in their original role as innocent and even righteous women. Luther provided them a home as women in their own right and thus gave them (back) a home in the Bible text.

First his interpretation of Dinah (Genesis 34). The narrative is extremely reticent to reveal anything about Dinah, merely stating that "when Dinah, the daughter Jacob had with Lea, once went out to visit the daughters of the land, Shechem, a son of the local emir . . . , saw her, took her, lay with her and violated her" (Genesis 34:2). Through the narrative, Dinah is the passive victim with various males as actors: her rapist, Shechem, her grieving father, Jacob, her angry brothers, Levi and Simeon, and the Shechemites, who were the hosts of Jacob and his people. In the narrative, Dinah primarily is "daughter of Jacob" or "sister" of her brothers and otherwise practically absent. By contrast, Luther offers an interpretation that gives Dinah a dignified life and future. According to Luther, Dinah is also "daughter of Leah whom she bore to Jacob," and he opens his commentary by discussing her age. Counter to tradition's tendency to see Dinah as consenting to the deed, he continually stresses that Dinah is but a child of around 12 years old, innocent of the violation and rape of her. To Luther, there is no doubt that she is a sexually immature girl who was raped and violated by Shechem, the son of the local emir. While medieval interpreters saw Dinah as symbolizing "the sinful soul who strays beyond its proper boundaries through boldness, pride and curiosity," Luther read the story as cautioning young girls from going out alone in a world that was too dangerous for lone young females to fare in. Most importantly, (1) he deems rape of such a young girl a capital sin—worsened by the fact that the rapist and his family tribe show no remorse and do not apologize, thus not acknowledging the violation; and (2) he deems Dinah an innocent victim of sexual sin and gives her a future life by imagining her restored by and to her family, living as the housewife of her family home. Both the narrative and Luther's interpretation contain so many layers that I cannot go into here, so let it suffice to end by saying that Luther adds empathy and pastoral care to the victims, including the females in a narrative that is silent about them. He adds a happy ending, giving Dinah a safe place, a home where she is secured a human life—not abandoned as human trash.[15]

Regarding Mary Magdalene, Luther does something similar vis-à-vis the tradition since Gregory the Great. Whereas Gregory conflated all Marys, except for the Virgin Mary, with the unnamed women of the NT, into one single figure and coined, or more correctly framed, this figure as Mary Magdalene, the harlot, Luther renders Mary Magdalene an honorable woman. Luther is aware that the woman of Luke 7: 36–50 is unnamed but chooses to keep naming her Mary Magdalene while restoring her as faithful to God. Instead of being "a woman in the city, who was a sinner" according to Simon the Leper's pejorative slander that for the basis from a centuries-long tradition, Luther, uninterested in her supposed sins, restores Mary Magdalene as a true disciple of Jesus who affirms his theology of grace.[16] Luther deems the rich Simon unrighteous and gives Mary Magdalene a safe place in a tradition that otherwise is obsessed with how to understand her loose hair (the text does not mention loose hair), her enjoying in a public meal with males (the texts does not have her eat), and her tears as symbols of her sinfulness.[17] Hence, from being driven away from her place as the main witness of the resurrection to a place of shame, Luther gives Mary Magdalene back her place as a true disciple. She gets back her place (which I am describing as a "homing") in Christian history as a human being.

In the following, I shall give two brief samples of Scandinavian creation theology—represented by Grundtvig and Løgstrup. In my view, they both continued Luther's perception of everyday life as God-given and God-created life where every person could find his or her home. Both of these Danish theologians were decided followers of Luther's theology, each of them giving it his own bent according to the immediate context. What is particularly interesting in this context is that they both offer creation theologies that could be termed proto-feminist if one, as I do, defines feminism openly as shared humanity.

N. F. S. GRUNDTVIG: HOMING THE
FEMALE IN EVERY HUMAN BEING

Grundtvig takes up Luther's esteem for the female side of humanity and the church. Post-Luther Protestantism had ignored the extremely experiential and sensual sides of Luther's theology and become either sterile and rational or pietistic. Grundtvig, however, re-found the sensual and female sides that matched his basic Romantic approach. He re-introduced the female element that, according to him, had been neglected by the church. Importantly, Grundtvig asserted that a true human being is both male and female, which to him is also the truth about Christ's humanity. If only male or only female, it is but half a human. Taken together, the male and female make a *whole* human being.[18]

I here refer to Grundtvig's famous *Women's Gospel* from 1842 to show how he operates in order to integrate what he understands as female and male features. In the first stanzas of the poem, he introduces the female/woman as mother of faith and utilizes the nuptial metaphor as a description of the relationship between God/Christ (bridegroom) and the community/congregation as bride with a true female character. Like Jairus' daughter and the woman who suffered from hemorrhages, the doubting believers should feel comfort with God. Finding the papal church particularly ignorant about women and untruthful about their role in both incarnation and resurrection, he lifts up central female figures such as Mary, the at once daughter of God and mother of the Savior, and Mary Magdalene, the female apostle who witnessed the resurrection. But even Eve is re-constituted as necessary for life in the garden of Eden—Eve was a gift to Adam (stanza 54), just as now the church without women would be like a wood without leaves (stanza 53). Interestingly, Grundtvig deliberates on the round breasts with which God created the woman—breasts created for not simply fleshly life but also for spiritual life and lust. After all, Christ sucked from female breasts, which points to the fact that breasts cannot mean or symbolize anything negative.

It is evident from this poem, as elsewhere in Grundtvig's oeuvre, that he, like Luther, is reconfiguring the church and the everyday life through recognizing women and the female as an integral part of God's creation and humanity. Parallel to Luther, Grundtvig does this by establishing family relations, divine and human, and thus creating a homeliness both universally and locally. Neither the church nor the world are homes for males only. In fact, they only constitute a sense of home when the female and the male are integrated in the human being, and though this might seem too binary to some, it should rather be seen as a cross-gendering perspective to being human and being at home in the human body.

K. E. LØGSTRUP: HOMING HUMANITY
IN COMMUNITIES OF TRUST

As an example of the shared humanity that already Luther fought for, and which to Grundtvig and Løgstrup were a given part of divine creation, I will conclude this essay by lifting up a few points from an article written during Germany's occupation of Denmark during World War II. The article was by Løgstrup, engaged in a heated discussion with his friend, the church historian Hal Koch. Unsatisfied with his friend's opinions on the politics of the occupation, Løgstrup accentuates the importance of humanness in living out a community life. A common life of ordinary people must build on trust (one hears an echo of Luther and his faith as trust), Løgstrup stresses, "in the folk life it is a matter of obeying the laws that are given with our life as humanity to create a common life where one can trust one another, and where one does not leave those persons who cannot manage on their own to their agony and fate."[19]

Løgstrup is adamant that people need to trust one another, not only when making solemn declarations but also when people are in need. People need to trust one another in times of war as in times of peace.[20] It is important for him to underline that spiritual life is more than simply showing interest in others. Rather, it is about a tension in every human being, a tension of opposites, he asserts. This leads him to state that one of life's laws, given with life as such, is that we must honor one another, "For a man's and a woman's honor is the trust we others have to his or her behaving humanely. If a human being behaves dishonorably, its life will dissolve."[21]

In this vein, he agrees with Luther: parents must educate their children to humanity by way of obedience in order for justice to prevail. A shared humanity is the goal, but it builds on an array of principles such as justice, honor, and trust—no less in the midst of war. As Løgstrup points out in an article on Christianity and faith in creation: "Without trust, a human being would not know what it means to talk to another human being. It would not be able to experience it, as truly that of talking to another person is to trust that what is said is understood as it is meant."[22] All people should be able to find a home, a safe place in the common life based on their shared humanity.

HOMING MY TEXT

In my view, it is of utter importance that we, like Luther and Trible, home women in Bible texts and tradition in order that we home them throughout history, in life, and ultimately in humanity. In line with Karen Barad, I see everything in this world to be entangled, and the way women are treated in Bible texts and tradition reflects the way they are treated in life and their place in humanity. When women are displaced in Bible texts and tradition, they are displaced everywhere in life, exiled from humanity. Luther had an eye for that when he in his universal theology of grace focus on inclusivity and an ordinary life in order to home women in Bible texts and thus to home them in humanity. In this brief paper, I have tried to show how the two Danish creation theologians, Grundtvig and Løgstrup continued Luther's vision toward strengthening a sense of people living as a shared humanity.

NOTES

1. See for example, Karen Barad, *Meeting the Universe Halfway: Quantum Physics and the Entanglement of Matter and Meaning* (Durham, NC: Duke University Press, 2007) and Karen Barad, *Agentieller Realismus: Über die Bedeutung materiell-diskursiver Praktiken [Agential Realism: On the Importance of Material-Discursive Practices]* (Berlin: Suhrkamp, 2012).

2. The erroneous assertion that Luther disparaged Copernicus has been debunked by Donald H. Kobe, "Copernicus and Martin Luther: An Encounter between Science and Religion," in *American Journal of Physics* 66, no. 190 (March 1998): 194. See also Terra Schwerin Rowe, "Genus Precarious: Luther in the Anthropocene," *The*

Alternative Luther. Lutheran Theology from the Subaltern, ed. Else Marie Wiberg Pedersen (London: Lexington Books/Fortress Academic, 2019), 336–43.

3. See the official homepage of the homeless in Denmark: https://husforbi.dk/hvad -er-en-hjemloes/, accessed June 9, 2023, for more information about the issue, including research on the sociological side of homelessness.

4. Trygve Wyller, "The Heterotopic Creation: A Short Contribution to a Subaltern Ecclesiology," *The Alternative Luther*, op.cit., 90.

5. Phyllis Trible, *Texts of Terror: Literary Feminist Readings of Biblical Narratives* (Philadelphia: Fortress, 1984), 2–3.

6. Trible, ibid., 4–5.

7. Beverly Wallace, "Hush No More! Constructing an African American Lutheran Womanist Ethic," *Transformative Lutheran Theologies. Feminist, Womanist, and Mujerista Perspectives*, ed. Mary Streufert (Minneapolis, MN: Fortress, 2010), 188–89.

8. Arnfridur Gudmundsdottir, "Let's be Loud! God in Context of Sexual Violence and Abuse of Power," *The Alternative Luther*, op. cit., 218.

9. The Lutheran World Federation, *Gender Justice Policy* (2013), 34. See further: https://www.lutheranworld.org/sites/default/files/2022-02/DTPW-WICAS _Gender_Justice.pdf, accessed June 15 2023.

10. Martin Luther, *Large Catechism* (1529), *The Book of Concord*, eds. Robert Kolb and Timothy Wengert (Minneapolis, MN: Fortress, 2000), 428.

11. Luther's relation to the Jews and the Turks is highly critiqued in the context of contemporary identity politics, as are his views on women. For an elaboration of Luther's inclusive theology vis-à-vis this critique, see Else Marie Wiberg Pedersen, "Luther as the Subaltern Precarious: The Banned, Excluded and Outlawed Eleutherius," The Alternative Luther, 19–38; and idem, "Radical Incarnation and Creative Ambiguity: Luther's View of Ministry and Gender," in *Studia Theologica. Nordic Journal of Theology* 73, no. 1 (January 2019): 4–22.

12. Ibid., 410.

13. See Luther's letter treatise, "To the Christian Nobility of the German Nation Regarding Its Christian Improvement" (1520), WA 6: 381–469. Incidentally, I deliberately refer to the German Weimar Edition, because I find so many mistranslations in the American Edition of Luther Works. I recommend, as an alternative English text, the translation by H. Ashley Hall of a later Luther text on the schooling of children: "To the Councilmen of All Cities in Germany, That They Establish and Maintain Christian Schools (1524), *The Annotated Luther 5: Christian Life in the World*, ed. Hans J. Hillerbrand (Minneapolis, MN: Fortress, 2017), 235–80. As Hall importantly states, "Every person in every vocation has the right, if not the obligation, to avail herself and himself of an education. Their education should not be overly constrained, but allow for playing and tussling," ibid., 241, which points to Grundtvig's thoughts related to his ideas of the high school for youngsters. See Else Marie Wiberg Pedersen, "Creation and Anthropology: N.F.S. Grundtvig as Humanist and Feminist," in *Dialog. A Journal of Theology* 60, no. 2 (June 2021): 137–44.

14. Thus, biblical scholarship is still divided on the question if Dinah is a victim or if she is complicit in the act narrated about in Genesis. See Monica Melanchthon's

eye-opening chapter, "Making Connections: Dinah, Luther, and Indian Women," *The Alternative Luther*, op.cit., 197–203, and notes 13–17. Parallel to that, Mary Magdalene has been stamped as a prostitute or a promiscuous woman since Gregory the Great co-read almost all Maries of the New Testament with the anonymous woman who anoints Jesus in Luke 7:36–50. See Surekha Nelavala's careful reading of the text and of other feminist comments to Luke 7:36–50 in her illuminating chapter, "Grace Alone! Alternative Subaltern Feminist Reading of the Muted, Sinful Woman I Luke 7:36–50," *The Alternative Luther*, 243–47.

15. As Luther gave this lecture the year after his beloved daughter, Magdalene, died at 13 years old, he struggled with the question how God could allow such atrocities to happen, finding no other comforting answer than this: the rape is the work of the devil. However disappointing this may seem to us now, it was a comfort to Luther in the context of the sixteenth-century harsh society that, though the atrocities are not those of God's work, God allows them to happen as trials of a rich elite group of people.

16. See Else Marie Wiberg Pedersen, "Sermons on Two Kinds of Righteousness 1519," *The Annotated Luther, vol. 2: Word and Faith*, ed. Kirsi Stjerna (Minneapolis, MN: Fortress, 2015), 9–24.

17. According to Nelavala, "Grace Alone!," 248, a few feminist scholars strongly questions how exegetes interpret the physical attributes of the anonymous woman as those of a prostitute. The result, however, is that many scholars still accept tradition's stamp of her as a prostitute, indeed, of her as Mary Magdalene the prostitute without further ado.

18. Cf. Else Marie Wiberg Pedersen "Creation and Anthropology: N.F.S. Grundtvig as Humanist and Feminist," *Dialog: A Journal of Theology*, 60:2 [2021], 137–44.

19. K. E. Løgstrup, *Folkeliv og udenrigspolitik* [*Folk Life and Foreign Politics*] (Copenhagen: Nyt nordisk Forlag, 1943), 15.

20. Ibid., 18.

21. Ibid., 9.

22. K. E. Løgstrup, "Kristendom uden skabelsestro" [Christianity Without Faith in Creation] *Vindrosen* 9, no. 7 (1962): 531.

PART III

Cosmos as Home

Chapter 10

Deep Inhabitations

Home and Cosmos in Scandinavian Creation Theology

Niels Henrik Gregersen

Scandinavian Creation Theology (SCT) has so far not developed a compre-hensive view of the intertwinement of home and cosmos. In his classic study *The Ethical Demand* from 1956, K. E. Løgstrup (1905–1981) laid out a phe-nomenology of close human interrelations. He showed how reciprocal trust is central to human living together and argued that ethical demands arise from the prior fact that we live in interdependency; we always have something of the life of others in our hands. Only later, Løgstrup and his student and collaborator Ole Jensen (1937–2021) developed their ecological thinking as part of an expansive theology and philosophy of creation.

What it means to have a home is a question that somehow lies between the fluidity of everyday communication and reflections on how the universe is pervasively present in the midst of human life. In what follows, I offer my own proposal for how to articulate the intertwinement of home and cosmos in the vein of SCT. My central point is that the expansive view of creation of SCT attends to creative processes that take place between natural and social domains of life, and consistently intersect what we are used to thinking of as separate realms. Homes are more than houses, and feelings of being at home are nourished by a broad awareness of historical and natural places. My argu-ment proceeds as follows. First, I point to a variety of homes and dwelling places within and outside of humanly constructed houses, while focusing on the interaction between human house-building and more-than-human aspects of reality. Homes are deep in materiality as well as in sociality, and homes are never fully insulated from the parts of the cosmos that we inhabit. Scientists thus refer to the "hospitability" of cosmos for life. Second, I go through seminal aspects of K. E. Løgstrup's cosmo-phenomenology, which points to the interplay between sensational qualities of world and our linguistic attempts to understand the world. Third, I suggest that resonance experiences constitute a phenomenological entry to understand why we feel at home in some places, but not necessarily everywhere. In this context, I discuss the relations of being home-sick in terms of a *nostalgia* that longs for lost, beloved homes, and *solastalgia*, a newly introduced term for the mental distress of losing the sense of home in environmentally destroyed habitats.

Toward the end, I bring in theological resources that move back and forth between a theology of creation and a theology of deep incarnation and inhabitation. From the perspective of the first article of faith, we are carried into a world that welcomes us, rather than being thrown into a foreign world, empty of meaning. So, what is the relation between being carried and being thrown? From the perspective of the second and third articles of faith, we see a similar tension between feeling at home where we are, and yet being on the move. Having developed the concept of deep incarnation elsewhere, I take up the concept of "deep inhabitation," suggested by Mary Emily Duba. I argue that the concept of deep incarnation has both a reference to a deep materiality of divine self-incarnation in the world of flesh, and a broad social inhabitation of Christ in the midst of our transitional homes.

We are indeed "homed by the universe" in a fundamentally passive sense of being carried and welcomed, but we should be aware that all concrete homes are transitional, and that our cosmic conditions are anything but idyllic. Certainly, planet Earth does offer multiple and constant resources of resonance to help us feel at home in the universe. Yet it also exemplifies destructive powers. Whether we like it, or not, death and destruction are part of the package deal of the way in which nature works. Illness and the annihilation of personhood, predator-prey cycles, to say nothing of the vast destructive force of tsunamis, earthquakes, and meteors, are part of reality no less than the life-promoting qualities of nature. As phrased by K. E. Løgstrup, "God's act of creation is terrifying in its splendor and annihilation; it exceeds our intellectual and emotional apprehension."[1] So, how can we be at home in a world that entails a wealth of resonance and a wealth of dissonance as well?

VARIETIES OF HOME: BEYOND THE NATURE-CULTURE DISTINCTION

We usually think of "home" as a house or apartment, in which we live and dwell. And that's how it is. We build, furnish, and decorate our homes so that they become comfort zones with relatively safe boundaries between "us" and the world "outside" of us. Houses are like skin that shelter our bodies while both regulating and allowing for movements of going out and coming home. This dialectic between home and horizon, closure and openness, relates not only to other people, but to sunlight and rain, cold and warm weather, insects and dust as well.

Human beings live in a wide variety of homes, some more temporary (like tents), some more stable (like houses). Usually we speak of home as an indoor thing but most people experience particular places in nature as part of our homes, insofar as they elicit feelings of resonance and belonging. Such outdoor homes are not "ours" in terms of ownership but they constitute a shared social-and-natural network, a field of the "commons" through which we interact with more-than-human beings. We would not be able to feel at home anywhere without the stability of rocks, solid ground, and other natural elements, nor would we feel at home without the sense of being connected to a flourishing of life around us. Indeed, nature is already part of the houses we live in, since they are built from timber and bricks, and from concrete and plastics too. Homes are examples of hybrids of natural elements, human craft, and machine work.

In his famous essay, "Building, Dwelling, Thinking" from 1951, philosopher Martin Heidegger captured an important sense of home, when he stated in his opening paragraph: "We attain to dwelling, so it seems, only by building."[2] The problem with this sentence is the "only." While houses are built for dwelling, comfort and delight, we do not dwell only by building. Even modern citizens who are living mostly as indoor people find dwelling places also in non-human nature such as gardens and parks. Even indoor people wish, if possible at all, to build their houses in places of natural beauty.[3]

However, we also use the term "home" in more comprehensive contexts, not restricted to the home life of families and individuals. We speak of our home too by designating our *origins*, with which we can identify ourselves as being somehow "at home." Likewise, we may (or may not) feel at home in particular *human cultures* (say, around the Mediterranean Sea), or may (or may not) feel at home in specific *religious traditions*, liturgies, and songs. We speak about our home countries, from which we can depart in travelling, and may later return to. Such homecomings can be quite cumbersome (which I will return to below). Likewise, we feel at home in our *native languages* that go back to our childhood rearing; yet we also use our first language(s) as the point of departure for learning new languages, in which we may later feel relatively comfortable. In addition to these historical and cultural senses of home, we have an even wider sense of home, pointing to the *natural space* to which we belong, as when we say that the kangaroo has its home in Australia.[4]

Does something like the latter characterize human dwellings too? Some would say "No," drawing a strict line between human beings and other living beings. Language teaches us better, however, for we speak about our sense of "belonging" to specific landscapes. We may feel relaxed in forests, stunned by the mountains, elated at the seaside, just as we may enjoy the open acres, and even resonate with flatlands of deserts. Here, the distinction between humanly constructed environments and natural habitats begins to dissolve. In the extensive literature on the experience economy, we likewise find the concept of "urban dwellers" who feel at home in specific parts of cities, say in Copenhagen or New York City, and enjoy the atmospheres of urban landscapes.

This wider understanding of home is presupposed in the very word ecology, where the "eco-" is derived from the Greek term *oikos*, "home." By contrast, the term "ecumenic" is derived from *oikoumene*, referring to whole orbit inhabited by humans only. When Gregory Bateson spoke of the "ecology of the mind," he was bringing the wide-scope term of *oikos* into the inner life of human longings, strivings, and worries.[5] What comes first: space or mind, is no longer easy to say.

BEING "HOMED BY THE UNIVERSE:"
SCIENTIFIC PERSPECTIVES

I use the past and present participle of "being homed" to suggest a *passive* sense of being somehow accommodated by the universe. "Being homed" articulates a fundamental sense of "being here," prior to the constructive sense of home-building but also prior to any scientific theorizing. The passive term of being homed runs contrary to the goal-setting actions of "homing in" on a target, as in the case of a missile. As rare as the passive participle form of "being homed" is in ordinary language, it is not unusual to speak of our "hospitable universe" from the perspective of contemporary physics and biology.[6] Evidently, the universe that we inhabit was here long before us, and so was planet Earth. Our planet has given room for life forms, each having and co-creating a multitude of habitats, specific to the agency of each organism. According to the prevailing view of the sciences of complexity and self-organization, the universe has exactly the life-enabling laws and self-organizing propensities that has made the emergence of life "well-nigh inevitable." As put by Stuart Kauffman: "The motto of life is not We the improbable, but We the expected."[7]

The reason behind this statement is that the universe harbors hospitable conditions for life, thus also creating the natural conditions for the subsequent building of habitats that takes place at every moment in evolution and human history. This is evident on our planet Earth, at least, but many scientists argue that it is probable that there is life elsewhere in the vast universe. In this volume Ted Peters encourages the Scandinavians to develop even more expansive theologies of creation that reflect upon on the likelihood of life, and intelligent life, on other planets outside the planetary system of the Earth.[8] On the one hand, any process of life will move "uphill," that is, go against the homogenizing tendencies of the Second Law of Thermodynamics (by reaping energy from the environment). On the other, the very capacity of local organisms to go against the degrading streams of general thermodynamics is based on the self-organizational propensities of basic chemical structures that underlie the reaping of energy essential to development and evolution of the individual organisms in their communities. There is an ongoing ecology of viruses, bacteria, and sponges no less than an ecology of mind.

Thus, biological agency is as central as the fact that life processes depend on, and in the end fall prey to, the inner vulnerability of complex biological structures. Decay and death are in this sense as old as creativity, but as long as the organism is at work, creativity takes the upper hand. As argued by the niche construction theory within Darwinian evolution, not only humans build houses and shape their environments but so do beavers, worms, and bacteria. Scientifically speaking, we are thus homed by the universe as the underlying (and often forgotten) basis for our own home-making. Furthermore, human home-building builds on a long evolutionary trajectory of niche construction, honed over time and exemplified by many other creatures than humans only. Accordingly, we may say that the predicament of human life is about *exploring* the universe to which we belong, even as we move on, charting new territories, looking for other options, and making decisions for how to make (parts of) this world *our* home. In this sense, we are concomitantly both "making homes" and "finding homes," in terms of using the generative platforms for life developed long ago, prior to us in time, but also spatially far more extensive than our humanly constructed homes and urban spaces.[9]

FROM SCIENCE TO PHENOMENOLOGY

Scientific descriptions of nature are important but cannot by themselves help us understand the universe as our home. Even if it is the case that "being homed by the universe" precedes and underlies the conditions for our continuous attempts at "home-making," one question is still nagging: To what extent can we, from a human perspective, speak about our world as a comfort zone, when we realize that the very ecospace that hosts us brings dangers upon us as well? Should we pretend to live in a paradise? No, that would be negligent, and anything but wise.[10] Should we pretend that we, as a human civilization, can live and act without worries about the risks that we are incurring on life on our planet? No, that would be unethical, since the unintended consequences of our actions threaten other life forms, and the life chances of future generations. So, what does it mean to say that we are homed by the universe, when there are also cracks in our trust in our cosmic habitat—cracks that remove from us the possibility of living in a thoroughly relaxed manner on our planet? In what follows, I wish to address this problem via delineating the contours of Løgstrup's ecophilosophy.

FROM HUMAN PHENOMENOLOGY TO COSMO-PHENOMENOLOGY: K. E. LØGSTRUP

Løgstrup worked as a phenomenologist, uncovering and analyzing typical forms of everyday human existence. At the same time, Løgstrup developed a vision for a cosmo-phenomenology that addresses how cosmic conditions impinge on human life. He often speaks of "the universe" but rarely refers to constellations of stars and solar systems. His point is rather that universal conditions of our cosmos appear recurrently in human experience, so that we cannot think cosmos away without thinking human life away. Programmatically, he wanted to develop a "descriptive metaphysics" without embarking upon a speculative metaphysics.

From the outset, he is addressing human beings as living and interpretative beings rather than as mere physical bodies. In the 1940s, he critiqued the subject-oriented phenomenology of Edmund Husserl for being caught in the epistemological framework of subject versus object, a framework of Kantian provenance. During the 1950s, Løgstrup developed Martin Heidegger's socially oriented phenomenology in new ways. He shared Heidegger's view of human existence (*Dasein*) as situated with other people (*Miteinander Dasein*), thus living in "interdependence." In an early book, *Kierkegaard's and Heidegger's Analysis of Existence and Its Relation to Proclamation* from 1950, he still saw Heidegger as an ally to the Lutheran view of the vocations of neighbor love in everyday life, which he put in contrast to Søren Kierkegaard's emphasis on human subjectivity and decision.[11]

Løgstrup, however, was a critical student of Heidegger. To Heidegger's "existential" or structural approach to phenomenology, Løgstrup added an ethical understanding of human life together, always imbued with reciprocal expectations and hopes. In a large number of original micro-analyses, he showed how human agents relate to one another in ethically loaded relations of interdependence such as trust and conversation, including the risk of misunderstanding and negligence. Hereby, he offered a phenomenological alternative to Heidegger's emphasis on the decisionist nature of human engagement.

Indeed, Løgstrup found the sense of ethics absent in Heidegger's work. These features came into a confluence in *The Ethical Demand* from 1956.[12]

Beginning in the 1960s, however, the importance of space came to the fore in Løgstrup's work, especially by pointing to the relation between ethics and ontology occluded in Heidegger's *Sein und Zeit* from 1927.[13] But it was not until 1969–1970 that Løgstrup declared Heidegger's idea of the ontology of time as a "a regional ontology of historicity," insofar as Heidegger consistently overlooked the human emplacement in non-human nature. This led Løgstrup to embark on his mature work, the four volumes subtitled "Metaphysical considerations," addressing language (1976), religion (1978), art (1982) and the relation between history and nature (1984).[14] Løgstrup understands the tasks of metaphysics to be descriptive rather than speculative, referring to aspects of reality that reoccur over time, albeit in empirical variations. Løgstrup's concept of "Metaphysics," we may say, is about what we cannot think away from reality without thinking the world and ourselves away.

ECOLOGY 1, 2, AND 3

Let me now introduce a grid of "three ecologies" by which I will attempt to describe the contours of Løgstrup's ecophilosophy. Ecological thinking is often, and for good reason, concerned with *non-human nature*: the "wild," "raw," and potentially "enchanted" world of non-human nature. Let us call this Ecology₁. These aspects are prevalent also in the work of K. E. Løgstrup. It is exactly the alterity and multiplicity of life forms that elicits a religious sense of wonder. Moreover, ecological thinking is naturally concerned about the *cultured nature*: The environment as cultivated through landscapes, gardens, cities, and new technologies via human stewardship and attempts at control. Let us call this Ecology₂. These themes feature prominently in the ecological thinking of the Scandinavian creation theology as well. In this chapter, however, I will focus on the aspect of a *human entanglement in and with nature*. Let us call this Ecology₃. The point is here that human experiences are so deeply enmeshed with nature, that human beings themselves are decentered, but also potentially re-capacitated as human agents.[15]

While Ecology₁ has been the focal interest of the ecological ethics in Scandinavian creation theology, also Ecology₂ has played a major role when emphasizing the inerasable role of human agency in dealing with nature. Ole Jensen, the leading ecotheological voice of SCT, has rightly pointed to the need for a human self-restraint vis-a-vis nature, ethically as well as politically.[16] What I will add to this concern is the concomitant need for a human struggling with nature as well. Certainly, nature is nowadays threatened by humanity, but natural systems henceforth constitute a constant source of danger to humanity, as we see it in the human fight against grand-scale disasters and small-scale diseases. Conditions of aging and illness as well as many disasters are not purely anthropogenic. Externally adduced *dangers* can't be reduced to humanly incurred *risks*.[17] As put by K. E. Løgstrup, "Today there are many Christians and religiously minded people who will not face up to the fact that there is physical suffering, disease and death which is impossible to understand as an effect of the evil in humanity. As if suffering, disease and death could be found only among humankind and not also in the animal world [. . .] We can argue about interpretations, we must bend before facts."[18]

It is important to keep in mind that we humans do not only plant, prune, harvest, and use natural habitats as testing labs for our human purposes. We are ourselves testing labs of natural selection too. Constantly, humans are pruned, gardened, and attacked by the pervasive forces of nature that do not stop at the human skin. We are here approaching the important but difficult-to-define themes of Ecology$_3$: our entanglement with nature in a pervasive dimension of our creatureliness.

LIVING BODIES ARE BODIES IN FLOW

By definition, pervasive features can't be defined, because they are ubiquitous. Nonetheless human nature entanglements can be described, even in the understanding of human personhood. I suggest that humans develop by absorbing resonances and overcoming dissonances as long as our life story goes. *Per-sona* in Latin means the crack in our masks or face open to the world through which sounds and tones (*sonae*) can flow in and out (*per-*), and therefore co-constitute our individual character. Accordingly, I propose to see human beings (and any other similar organism) as "persons" through which all the sounds and voices of the world flow, while we ourselves also give sound and voice back to the world, each from our individual perspective. If we try to think of all the things that have filled us up, it's not just other people, but also nature has left its footprints in us. The wind and the sunrays, the dog and its barking, the insects and their buzzing belong to our humanity. Sounds, smells, and sensual touches are part of our lives—whether we like the smells, sounds, and touches, or not.[19]

In the same manner, we carry nature within ourselves, since our bodies are *examples* of nature, whether we are aware of it or not. Nature is in us like bones and minerals, blood, and oxygen, etc. Why is our blood red? Because blood carries the iron content formed by stellar explosions billions of years ago. Similarly, we have the entire biological history of the species represented in our bodies in the small selection of the biological *genome* handed over to us at conception. But more than that, we carry with us on our skin and in our throats and stomachs a vast amount of DNA and RNA in our non-human *microbiome*, consisting of bacterial DNA, viral RNA, and fungal forms, without which we could not survive from day to day. In short, our bodies are formed as hybrids of different materials, physical elements, chemical compounds and biological systems. Even viewed as vital physical bodies (*Körper*), we are interwoven into natural networks, and even more so as living and interpreting bodies (*Leiber*).

CONTOURS OF K. E. LØGSTRUP'S ECOPHILOSOPHY

Now back to Løgstrup's ecological project, which dates back to end of the 1960s, before ecology was on the top of the international agenda. In his posthumous volume on the metaphysics of nature and history (1995, II, 1–145), Løgstrup made a principal distinction between seeing nature as a mere *environment* to human undertakings as opposed to seeing the universe as an ubiquitous *source* of human life. He found the modern understanding of human civilization as a "marginal existence" (somehow superadded to nature and enclosed from the universe), both delusional and dangerous. As he wrote in the end of the 1970s:

> The apprehension of our place in the cosmos is decisive for the culture we get. To deluded conceptions corresponds a deluded reality that begins to become dangerous, whether it is cause or effect. At the edge of the universe, we come to the edge with nature. Even economists, who otherwise takes pleasure in disillusioning the rest of us, have begun to disillusion the development for what it causes: pollution, a latrine of garbage, soil exhaustion, waste, social unrest (1995 II, 9).

Løgstrup coined the term "cosmo-phenomenology" for careful descriptions of how the universe manifests itself in the midst of human awareness of reality. If we take a closer look at his cosmo-phenomenological analyses, he starts out with features of *Ecology1*. The world of non-human species, so Løgstrup, each have their own characteristic form and shape; so also the world of colors, as well as the recurrent feature of dynamical self-organization in living organisms (1995 I, 133–194). Each of these features exemplify what Løgstrup calls "singular universals," that is, characteristic features of reality that are prior to particular human categorizations thereof but which nonetheless are apprehensible in concrete phenomenological analyses of *how* the non-human world of nature presents itself to humans. According to Løgstrup, such characterizations may differ from language to language but will always be recognizable from the point of view of other languages.

In terms of *Ecology*$_2$ and *Ecology*$_3$, Løgstrup uses a distinction between the physical body (in German: *Körper*) and the living body (in German: *Leiber*). As pointed out in the opening section of *Source and Surrounding*. "With our respiration and our metabolism, we are emplaced in the cycle of nature. With our sensation we are emplaced in the universe" (1995 I, 1; trans. rev.). By the "cycle of nature," Løgstrup refers to human interaction with nature as bodily *Körper* (Ecology$_2$), by "universe" he addresses the pervasive features of the world in which we are embedded and enmeshed (Ecology$_3$).

Løgstrup is of course aware that humans constitute a rare species not least by having "a sustaining consciousness" (1995 II, 23–28). Consciousness allows us to live in our own cultural worlds of language and understanding. "We do not live only in actual space, we also live in fictive space" (1995 II, 130). Our withdrawal from the universe is a precondition for the coming into existence of language and understanding, hence of cultural worlds of fictitious space (1995 II, 33). Nonetheless, Løgstrup argues that the fictive space (which allows us to withdraw from nature, sheltered by human culture) draws from our sense of the openness of space too, prior to particular cultural frameworks. Moreover, our perceptual and conceptual withdrawals from the environment find their analogues in non-human nature. "A primary condition [for withdrawal] is that the sensing organism, whether it is animal or human being, must be capable of moving freely in its surroundings" (1995 II, 33). This applies to humans as well as to mosquitos and lions. An additional precondition is the fact that all living organisms are open systems that rely on an influx of energy. "The organism has its needs which can only be satisfied and fulfilled by what belongs to its surroundings" (II, 33–24).

In this sense, the reaping of energy from other organisms sets a distinction between the organism itself, and what is outside of it. In continuation of this biological view, it can be added that such reaping of energy from the environment cannot but have some violent form, be it from a human omnivore or a vegetarian, an ox or a virus needing a host cell in order to spread. The whole world of Ecology$_2$, with its many forms of friendly symbiosis and organism-centered fight for survival, should not be seen a human prerogative only. As a matter of fact, biological organisms (including ourselves) do not live in a peaceful kingdom, and we can't if we are to survive.

At this level of Ecology2, Løgstrup is highly critical of the unbridled human egoism, or the human "speciesism," as later dubbed by Ole Jensen. Løgstrup repeats his earlier point: "With our respiration and our metabolism, we are emplaced in the cycle of nature." But note now how Løgstrup continuous his argument: "It is as conscious beings, and not as living beings, that we have broken out of this systematic unity. The risk, which the reduction of instinct contains, is that we as conscious beings become inconsistent, incompatible with ourselves as living beings" (1995 II, 43). The ecological crisis is thus the manifestation of the fact that insatiable human needs threaten to destruct the very natural basis for the fulfillment of human needs for survival and flourishing. Yet, as he remarks, "only by our consciousness can we save ourselves from the threat that originated from our consciousness" (1995 II 43). We can, in other words, not solve the ecological crisis if we don't take up our specifically human responsibilities.

In other aspects, the agential repertoire of Ecology2 does not set the human species apart from other living beings. In satisfying our everyday needs we have nature in front of us, just like it is the case for other creatures in their environments. The problem lies in the unbridled greediness of human appetites that has been reinforced by our cultural conceptions of what constitutes a good life: travelling more, eating more, using more of the easiest available energy, etc. "Need is pushiness, conquest, greediness, destruction of opposition" (1995 II, 44). At this point, Løgstrup highlights the importance of human self-restraint, the need for tempering the aggressiveness inherent in approaching reality via our needs. Ethically, self-restraint correlates with need, so that human beings "become cultural beings and acquire history [in] restraint in all its variations, shame and shyness, respect and recognition, bashfulness and modesty and more" (1995 II, 44).

Let me now approach aspects of Ecology3 in Løgstrup's work. Løgstrup argues that we are not only dependent on our natural environment to survive, we are also fully dependent on the universe for living our existence in sensation and sensitivity. Living in sensation, however, stands in a remarkable contrast to living in needs: "As aggressive as the need is, so unaggressive is sensation" (II, 44). Løgstrup's cosmo-phenomenology of sensation is highly original, therefore also contested—and in my view contestable too. So let me declare that in what follows, I present the gist of his phenomenology of sensation, only insofar as I myself find them persuasive. His basic argument is that in sensation we have an immediate (or better: involuntary) presence of the universe in us. Human life is not only about fulfilling needs, or about finding our place in nature by understanding ourselves and nature as being "out there." To live as a human is also to be engulfed in sensation of what is not ourselves but nonetheless present in us in a penetrating and uncontrollable manner.

According to Løgstrup, our life in *sensation* goes deeper than, and differs from, an organism-centered *perception* of something in the outer world. Sensation is not like scanning a territory instrumentally for that which may become prey for our appetites as epistemological predators. Sensation is what constitutes our experiential world deeper than any concrete perception of something just being "out there." Seeing, hearing, and being touched *is* with us, and we are *in it*. Seeing is a primary fact, before we begin to explain the light as coming from the sun and being transported through our eyes. Hearing a noise is prior to the question whether the noise comes from a thunder or a jet plane. We feel a touch involuntarily before we begin to perceive the touch as friendly or invasive. When we see a deer in the back of the garden, we are co-present with the deer in sensation and the deer is present in my sensation, even though my body is situated twenty meters away, and whether or not I know about its exact species, age etc. When we see the ocean, we are engulfed by the sea, and the sensation of the sea is present in us.

Here some examples of my own: Anyone who has seen movie *The Andalusian Dog* by Salvador Dali and Luis Buñuel from 1929 will recognize the experience of distancelessness in sensation. In one scene, a fully open eye fills out the screen; subsequently a knife silently and slowly comes in from the one side of the eye, cutting through to the other side of the eye. Few people can see the scene without squinting the eye. The eye on the screen is present in my own eyes. Similarly, when we are going to a concert, the sounds and rhythms are present in our ears and bodies prior to any description of the music.

Løgstrup's phenomenology of sensation is a critique of a universalized hermeneutics, such as the tradition of Heidegger and Gadamer, on the one hand, and of the empiricist view of discrete sense-data within the philosophy of positivist empiricism, on the other. "Sense data, to which according to the sense data theory we should find ourselves at a distance without the understanding, do not exist" (1995 II,13). Løgstrup admits, however, that we never have sensation in pure form. Sensation is always experienced in us within the limits of bodily distance and conditioned by language and understanding. But *what comes to us* by hearing and seeing *is present* in us. Sensation is not a raw material or foil for understanding and intervention, nor is it a set of itemized sense data, for what is sensed comes to us in its own form prior to our conceptualization: "reality is ever present" (1995 II, 3).

In Løgstrup, sensation (the presence of the universe in us) and human understanding (based on withdrawal) are always at odds with one another, even though both work in tandem in human experience. "Sensation lacks distance. The seen and heard are at a distance from our body but not at distance from our sensation. The ship we see out on the ocean, the dog's bark down in the village are far away from our body but not from our vision and hearing" (1995 II, 6). Understanding differs from sensation by withdrawing from what is seen and heard, and by wanting to bring what is seen and heard into a shared human world ("common possession"). There is always a particular effort involved in understanding things, whereas sensation comes to us effortlessly: "in sensation, we are totally powerless in the face of the universe" (II, 6).

THE WONDER OF "BEING-HERE" AND
THE EXPERIENCE OF RESONANCE

Let us now move back to our initial considerations about the feeling of being homed and emplaced. What is the relation between our (sometimes terrifying) powerlessness in front of the universe, and our feeling at home somewhere but not everywhere? Being homed by the universe is about being allowed to exist and thrive. Yet feelings of being at home arrive only within an organismic and human perspective. Phenomenologically speaking, feelings precede what may subsequently be schematized, for example in psychological or sociological measurements.

Newborns and small children experience their world within a symbiotic sphere. Adults, too, sometimes experience the wonder and puzzlement of existence in the brute sense of "something being there," before we begin to make distinctions between "us" and the external world, between "home" and the outside. Infants and children develop their sense of world and self from the experience of living in an undifferentiated environment. But, as I said, also grown-ups are regularly stricken by a pre-schematized sense of "something being there"—without knowing exactly what it is, and how to relate to it from our point of view. This sense of "something appearing" is prior to any objective conceptualization or subsequent subjective view. This experience does not build on theory or thought but comes with primary experience. We begin as creatures floating in surroundings that include ourselves, similar to a fetus in a mother's womb.

The German sociologist Hartmut Rosa takes his point of departure in such uncoded awareness of something "being there," before he undertakes a resonance-based theoretical interpretation of feelings of home.[20] Resonance experiences are mental attunements between self and world. Seen from a physical perspective, resonance exists everywhere, because sonar and magnetic relations are ubiquitous in nature (measured in Herz, Gauss, etc.). Being a sociologist, the physical ubiquity of objective resonance relations does not stand in the foreground of Rosa's sociological and cultural analysis of home. The reason is that from a human perspective, we always experience resonance in particular constellations such as musical tones and tunes, the softness or solidity of the ground on which we walk, or bodily gestures of others that invite us into positive reverberations between us and them. In Rosa's analysis, there is always an affectivity preceding our emotional attunements. Moreover, the interplay between being affected by the world and our emotional responses has transformative effects on us, and usually they are difficult to control in advance. Thus, we have four dimensions of resonance experiences: affectivity, emotional response, transformation, and uncontrollability.[21]

But what about feeling the world as our home? Well, the very category of home will always be limited. We think of some specific places as home, without claiming that everything in space and time feels like a home to us. As put by Rosa, "Home is the idea that there exists a part of the world (*Weltausschnitt*) that responds to us and with which we enter into resonance experiences."[22]

Rosa distances himself from a too backward- and identity-based view of home, centered around territoriality. A reason may be a particular German worry of *Blut und Boden*-thinking that was prevalent in Nazism. However, also in the current polarized United States, we find the *Stand Your Ground*-movement, in which some citizens claim the absolute right to protect one's home against unrecognized strangers, if needed by guns, if needed even unto death. Instead of these combative attitudes, Rosa suggests to we should aim to find "new homes," in the sense of particular "places, in which resonance is possible—the places, where one's voice can be heard and find a response."[23] His proposal is as follows: Find the people with whom you can resonate and who bring forth your own voice! Find the music that fits to you! Find a work and a material world that speaks to you and bring yourself to speak! While Rosa is well aware that the longing for coming home is deeply connected with child experiences, and hence never to be deleted, he nonetheless opts for a more dynamic view of finding places and homes that facilitate resonance experiences, and thus make us feel less alienated from the world.

What I find revealing in Rosa's proposal of bringing home and resonance theory together is the way in which the sense of "finding" a home goes together with a dynamical "looking out" for homes. The feeling of home bases itself on the potentials of resonance relations already offering themselves to us in many "axes of resonance," including nature and culture, religion and art but also more pedestrian forms of being together, among family, friends, and colleagues, for example. Thus, resonance theory is able to explain why feelings of home are not a social construction out of the blue but appear in the interface between natural and cultural space. I believe that a similar dialectic can be found between *nostalgia*, the sense of being "homesick," and *solastalgia*, the sense of having lost places of home even when coming home.

BETWEEN NOSTALGIA AND SOLASTALGIA

The term *nostalgia* is generally used to describe affectionate remembrances for a past place or period. Etymologically, it is derived from the Homeric term *nostos* meaning "homecoming," and *algia,* meaning "pain" or "sorrow." Nostalgia is about a sentiment that is related to lost times, and to loved homes of the past. More recently, ecophilosophers have introduced the term *solastalgia* for the emotional loss of natural space, caused by environmental degradation.

The Australian ecophilosopher Glenn Albrecht suggested the term as late as 2005, combining the Latin words *solacium* (comfort) and the Greek *algia* (pain, suffering, grief). His point was that "disorientation, memory loss, homelessness, depression and various modes of estrangement from self and others" are part of an emotional or existential distress caused by environmental degradation. "Solastalgia is not about looking back to some golden past, nor is it about seeking another place as 'home.' It is the 'lived experience' of the loss of the present as manifest in a feeling of dislocation; of being undermined by forces that destroy the potential for solace to be derived from the present. In short, solastalgia is a form of homesickness one gets when one is still at 'home.'"[24] Examples of such pain of place is when people find themselves placed in natural habitats which in the meantime have been destructed by drought or flooding, by mining or volcanos.

Since then, the term solastalgia has given rise to empirical investigations of the eco-anxiety caused by the down-break of lived natural-human resonance relations.[25] It seems to me, however, that the feeling of solastalgia is the same, regardless of whether the desolation is caused by long-time environmental deterioration, by sudden disasters, or by human warfare. How is it to live in Mariupol in Ukraine after the endless Russian shelling of the cities in 2021, or in Bakhmut in 2022? How is it to experience the destruction of the great Kakhovka Dam in June 2023, leading to flooding of cities and landscapes in southern Ukraine? I suggest that the connection between human homes and natural conditions is so deep that it makes up an experiential unity, be it in term of homesickness (nostalgia) or in terms of destroyed homes (solastalgia).

THROWN OUT INTO A FOREIGN WORLD, OR CARRIED INTO AN ACCOMMODATING WORLD?

How may all of this inform our thinking of home from the perspective of an expansive creation theology like SCT? Let me address this question by contrasting two typical attitudes to the world in which we may understand our place in cosmos: Are we *thrown* into an empty world without intrinsic meaning, or are we *carried* into an accommodating world that somehow expects us and welcomes us.[26]

The first basic attitude to the world of nature is to treat it as radically different from us so that we as humans find ourselves *thrown out* into a foreign territory. In consequence, we have to conquer the world in order to be able to gain zones of safety and authenticity in an indifferent if not hostile universe.

This was the world story narrated by the Gnostics in the early church (many of them understanding themselves as the genuine spiritual Christians). It was also the story told by evolutionary biologists such as Jacques Monod, George Gaylord Simpson, and Richard Dawkins in the latter half of the twentieth century.

Another basic attitude is that we are *carried into* the world, somehow welcomed into a shared world of being-and-becoming. In this view, the world is handed over to us as a gift to be enjoyed. At its core, the world is constituted as a being-together with one another, and even if we sometimes compete with one another about space and livable futures, we are, at a still more fundamental level, enlivened by encountering one another and non-human creatures as well.

I'm here speaking of basic faith commitments associated with overarching interpretations of reality, social and natural. Yet, in lived practices the two attitudes are often blended. Most of us, regardless of faith commitments of a religious or anti-religious provenance, are able to recognize from our own experience periods of emptiness and periods of living an engaged life. The difference is not just about having negative versus positive experiences with the world. The real difference is how we see what comes "ontologically" first, and what we expect to be carried through to the final end.

From the perspective of "emptiness first," the world is basically empty and pointless. Everything ends in tragedy and death, even though it may still be possible to experience pockets of meaning in the midst of a life history, either by sheer luck and happenstance, or as a result of a helpful social construction that improves life, at least for the successful ones. From the perspective of "fullness first," the world is basically a place made for flourishing and accommodation, even though any believer will encounter aspects of reality that seem to be at odds with the basic attitude of being welcomed. In Løgstrup's view (1995 I, 267–68), the irreligious attitude will have to face the problem of "nihilodicy" when experiencing ever new examples of goodness and welcome; conversely, the religious attitude will have to cope with the problem of "theodicy" in face of evil and ugliness.

This distinction between thrownness and being carried into the world points to a fundamental difference between Martin Heidegger's interpretation of human existence and K. E. Løgstrup's philosophy of creation. According to Heidegger, humans (*Dasein*) are thrown out into a foreign world (*Geworfenheit*), in which we have to make our own individual or authentic decisions (*Entscheidungen*) and project our lives into the future (*Entwürfe*) in front of death as the ultimate condition of life (*Sein zum Tode*). Løgstrup argued that Heidegger's decisionist view of *Dasein* expresses only a small portion of human existence, and that Heidegger's ontology was in reality only "a regional ontology of historicity," that is, of human self-determination.[27]

Without knowing the work of Hannah Arendt, Løgstrup's understanding of the place of humanity in cosmos is close to her view of *natality*, by which she argues that we are born to live rather than born to die. We are born with the gift of natality; we are birthed before we die, and during our lifetimes we use the resources of our own givenness when channeling our lives in *labor* (in order to maintain bodily survival), in *work* (when reshaping our conditions), and in *action* (by setting political goals for social life).[28] In this view, the world is not a foreign place, but we are rather "carried into" the world before we begin construct our houses, roads, and bridges—all that which Heidegger defined as the human conditions for dwelling and thinking. Speaking in terms of creation theology, we are welcomed into the world by God as the transcendent source of all reality and possibility, who forever remains present in the immanence of creaturely structures and agency.

CREATION THEOLOGY INTERSECTING HUMAN AND COSMIC HOMES

The expansive view of creation is part of a common Christian understanding of life as a gift, and not only something that is given "out there" without intrinsic meaning. In his *Small Catechism* from 1530, Martin Luther offered a particularly revealing expression of the first article of Christian faith. "I believe that God has made me together with all creatures; that He has given me my body and soul, eyes, ears and all my members, my reason and all my senses, and still preserves them; that He richly and daily provides me with food and clothing, home and family, property and goods, and all that I need to support this body and life; that He protects me from all danger, guards and keeps me from all evil; and all this purely out of fatherly, divine goodness and mercy, without any merit or worthiness in me." In this view, human beings are not isolated from the cosmos, for the divine creativity takes place in "me together with all creatures." Moreover, the life of any human being is intertwined with the external world in terms of human sensation and understanding, "eyes, ears and all my members, my reason and all my senses." Finally, we are embedded in social life "with food and clothing, home and family, property and goods, and all that I need to support this body and life." And religiously speaking, all this happens "purely out of fatherly, divine goodness and mercy, without any merit or worthiness in me." The world is at once something pre-given and a gift to be re-actualized and absorbed in a fundamental gratitude for our past and present life, and in a trusting attitude toward the life ahead of us.

FROM DEEP INCARNATION TO DEEP INHABITATION . . . AND ONWARD

Life begins in a surplus, not in a deficit. This basic affirmation of the world is not expressed in the first article of faith only (on creation), but also in the second article of faith (Christ), and the third article (Spirit).

In Christian faith, the love of God does not only refer to a divine character beyond the world, active in a benevolent creativity, but also to a divine sharing of the life conditions of creatures "from within." "For God so loved the world (in Greek: *kosmos*) that he gave his only Son" (John 3:16), and "God did not send the Son into the world to condemn the world, but in order that the world might be saved through him" (John 3:17). This passage takes up the motif of the divine fatherly love of creativity, but now continued in a new and radical form in the divine self-incarnation of the eternal "Son," Word," or "Wisdom" of God. Divine love does not stand aloof but enters and conjoins the material human world.

In the prologue to the Gospel of John, we find the central expression that the divine Word/Wisdom "became flesh and lived among us" (John 1:14). Here, two aspects of the doctrine of incarnation are combined. First, we have the divine affirmation of the material world, as already created by God. What is said in John 1:14 is that God in Jesus Christ takes the world of creation into Godself ("the assumption of the flesh"), even to the point of suffering. Second, we have the sense of Christ inhabiting the social world, in which we have houses and habitats; but also here, I would add, God indwells the world even in the ruins of the destructive powers of nature and human evil-doing.

Now the cosmic and radically material aspect of divine self-incarnation is emphasized in the proposal of "deep incarnation."[29] This view of incarnation is at once in "high" in Christology (insofar as it is about the eternal divine Word conjoining the world of creation) but at the same time "low in materiality," insofar as God conjoins with, embraces and absorbs the innermost core (*radix*) of all created reality—from the core of matter to the core of creaturely suffering. Deep incarnation is thus a radical view of incarnation, insofar as God went into the depth of all material beings. Humans share the conditions of "all flesh"—dust and grass, flowers and foxes, life and death, order and disorder, blessing and annihilation. Not only was the cross of Jesus the consequence of God's self-embodiment, but it was the fulfilment of God's solidarity with "all flesh" that inevitably will end in death (cf. John 19:30: "It is fulfilled"). Relating to Løgstrup's emphasis on the built-in cruelty of creation, deep incarnation views the incarnation as God's own response to the fact that splendor and cruelty are combined in divine creativity. The incarnate God is the co-suffering God who absorbs pain and includes pain in the divine life itself. Thus, the divine joy of living amongst us is internally related to the divine pain of living with and suffering together with dislocated creatures.

Moreover, the deep incarnation of "living among us" includes the fluid social nexuses of life and habitats. In this volume, Mary Emily Duba has helpfully proposed the term "deep inhabitation" for the way in which our sense of home is connected to manifold natural relations that are part of social habitats.[30] The deep inhabitation of Christ refers to an accompanying presence of the divine in the midst of our broken inhabitations. The ubiquitous divine inhabitation takes places in the midst of our always limited inhabitations, which always blend and intersect features of natural and social processes, much like influx and efflux.[31]

In this perspective, it is important not to reify and bolster our homes, as if they (and we) were stable forever, and as if our homes are simply our own creations. As noted by Miroslav Volf and Ryan McAnnally-Linz, "The arc of John's prologue ends, formally, where Exodus ends: with God dwelling among the people. . . . God and the people are at home with one another in an irrevocable but still only anticipatory way."[32]

The reference to the "anticipatory way" is not part of John's prologue on incarnation, I would say, but it is part of the larger story of John (chapters 14–17). The anticipation is what happens in the transition from the incarnate Christ (who is irrevocably present) to the sending of the Spirit, or Comforter. In the words of Michael Welker, the Spirit is "the mobile presence of God" that always drives us forward, while affirming the intrinsic value of what was and is.[33] In this sense, we may say that we are not only settlers and dwellers but also travelers on the way to find new homes beyond the destruction of our existing homes, and the annihilation of our own life trajectories.

From the perspective of SCT, too, the transitory character of all life is the reason why its proponents do not reduce the Christian faith to a first article Christendom. SCT's expansive view of creation is not expansionist in the sense of replacing Christology and pneumatology with a creation theology that speaks of stability. However, SCT does argue that one can't understand the Christian message without a strong creation theology as its interpretative horizon. But more than, SCT insists that we should never think of redemption and fulfillment by taking leave of our embodied and social existence in some soulish afterlife. Our lives are always enmeshed with the cosmos and chaos of the world of creation. We are indeed to be saved—*with* the universe but not *from* the universe.

NOTES

1. K. E. Løgstrup, *Metaphysics. Volume I-II*. Translation and with an introduction by Russell L. Dees (Milwaukee, WI: Marquette University Press, 1995), Vol I, 272.

2. Martin Heidegger, "Building, Dwelling, Thinking" in *Poetry, Language, Thought*. Trans. Albert Hofstadter (New York: Harper Colophon Books, 1971), 143–59 (143).

3. See Derek R. Nelson, "Belonging, Comfort, and Delight: An Invitation to Home and Scandinavian Creation Theology," in this volume.

4. The kangaroo example is from *Cambridge English Dictionary*, which lists the meaning of home as "a place of origin, or a place where a person belongs."

5. Gregory Bateson, *Steps to an Ecology of Mind: Collected Essays in Anthropology, Psychiatry, Evolution, and Epistemology* (Chicago: University of Chicago Press, 1972).

6. Rodolfo Gambini, *Hospitable Universe: Addressing Ethical and Spiritual Concerns in Light of Recent Scientific Discoveries* (London: Imprint Academic, 2018).

7. Stuart Kauffman, *At Home in the Universe: The Search for the Laws of Self-Organization and Complexity* (New York: Oxford University Press, 1995), 43 and 45.

8. Ted Peters, "At Home in the Universe," this volume.

9. Niels Henrik Gregersen, "The Exploration of Ecospace: Extending or Supplementing the Neo-Darwinian Paradigm?" *Zygon* 52:2 (2017), 561–86.

10. See Jakob Wolf, "At Home in the Universe?," this volume.

11. K. E. Løgstrup, *Kierkegaard's and Heidegger's Analysis of Existence and its Relation to Proclamation*. Trans. Robert Stern, Christopher Bennett, Jessica Leech, Joe Saunders, and Mark Textor (Oxford, UK: Oxford University Press, 2020).

12. K. E. Løgstrup's *The Ethical Demand. Introduction by Hans Fink and Alasdair McIntyre* (Notre Dame, IN: University of Notre Dame Press, 1997).

13. K. E. Løgstrup, "Ethik und Ontologie" (1962), translated as "Ethics and ontology" in an appendix to a new revised edition of K. E. Løgstrup's *The Ethical Demand* (Notre Dame, IN: University of Notre Dame Press, 1997), 265–94.

14. Løgstrup's four-volume metaphysics is partly translated in K. E. Løgstrup, *Metaphysics. Volume I-II*. Trans. Russell L. Dees (Milwaukee, WI: Marquette University Press, 1995).

15. The typology of the three ecologies I owe to my colleague in anthropology at the University of Copenhagen, Cecilie Rubow, see "Økoteologiske udfordringer." *Kritisk forum for praktisk teologi* 40 (2020), 53–63. Cecilie and I will together lead a common project, *Carnal: Eco-ethical Articulations of Body, Meat, and Flesh*, funded by the Velux Foundation for 2024–2027.

16. See Ole Jensen, *Unter dem Zwang des Wachstums. Ökologie und Religion* (München: Chr. Kaiser Verlag, 1977), and Ole Jensen, "Creation Theology and the Confrontation with Speciecism: Memories and Reflections," in *Reformation Theology for a Post-Secular Age: Løgstrup, Prenter, Wingren, and the Future of Scandinavian Creation Theology*, eds. Gregersen, Niels Henrik, Uggla, Bengt Kristensson, and Wyller, Trygve (Göttingen: Vandenhoeck & Ruprecht, 2017), 147–56.

17. See Mikkel Gabriel Christoffersen, *Living with Risk and Danger: Studies in Interdisciplinary Systematic Theology* (Göttingen: Vandenhoeck & Ruprecht, 2019), with an extensive coverage of the sociological and theological literature.

18. K. E. Løgstrup, *Metaphysics* vol I, 271. In what follows, I refer to Løgstrup's *Metaphysics* in parentheses in the main text.

19. Niels Henrik Gregersen, "Resilient selves: A theology of resonance and secularity." *Dialog: A Journal of Theology* 59: 93–102, 2020; https://doi.org/10.1111/dial .12568

20. Hartmut Rosa, "Heimat als anverwandelter Weltausschnitt. Ein resonanztheoretischer Versuch." In *Heimat global: Modelle, Praxen und Medien der Heimatkonstruktion,* eds. Costadura, Edoardo, Ries, Klaus and Wiesenfeldt, Christiane (Bielefeld: transcript Verlag, 2019), 153–72, p. 154: "Da ist etwas! Und dieses 'da ist etwas' geht dem 'Ich' und der Welt voraus. Daraus entwickeln sich dann sozusagen ontogenetisch ein erfahrendes Subjekt und eine erfahrene Welt."

21. See Hartmut Rosa's main work, *Resonance: A Sociology of Our Relationship to the World* (Cambridge, UK: Polity Press, 2019), and Hartmut Rosa, *The Uncontrollability of the World* (Cambridge, UK: Polity Press, 2020), 15–18.

22. Rosa, "Heimat als anverwandelter Weltausschnitt," 167.

23. Rosa, "Heimat als anverwandelter Weltausschnitt," 170.

24. Glenn Albrecht, "'Solastalgia': A New Concept in Health and Identity," *Pan* 2005:3, 41–55 (43 and 45).

25. L. P. Galway, T. Beery, K. Jones-Casey, and K. Tasala, "Mapping the Solastalgia Literature: A Scoping Review Study." *International Journal of Environmental Research and Public Health,* 2019; 16(15):2662, https://doi.org/10.3390/ ijerph16152662

26. I'm here inspired by Hartmut Rosa, "Geworfen oder getragen? Subjektive Weltbeziehungen und moralischen Landkarten." In *Weltbeziehungen im Zeitalter der Beschleunigung. Umrisse einer neuen Gesellschaftskritik* (Frankfurt am Main: Suhrkamp, 2012), 374–414.

27. K. E. Løgstrup, "Historicitetens rolle i Heideggers værenstænkning," in *Ophav og omgivelse. Metafysik III* (København: Gyldendal, 1984), 207–27 (not translated into English).

28. Hannah Arendt, *The Human Condition. Second Edition* (Chicago: The University of Chicago Press, 1998 [1958]), 22–78. See Elisabeth Gerle, "Who Does Not Want to Have a Family? Home and Family, Reality and Ideal," in this volume.

29. Niels Henrik Gregersen, "The Extended Body of Christ: Three Dimensions of Deep Incarnation." In *Incarnation. On the Scope and Depth of Christology*, ed. Niels Henrik Gregersen (Minneapolis, MI: Fortress, 2015), 225–54. See the excellent analysis in Joseph Lenow, "Christ, the Praying Animal: A Critical Engagement with Niels Henrik Gregersen and the Christology of Deep Incarnation." *International Journal of Systematic Theology*, 2018, 20: 554–78. https://doi.org/10.1111/ijst.12312.

30. Mary Emily Duba, "Living on Borrowed Ground: Inhabitation as Lived Theology," in this volume.

31. I here think of the organismic perspective of Jane Bennett, *Influx and Efflux: Writing up with Walt Whitman* (Durham, NC: Duke University Press, 2020).

32. Miroslav Volf and Ryan McAnnally-Linz, *The Home of God: A Brief Story of Everything* (Grand Rapids, MI: Brazos Press, 2022), 74.

33. Michael Welker, *God the Spirit* (Minneapolis, MI: Fortress Press, 2014).

Chapter 11

At Home in the Universe?

Jakob Wolf

THE UNIVERSE AS A PROBLEMATIC HOME

It is a widespread idea today that the universe or the Earth should be understood as our home. According to this view, the relationship between the universe and humanity is basically harmonious. Many publications have promoted this idea since the 1980s. John Barrow published *The Anthropic Cosmological Principle* in 1986 and Stuart Kauffman put out a book in 1995 with the title *At Home in the Universe*.[1] "Earth, Our Home" is a headline in the preamble of the UN document *The Earth Charter* from 2000. Those are just three examples among many. This idea has played a major role even today in the ecological movement and thinking that began in the 1960s. Humanity is an integrated part of the ecological systems that constitute life on Earth.

The idea of Earth as our home opposes the idea that humanity is not a part of nature. According to this opposing view, humanity is a subject that confronts nature as a foreign object. Earth is not our home, but a hostile or indifferent environment, where each person has to build their own home by their own means. We are strangers on planet Earth. The Earth is seen somewhat like the moon: an unfriendly place that we could inhabit only by means of our own technology.[2] The ecological crises, which we have experienced the last 50 years, have convincingly falsified this idea.

The idea of the Earth as our home is however not unproblematic. It tends to emphasize too strongly the harmony between humanity and Earth. There is a very powerful tendency today to paint a sweet and rosy picture of nature, which is not completely comprehensive. This of course has to do with the change in the balance of power between human beings and nature. Today human beings are the masters of nature and have become a deadly threat to nature. Not too many years ago, human beings needed protection against nature. Today, it is nature that needs protection against human beings. Ecologically informed thinking about nature has a tendency to see human beings as evil and ugly and nature as good and beautiful. This thinking oversimplifies the problem of the relationship between nature and humanity. Nature is not only unambiguously good and life promoting. It is also evil and destructive. One species lives by eating another. Diseases and natural disasters kill millions of peoples and animals. Meteor falls cause massive destruction of life. The universe also displays random violence. Shakespeare puts it this way: "As flies to wanton boys are we to the gods; they kill us for their sport." Murder and torture is not at all forbidden in nature. Animals torture and kill each other, and nature tortures and kills human beings.[3]

It is realistic to say that it is a *question* whether we are at home in the universe or not. Hence, the question mark in title of this article. Einstein was once asked: "What is the most important question you can ask in life?" His answer was: "Is the universe a friendly place or not"? It is realistic to say that nature is ambiguous, and that the relationship between man and nature is problematic. The universe is a place that makes it possible for us to live and thrive *and* an uncanny and hostile place. What is at stake here is of course the problem of "physical evil" as Leibniz named it.[4]

THE IDEA THAT THE UNIVERSE IS
OUR HOME IS PHILOSOPHICAL

Secular thinking has nothing to say about the problem of evil. It hardly recognizes it at all. Many would say it makes no sense to talk about evil in relation to nature. Nature is neither good nor evil. It just *is*. Scientifically seen you may say so, but not phenomenologically seen. Our involuntary experience of the cat's behavior, when it tortures the mouse before killing it slowly, is that what takes place is evil. Of course, it does not make sense to say the cat is evil, but some might say that it is evil that nature is structured such that the cat tortures and eats the mouse. The arrangement is evil. To state that we are at home in the universe without dealing with the problem of evil is untrustworthy.

The idea that the universe is our home is not just a scientific theory, it is a philosophical idea. Ideas about the universe as a whole and man's position in the cosmos are philosophical. I think it is obvious that, for example, Barrow's and Kauffman's endeavors are science with an agenda. They play to the desire that science would confirm our ideas about a harmonious relationship between humanity and the universe. Ideas about an "anthropic principle" or "self-organization" and "emergence" are heuristics or metaphysical ideas rather than scientific theories. Self-organization and emergence are only descriptions of processes in nature; the concepts do not indicate causes. Self-organization and emergence are *spontaneous* processes; but when something happens spontaneously, it means that it happens without a cause. Nothing is scientifically explained by these concepts. Furthermore, science is by definition not normative, but the term "Home" is ethical. It does not just describe our situation; it also says we should take care of our home and not demolish it.

When it comes to philosophical ideas about the cosmos, then, theological reflections are relevant as a possible source of clarification. The idea that the universe is created is not a specific theological idea. It is natural theology. It is a philosophical idea along with other philosophical ideas about the cosmos. The idea is based on our involuntary experience that we live in surroundings that we have not ourselves created. We are thrown into a situation with certain conditions, on which we have had no influence. Before we entered life, we were not asked whether we agreed to terms and conditions that we would be born in a certain place at a certain time, and we shall after a long or short time die. We live under the condition that we cannot force anybody to love us, even though it is a matter of life and death to us whether we are loved or not. We were not asked whether we agreed on living in a world with stars, moons, elephants, dogs, roses, stinging nettles, or viruses. We do not experience these conditions as coincidences that we can simply ignore. We react spontaneously to natural evil with anger and despair, and we react spontaneously with gratitude to all the good gifts life gives us. Feelings of despair and gratitude however relate to somebody. Somebody is responsible. In these feelings, we interpret the universe as created by "somebody."

The problem of evil has been discussed thoroughly in the theological tradition. I think that theology can contribute with universal fundamental reflections to the question whether we are at home in the universe or not.

THE PROBLEM OF EVIL IN THE
CHRISTIAN TRADITION

Many theologians today embrace the idea of Earth as our home. It corresponds smoothly with the idea that we can feel at home in the universe, because it is God's creation. God has created the universe as a home for us.

This idea is however not completely unambiguous, even in theology. Our true home is according to classical Christian theology not in "this world" but in heaven, in a coming world. Eschatology is an important part of Christian theology. Moreover, in as far as Gnosticism influences theology, "this world" is considered a thoroughly evil place.

In Christian theology, there is always a tension between creation and salvation. If Christian theology is only about apocalyptic salvation, then the created world tends to be deprived of any intrinsic value. If you live in an atmosphere of believing the second coming of Christ is near, then the created world is not too important. It is soon to disappear. This was not just the case in early Christianity; also, later on Christians preached the indifference of "this world," to be a Christian is to forsake "this world."[5]

Augustine delimited gnostic ideas from Christian theology by saying that God's creation is basically good, but the universe is a *fallen* creation. This idea about the universe as a fallen creation is a brilliant comment to nature's ambiguity. It neither betrays the fact of nature's evilness, nor its goodness, and it corresponds to our spontaneous expectation that creation is good. We see evil as a lack of goodness, we see meaninglessness as a lack of meaning, and not vice versa; goodness is not a lack of evilness. There is an ontological ranking between good and evil.

The problem of evil has been dealt with in the theological tradition by presenting theodicies. Theodicies are attempts to defend God against the accusation that he is the cause of evil. God is almighty and good, consequently he must be held accountable for the existence of evil.

Augustine tried to defend God by saying, humanity is the cause of evil, not God; God is innocent. Evil entered the world through the free human will. Humanity was created with a free will but used it to do evil instead of good.

It is interesting to see how the free will argument is given a cosmic dimension in modern process theology. Not just human beings have a free will; nature also has a kind of free will. According to modern science, quantum physics and Neo-Darwinism, nature is not just tyrannized by causality; contingency also plays a role in the progress of nature. This is interpreted in process theology as a kind of free will; nature has the opportunity to choose among different options. When God creates, he does not use a dictatorial power; he tries to inspire and lure nature to make the right choices. He does not always succeed.[6]

Is the free will defense however a defense that holds up in court? Not entirely. Surely, man causes a lot of evil. People fight and torment each other at a large scale, though they might as well not do so. However, as already Augustine himself realized: If humans were created as perfect creatures, why should they use their free will to do evil? That is not at all evident. And, if humans were not created as perfect beings, it is God's fault, and then God is the actual cause of evil.[7] Free will is only a condition for evil, not a cause. In the myth of the fall in Genesis, Eve's free will is not the cause of the fall; it is the temptation by Satan. But is the argument that Satan is the cause of evil a good one? Not entirely, because the consequence is that there are two

Gods fighting each other. But there is only *one* God. The snake, a metaphor for Satan, is a creation of God.

Another problem with the free will argument is that it is not convincing that humanity is the cause of *all* evil. Humanity is not the cause of physical or natural evil. Cosmic random violence of all kinds: natural catastrophes, deaths, nature's cruelty, etc., are surely not caused by humanity alone, but are given, created conditions for life. If you say that humanity is the cause of all-evil, you portray humans as somehow almighty, creating volcanic eruptions, earthquakes, tsunamis, etc.

The free-will argument may shed light on the paradox of moral evil. Why do human beings use their free will to do evil instead of good? That is a true mystery, and unexplainable mysteries are dealt with in myths. However, the myth of the fall has nothing relevant to say about natural evil. When Christians try to explain natural evil by the myth of the fall, they are guilty of intolerable, untrustworthy speculations. Natural evil, suffering, shall prevail even if everybody were saints.

The idea of humanity as the source of all evil is somehow misanthropic. In ecological thinking, you sometimes meet the same misanthropy. Humans alone cause all evil. They are like a cancerous tumor in nature. Augustine's final answer to the problem of why man uses his free will to cause evil is *predestination*. This is of course not a good defense for God, because then God is the cause of evil.

If, with Leibniz, you do not limit evil to moral evil, you may ask how evil is defined. My definition is, that evil has to do with suffering, physically and spiritually, and the destruction of life and life opportunities. Evil is what *really* hurts. Not all suffering is evil. When a woman gives birth to a child, she suffers, but this suffering is not evil. It has a good purpose. It is a mean for goodness, promotion of life. However, if the woman loses the child, it *really* hurts; it is a purposeless destruction of life.

Another type of theodicy is to say that evil merely *seems* to be evil, but in reality it is good. Evil is an instrument to produce goodness. The world is a "vale of soul-making."[8] If there were no suffering in the world, people would not grow morally and spiritually. But is that a satisfying defense? Not entirely; surely, we mature through suffering, but a lot of suffering is nothing but pure destruction and annihilation. It does not contribute to the amount of goodness in the world at all. The experience of tragedy and absurdity is basic to human life.

Leibniz has still one more defense for God. You cannot blame God for physical evil; he has done his creating work as well as he can. We live in the best of all worlds. Leibniz's idea is, that as a creator of a universe, you have different options. A universe is put together by different parts. You can assemble these parts in different ways. Because God is omniscient, he knows all the different universes that are possible,[9] and because he is good, he chooses the best possible world for us to live in. This best possible world does, however, have some unfortunate side effects. Gravity, for example, which is a very important part of our universe, has the effect, that when there is an earthquake, heavy things may fall on your head and mutilate or even kill you. However, this is as good as it gets. Do not blame God. However, since God is almighty, is he not then really able to do it better? Thomas Aquinas thought so. And Christianity does in general think God is able to do it better, when Christianity teaches, that after this world, God shall create "a new heaven and a new earth," and here "there will be no more death or mourning or crying or pain, for the old order of things has passed away" (Rev 21:4).

A typically modern theodicy is to claim that God is not almighty. God wants to annihilate evil, but he does not have the power. The process theologian Ian Barbour says it directly: "By rejecting omnipotence the process philosophy makes it clear that God is not directly responsible for evil."[10] This is just one example among many. The Jewish philosopher of religion Hans Jonas was one of the first to launch the idea of God's impotence.[11]

I think it is impossible to deny that God is omnipotent. If you deny God's omnipotence, you deny the concept of God all together. A God who is not omnipotent is no God. As Kant says: The sentence, "God is omnipotence" is an analytical sentence. Omnipotence is part of the definition of God.

However, it is of course possible to discuss what omnipotence means. Some hold, that it does not mean that God is able to do everything. As a completely abstract statement, it contains a contradiction, because it is then possible, that God is able to create a stone, which is so big, that he is not able to lift it. I completely agree that it is in vain to discuss the concept omnipotence in a purely abstract way, but I think that God's omnipotence cannot mean, that his power is less than a creative power, which creates and upholds everything there is. Luther interprets omnipotence in this way: "What I call God's true omnipotence is not a power, which is able to do many things, but does not do them; it is the actual power, which causes everything in everybody; it is in that way the scripture calls him almighty."[12]

I find this to be a reasonable understanding of God's omnipotence. This interpretation does not get lost in abstractions, and it does not make God smaller than he is. I agree with Luther, that any interpretation of omnipotence that attributes God less power than causing all that happens concretely is to ridicule God.[13]

When the father of process theology Alfred Whitehead claims that God is not a heavenly creator, a demiurge, but *"the fellow sufferer who understands,"* I think this is God reduced to nothing but a human projection.[14] It is true that God is not almighty in his incarnation in Jesus from Nazareth. In his incarnation, God renounces his omnipotence (*kenosis*[15]). However, his incarnation in Jesus does not mean, that he renounces his omnipotence as creator *(tzimtzum*[16]*)*. If you draw that conclusion, you misunderstand the idea of the incarnation as *kenosis*. If the consequence of incarnation were the renunciation of omnipotence in general, the universe would immediately disappear into nothingness. The almighty incarnates himself as powerless. That is the essential Christian paradox.[17]

When you reject the thought that God is almighty, you very often actually reject the idea that God has created the universe all together. Creation means creation out of nothing, *ex nihilo*, and anyone who is able to create out of nothing is almighty. Some theologians try to avoid blaming God for physical evil by saying God has only created all the good things in the universe. Woody Allen was once asked whether he believed that the universe was created by God or not. After pondering a long time, he answered: "I believe God has created the universe, except for some parts of New Jersey." Either God has created everything or nothing, there is no middle ground.

The conclusion about theodicies is that they all fail.[18]

Who, then, is responsible for physical evil? Certainly, human beings are not. The only plausible answer is *God*. God does not just overwhelm us with endless good gifts; he also causes evil, suffering, destruction, and death at a large scale. Løgstrup is convincing to me on this matter. He writes, "God's act of creation is terrifying in its splendor and annihilation; it exceeds our intellectual and emotional apprehension."[19]

So many theologians do not draw this conclusion. Løgstrup is at this point an exception among theologians. They deny that God can be the source of evil. Among people in general you often hear the statement, that the reality of evil excludes the existence of God. I do not agree with the conclusion in this statement, but I do agree with the insight, that the reality of evil is God's problem. People articulate what is obvious. At this point people in general are better theologians than many professional theologians are.

There is a biblical scripture that criticizes theodicies and supports the idea that evil is God's problem: *The Book of Job*. Job is a man who has many gifts, ten children, wealth, good health etc. but this is all taken from him. His children die from a storm, all his cattle are killed, he becomes ill, he gets malignant boils all over the body, and ends up in an ash heap scraping his sores with a broken piece of pottery. Who is guilty of all this evil? In the original "Job's poem," which lacks the framing narrative added later, Job very clearly proclaims that he is innocent, and he violently accuses God. His friends try to convince him that he is himself guilty. The disasters that befall him are punishments for sins he has committed. God is just. Job vehemently opposes his friends' view. God is the guilty one, he says. When God finally enters the conversation in the end of the poem, he rejects the theodicy of Job's friends. They are not honest; they are just trying to flatter God. God does not want to talk to those hypocrites. He does not want to be defended. He wants to talk to Job because he is honest. And what is God's answer to Job? What is God's defense? Literally hundreds of commentators have tried to figure that out. But there is no general answer.[20] There is only a personal existential answer. God's answer to Job is the result of a personal discussion and intense meeting with God. "I had heard about you with my own ears, but now I have seen you with my own eyes" (Job 42:6).

It is not the task of man to defend God, but to accuse God.

In Kierkegaard's book *Repetition* the main character, "the young man," expresses the same thought: "Speak up, then, unforgettable Job, repeat everything you said, you powerful spokesman who, fearless as a roaring lion, appears before the tribunal of the Most High! . . . Complain—the Lord is not afraid, he can certainly defend himself. But how is he to defend himself, when no one dares to complain as befits a man."[21]

GOD AS CREATOR AND THE GOSPEL

To me this is an extremely important point. It should not be repressed or just whispered but said aloud. If we want to speak trustworthily about God and his creation, the universe, we cannot just speak of the universe as an unproblematic home for us, and of God as the source of all goodness. So many philosophers and theologians do that.

The reason why theology reduces God to the loving father, the "*Abba*" of Jesus, is of course, that this is what the gospel preaches. However, we have to distinguish between what the gospel preaches, and how we experience living in God's creation. The backdrop of the gospel is the created universe in which we live. The gospel *preaches* that God is love. It does not present it as a matter of fact. It is an assertion you may *believe,* not knowledge. Certainly, many facts point in another direction. If Christian preaching does not highlight what the backdrop of the preaching is, it becomes untrustworthy sweet talk about a loving Father in Heaven. As a piece of graffiti says: "Jesus is the answer—what is the question?" To me it is so important that we make clear, what is the question? The question is: Is God good? The answer is: God is good. However, this answer is nothing but an abstract phrase if it is not heard by a person who is deeply contested by the question: Is God good?

It is an obvious fact that the created universe is not just friendly to us, hence it is a fundamental theological question: What is the relationship between God as creator and God as the father of Jesus from Nazareth, God as ambiguous and as unambiguous? It is understandable that the Gnostics solved the question by claiming there are two Gods, the creator God and the father of Jesus, but it is also obvious that this answer is not valid. It is also obvious that you cannot just say that God is both ambiguous and unambiguous. That is nonsense. Such a statement violates the principle of contradiction as Aristotle formulated it: Contradictory propositions cannot both be true in the same sense at the same time.

Is it possible to say anything meaningful about this apparent contradiction between God as creator and as the loving Father?

At this point Løgstrup refers to Luther's distinction between God's *opus alienum* and God's *opus proprium*. He uses this distinction in his own way as a distinction between creation and the Kingdom of God.[22] Usually Luther uses the distinction to characterize the distinction between the Law and the Gospel.

Luther is a master of thinking in contradictions; this makes his thinking remarkably realistic because life is full of contradictions. Luther's point is that not all contradictions are mutually exclusive. The creation and the Kingdom of God do exclude each other because they are both the works of God. They do not violate the principle of contradiction, because they manifest the work of God in different senses, in the sense that it is God's *foreign* work or God's *proper* work. The expression "God's foreign work" is brilliant. It says that if you believe God reveals himself in the gospel, he hides himself in his other works. When we know God as he is through his proper work, he seems foreign to us in his other works.

The distinction between *opus alienum* and *opus proprium* corresponds to Luther's distinction between *deus absconditus* and *deus revelatus*, the hidden and the revealed God. We may use this distinction as further clarification of the apparent contradiction between God as the creator and as the Father of Jesus.

Christian belief is a belief in the incarnation. God has incarnated and revealed himself in the life and preaching of Jesus from Nazareth. The message of the gospel is, that if you want to know who God *really* is, look at Jesus, he is God's self-portrait, "the image of the invisible God" (Col 1:15). This means that God is hidden everywhere else. Nowhere else do you see who God truly is. Hiddenness is the backdrop of revelation. Hiddenness and revelation are not contradictions; revelation presupposes hiddenness. God's revelation does not mean we do not know anything about God, before he reveals himself. We know him, because we live in a world that is created by him—but we know him as hidden.

Incarnation does not mean that God enters into this world from another world. That is Gnosticism. God is always present and recognizable in his creation as "the power to exist in everything which exists" (Løgstrup). God is omnipresent (*ubiquity*) (Luther). The backdrop of God's incarnation in Jesus from Nazareth is that he is already incarnated in everything as the power of being in everything (*creatio ex nihilo et continua*). God's incarnation in a human being is possible because he is already incarnated in everything as the power of it's being. The difference between God's incarnation in everything and in Jesus is, that he is hidden as incarnated in everything, and revealed as incarnated in Jesus.

If God hides himself in his creation, it may not be a contradiction, that he reveals himself as love in the life and preaching of Jesus. Hiddenness means, that you cannot conclude from what is happening in nature and history to who God is. You cannot conclude, that because God's creation is ambiguous, God is ambiguous. To be hidden is to be incomprehensible, undefined. It is impossible to put a predicate on God. God has not defined himself as hidden, only as revealed, in his Word.[23]

God's incarnation is an expression of God's love to humanity. God wants to meet and communicate with human beings, and this is only possible if God becomes one. We cannot communicate with the undefined infinite.

Luther's distinction makes it possible that the God of creation and the God of the Gospel is the same. Jesus does not preach a new God. His God is the creator God of the Old Testament.

The distinction between the hidden and the revealed God does not violate the principle of contradiction; because it is not in the same sense that God is hidden and revealed. He is hidden in the sense that we experience God in his creation, and he is revealed in the sense that we believe in the gospel.

Often there is no contradiction between experience and belief. The created world is full of good gifts. However, when we experience evil in the created world, experience and belief contradict each other. The relationship between the hidden God and the revealed God is not essentially a difference in time: God is simultaneously hidden and revealed. And again, that is not a violation of the principle of contradiction. Contradictory propositions can be true at the same time if they do not contradict in the same sense. A table cannot at the same time be blue and yellow, but it can at the same time be blue and square, because it is in relation to color, it is blue, and in relation to form, it is square.[24]

As long as this world exists, a conflict between belief and experience shall persist. That is why we talk about belief and faith and not knowledge. We know that $2+2=4$, that shall not be contested. We do not know in the same sense that God is good, because that is constantly being contested. That is the reason why faith always must be renewed. The service is repeated Sunday after Sunday. Faith is always a fighting faith. Belief in the gospel does not provide us with an explanation of evil. When faith seizes us, we do not exclaim: Oh, now I understand why evil exists! When God reveals himself to faith, not everything is revealed. The essentials are revealed: *God is love*, but it is not revealed why evil persists. As long as this world exists it shall be hidden; eschatologically however all hiddenness shall disappear: "then we shall see face to face" (Corinthians 13:12).

THE PROBLEM OF EVIL IS UNIVERSAL

This explanation of the problem of evil is closely connected to the European, Christian tradition, but it does not delimit the problem as a specific Christian problem. The problem of evil is universal. You will find that all religions and philosophical systems deal with the problem. It was brilliantly formulated already by the Greek philosopher Epicurus (341–270 BC): We have three sentences, which are all true: God is almighty, God is good, evil exists. This poses a problem, because not all three sentences can be true at the same time. The problem is unsolvable according to Epicurus.[25] The way the Christian tradition deals with the problem is not very different from all other traditions. Even the distinction between the hidden and the revealed God is to be found in all major religions.[26]

A universal formulation of the problem of evil could be, that it manifests the problem whether life is meaningful or meaningless. The existence of evil is a challenge to everyone. Does my life make sense when random violence kills my loved ones? When this happens, everyone poses the question: Why? And we keep asking the rest of our lives. You could say that we persistently wrestle with the hidden God. And as the patriarch Jacob, who wrestled with God, said to God: "I will not let you go unless you bless me (Genesis 32:26)"—so do we. We want an answer. We want an assurance that life is meaningful despite evil. We want to believe that life is basically unambiguously trustworthy, in spite of the hostility and ambiguousness it sometimes confronts us with.

CONCLUSION

Is Earth our home? My answer is: It certainly is. We do not have any other home. We are not essentially disembodied souls who truly belong in a platonic world of ideas or some spiritual paradise. The pictures from Apollo 8 of our blue planet were convincing evidence that planet Earth, the planet of life and colors, is our true home. It is here we belong and nowhere else in the vast and unfriendly universe. This home gives us marvelous opportunities to live and thrive and experience beauty and wisdom. It would be the ultimate crime of man to exploit this home and destroy the possibility of a rich life to flourish. We are faced with a radical ethical demand to protect and take care of all the life that inhabits planet Earth.

We should, however, not confuse our home with paradise. We should not overlook the ambiguity of nature. It is extremely important that we have a realistic view of our home. Otherwise, we shall face the challenges that meets us in a false perspective.

The ethical demand to take care of our home planet is, for example, not unproblematic. Often the only way you can take care of some life is by destroying other life. Genuine ethical problems in this world are all about ethical dilemmas. We shall always to some degree fail ethically. It is impossible to live a true ethical life without forgiveness. Furthermore, living in this home creates despair and hopelessness, because experiencing evil is unavoidable. How do we keep our trust and hope alive? To really feel at home in the universe it is not enough to see the universe as a created home for us; you must also be confident that behind the ambiguity of the universe there is a unique love, which in the end penetrates everything.

NOTES

1. J. D. Barrow, *The Anthropic Cosmological Principle* (New York: Oxford University Press, 1986) and Stuart Kauffman, *At Home in the Universe* (New York: Oxford University Press, 1995).

2. Today billions of dollars are being spent on trying to go to Mars. Sometimes you hear the reason for doing this is, that we may in near future have to colonize other planets to survive, because we will then have exploited planet Earth to a degree where it has become inhabitable to us. The backdrop for this thinking is actually that Earth is not our home, and we are not obliged to take care of it as such. There is a planet B.

3. This reality is what made the Danish film director Lars von Trier claim in his movie *Antichrist*; nature is the "Church of Satan."

4. It was Leibniz who coined the concept "Theodicy" classified evil as moral, physical and metaphysical. Moral evil is evil caused by man's free will, sin. Physical evil is suffering caused by nature. Metaphysical evil stems from the fact that creation necessarily is imperfect. If it were perfect, you could not distinguish between the Creator and the created. See Leibniz, *Essais de Théodicée. Sur la bonté de Dieu, la liberté l'homme et l'origine du mal. Suivi de la monadologie. [Par] Leibniz. Préface et notes de Jacques Jalabert* (Paris: Montaigne, 1962).

5. Scandinavian creation theology wants to highlight the intrinsic value of the created world. It is a purpose in itself, and not just a means for something that is external to creation. For example, the world is not just created as a place for salvation. This does not mean that the aspect of salvation is unimportant to creation theology. It is important, because suffering and evil is a persisting reality in creation. Salvation means in Løgstrup's creation theology, that we are saved, not *from* this world, but *with*

this world. Salvation has cosmic implications as by Paul. Salvation is "resurrection of the flesh," a not just a salvation of an unembodied soul.

6. The combination of natural science and theology in process theology is not valid. Natural science is per definition atheistic. God cannot be introduces as a cause in continuation with natural causes. As Kant pointed out, it is a category mistake to introduce God as a first cause among causes.

7. John Hick, *Evil and the God of Love* (Norfolk, VA: Collins, 1966), 68.

8. Hick, 208.

9. Leibniz anticipates the theory of the multiverse.

10. Ian Barbour, Religion in an Age of Science (New York: Harper & Row, 1990), 264.

11. Hans Jonas, "The Concept of God after Auschwitz: A Jewish Voice" in *Journal of Religion*, vol. 67, no. 1 (January 1987), 1–13.

12. "Omnipotentiam vero Dei voco non illam potentiam, qua multa non facit quae potest, sed actualem illam, qua potenter omnia facit in omnibus, quo modo scriptura vocat eum omnipotentem" (WA 18:718).

13. "—alioqui ridiculus foret Deus" (WA 18: 719).

14. Alfred North Whitehead, *Process and Reality. An Essay in Cosmology* (New York: Free Press, 1978).

15. cf. Phil 2, 6.

16. Hans Jonas uses this concept from the Jewish Lurianic Kabbalah to argue, that God withdraws his almightiness from creation all together (Jonas 1987).

17. As Kierkegaard said: Christianity is all about the absolute paradox: Christ being fully human and fully God. As human Christ is vulnerable and powerless, as God he is almighty (*Philosophical Fragments* Chap.3).

18. cf. Kant's essay on theodicy: "*On the Failure of All Philosophical Trials in Theodicy.*"

19. Løgstrup, K. E. 1995, p. 272, *Metaphysics*, Marquette University Press, Milwaukee, WI.

20. If there were, *The Book of Job* would be trivial literature.

21. Kierkegaard, S. *Repitition*, Princeton,1983, p. 198.

22. Løgstrup 1995, p. 174.

23. " . . . neque enim tum [as such, as hidden, JW] verbo suo definivit sese" (*WA* 18: 685).

24. Luther's distinction was misunderstood by Karl Barth and many others, They thought his distinction created an intolerable discord in the concept of God. It is impossible that God simultaneously cries over death and fights it in the gospel *and* causes life, death, and everything in everybody and everything in the creation. However, this is only intolerable if God reveals himself both in his creation and in his incarnation in Jesus from Nazareth. Barth and so many others overlook the meaning of "hidden." Luther does not create a discord in God; he prevents a discord in our understanding of God.

25. Epicurus' conclusion was, that the Gods could not care less. He encouraged his student to stop speculating and cultivate his garden.

26. Smith, Houston. 2001, *Why Religion Matters*. Harper, San Francisco, p. 237.

Chapter 12

At Home in the Cosmos

Ted Peters

It is one thing to exist in a context. It is quite another to feel at home in one's context. It's still another to invite guests to feel at home in our home. We know we're home when we feel centered, connected, and comforted.

Victor Hugo (1802–1883), remembered for *Les Misérables,* compares a house to a home.

A house is built of logs and stone,

Of tiles and posts and piers.

A home is built of loving deeds

That stand a thousand years.

A loving home can stand for a thousand years. Can it stand for a thousand light years? For 13.7 billion years and counting?

A home can be the house we live in. It can be our hometown. It can be the farmland of our ancestors, where you or I were born. We can feel at home in the context of our culture, our native tongue, or the songs we sing. Against the backdrop of outer space, Earth is our home.

Can we imagine a connection between our home and places we've never visited? Can we imagine turning our house into a home for those visiting from far off places? Can we imagine hosting a family dinner with guests from a planet orbiting Proxima Centauri? Can we imagine loving aliens, aliens from across the border or across the galaxy? "You shall also love the stranger" (Deuteronomy 10:19).

If we are to feel at home in the cosmos as well as in our hometown, we might ponder the cosmic scope of family love. After all, God loved the whole cosmos (John 3:16:).

Scandinavian Creation Theology (SCT) "does not picture the world as a cold and hostile place—instead it is our home," writes Bengt Kristensson Uggla elsewhere in this volume. "This means that Christian faith does not promote the Church, the 'Christian home' or the 'heavenly home' as a privileged place where we belong—in separation from the world we share with all living creatures."

All creatures? Only terrestrial creatures? Or might extraterrestrial creatures be included? More than creatures. How about the very physical cosmos itself in all its unfathomability, magnificence, and grandeur? Can we love the cosmos as God loves it in John 3:16? Can we think of ourselves at home in the entire cosmos? Let's try this thought on for size.

Here is the task at hand. I wish to show that the resources exist within SCT to prepare for communication with new space neighbors and to invite extraterrestrials to our hometown for a covered dish potluck dinner.

CREATION *WITHOUT* COSMOS AND *WITH* COSMOS

To think of our created world as our home is central to the renaissance of Scandinavian Creation Theology. Christians are not to be considered as aliens in the world. Nor do we think of Christians as mere pilgrims on their way to another world. The world is God's creation. This is where God has placed us and wants us to be. To live an ordinary human life among other living creatures involves participating in God's life.[1]

Now, I ask: does God's creation include the cosmos or not? By "cosmos" I mean the physical world with its own natural history that is studied by our natural scientists. In a previous treatment of SCT, I pitted Regin Prenter against Niels Henrik Gregersen on this issue.[2] Prenter gives us creation without cosmos, whereas Gregersen gives us creation with cosmos. I recommend synoptic vision: both the eye of faith and the eye of cosmos.

On the one hand, one-eyed Prenter relies exclusively on what he knows theologically about our home in God's creation. He need not anticipate learning new things from telescopes and microscopes. The model for relating faith and science Prenter adopts is what Ian Barbour calls *independence* and I label the *two-language model*.[3] "There is no real problem with respect to the relationship between natural science and faith in creation. The two do not deal with the same questions, unless one or the other fails to keep within its own proper field."[4] The theology of creation can learn nothing relevant from scientific cosmology. With this as a theological method, it would be difficult to forecast how future discovery of new galaxies or communication with extraterrestrial creatures might impact our understanding of Earth as home.

On the other hand, two-eyed Gregersen takes advantage of both faith and science. The "Book of Nature" runs "parallel to the Book of the Bible."[5] Just as theologians interpret the Bible, scientists interpret nature. With one eye Gregersen reads the Bible. He reads the Book of Nature with the other eye. Or, more likely, he gives both eyes to both alternatingly.

When assessing the significance of autopoiesis within biogenesis, Gregersen notes with amazement that God has created creativity within creation. "How could one from an informed Christian perspective think consistently about God's relation to a universe that seems to be self-organizing, if not self-creative? Could it be that God has so created the material world that it has an innate ability to form life out of matter and thus give rise to new emergent phenomena such as perception, feeling, and consciousness?"[6]

Gregersen's notion of divine creation includes the cosmos. I propose that Gregersen is taking two giant steps forward here. First, methodologically, he is stepping beyond the perceptive horizon of the eye of faith to see things through the eye of science as well.[7] Second, what he comes to see through the eye of science—creativity within nature—then qualifies if not edifies the doctrine of creation he sees through the eye of faith.

Gregersen is by no means alone in asking science to contribute to theology. Sweden's former Archbishop Antje Jackelén illustrates such a method that leads to a faith-informed theology of nature. According to Jackelén, theology's vision of creation approaching new creation "can be reconciled with the findings from the field of natural sciences, but it cannot be derived from them."[8] A theology of nature incorporates scientifically procured knowledge, but it rests first on special revelation as reported in Scripture.

Might a method such as Gregersen's or Jackelén's provide a launch pad for rocketing toward what we earthlings might yet learn about cosmos? Might we learn that creativity within extraterrestrial civilizations has contributed to the direction some parts of our cosmic history are taking? Might extraterrestrial histories someday become meaningful to us when our astronomers and astrobiologists inform us of them?

For us to feel at home not only on Earth but also in the cosmos, we will need a basic commitment to loving God's creatures we have not yet met. Whatever love we can muster must expand beyond Earth to those we have yet to communicate with elsewhere in our galaxy and the universe beyond. How can we think about love on such a scale?

LOVE IN THE HOME AS *CARITAS*

Don Browning and I argued over two things. One argument ended in a stand-off. The other argument he won.

As a seminarian I had read Don S. Browning's book nee dissertation, *Atonement and Psychotherapy.* I loved it. I looked forward to studying with Professor Browning when I would later work on my doctorate at the University of Chicago Divinity School. While taking his courses at Chicago, we did become friends of a sort.

Two decades after my graduation, Don became principal investigator for a Lilly Endowment grant on "The Family, Religion, and Culture." Don invited me to join his team of scholars. My contribution was later published as *For the Love of Children: Genetic Technology and the Future of the Family.*[9] Don along with Ian S. Evison coauthored the foreword.

By this time, Don had succumbed to the charm of evolutionary psychology, a child of the selfish gene theory within sociobiology. "The genes hold culture on a leash," claimed E. O. Wilson, whom Browning admired. "The leash is very long, but inevitably values will be constrained in accordance with their effects on the human gene pool."[10] What is being said here is this: the creativity of culture can be explained by appeal to the selfish gene.

Don believed that genetic determinism within evolutionary theory could help explain family and home life. I thought then and still do that genetic determinism is pseudoscience. This is because the creativity of culture exhibits grand epigenetic traits that cannot be reduced to biology. I believe this despite the fact that sociobiology's progenitors occupied professorships at Harvard and Oxford. I applauded Don for taking science into this theology, but booed when he selected bad science rather than good science. Don and I simply agreed to disagree on evolutionary psychology's value. The argument ended in a standoff.

Our other argument is relevant to the question we are asking here: can we earthlings feel at home in the cosmos? This second debate had to do with the kind of love in the home that makes a family a family.[11]

I spouted off the value of love understood in Greek as *agape*. This kind of love comes to its highest expression in self-sacrifice, in giving one's life for the neighbor (John 5:13). God's love for the cosmos in John 3:16 is *agape*.

Don Browning was not favorably impressed. He sharply criticized me. "Ted, that *agape* stuff is just Protestant heroics and histrionics. Some sort of super-love. That's not the way love works in real life. Get realistic!"[12]

I was aghast.

"What we need," Browning continued, "is love understood in the medieval Latin sense of *caritas*. Thomas Aquinas understood love. He really understood how love works. This kind of love begins with intimacy in the family at home. Sociobologists call it *kin altruism*. Then, in the form of mutuality-in-community, love spreads to the neighborhood, the town, the country, and the world. Loving the stranger is an application of loving that we all learned first at home. Kin altruism is prerequisite for inclusive fitness."[13]

I balked. Well, at first I balked. But then I began to look again at the dynamics of love that are observable in human experience. After observing, I concluded that Don Browning was right. Love begins experientially with the intimacy of home life. Whether we label it, "kin altruism," or not is beside the point.

Those of us who grow up with compassion for the needy combined with a passion for justice are expressing something we learned very early in our family life. Whether we label it, "inclusive fitness," or not is beside the point. From family to the world including the enemy is the direction the love arrow flies. I concede: Don S. Browning was more helpful than me on this particular point. He writes,

> Christian love is more than love of kin, however. It entails in principle loving all humans, including the stranger and the enemy. The point of my argument, as it was with Aquinas, is that love of the other—even the nonreciprocating stranger and hostile enemy—builds on and extends the natural entanglements of self-regard and other-regard embedded in kin altruism. God's grace does not suppress kin affections; it builds on and extends these natural affections to include the other, be it non-kin neighbor, stranger, or oppressive and angry opponent. Extending this natural affection, with the help of God's grace, requires acts of self-sacrifice, but this sacrificial love builds on natural affections. It does not function to extinguish them.[14]

First, *caritas*. Then, *agape*. That's how we experience love. That's how we absorb love and subsequently exhibit the virtue of charity.

How is this relevant to the question: could we feel at home in the cosmos? It has to do with the expanding context of meaning. Intimate love at home with the family expands its context to the neighborhood, the hometown, the nation, the world, and then to the cosmos. The cosmos? Might that be too big of a stretch? Well, let's stretch.

THE EXPANDING CONTEXT OF MEANING

With the universality of Christian love in mind, let me turn to the hermeneutical concept of the expanding context of meaning. I will rely here in large part on the philosophical work of Hans-Georg Gadamer and theology of history propounded by Wolfhart Pannenberg.[15]

Meaning is contextual. Fragments of meaning have their contexts, even if the context is not immediately obvious. Further, each context has its more comprehensive context. Now, where might this take us? Like building a Lego house, we start small but end up large.

Let's start with a word. What does each word mean? To grasp a word's specific meaning, we must understand its place within the sentence. Yet, the meaning of the sentence is dependent on its context within the paragraph, which in turn is dependent upon the meaning of the book in which it is a part. Further, the meaning of a book is dependent upon its genre and even its epoch. Each epoch is dependent upon its context within the broad sweep of history, which finally is determined by its place in the consummate whole which is the totality of reality.

The totality of reality does not exist anywhere now. Why? Because it's not done yet. History is not complete. There is yet no whole to history. What we experience on Earth is a finite set of parallel yet overlapping histories we know as traditions. Despite attempts by the United Nations and other ecologically conscious do-gooders, stimulating a sense of planetary unity remains but an idealist's dream.

Only when history becomes a whole in God's eschatological new creation will the precise meaning of your and my experience at this moment be determined. Only then will the meaning of everything that has happened on Planet Earth be determined. It takes the whole of reality to determine the meaning of each part. It takes the future of reality to retroactively determine the meaning of present and past events.

GOD OF CREATION AND CONSUMMATION

When we begin addressing the question of the totality of reality, we are asking about God. At least, according to Wolfhart Pannenberg. "It belongs to the task of theology to understand all being (*alles Seienden*) in relation to God," writes the late Munich theologian; "so that without God they simply could not be understood. That is what constitutes theology's universality."[16] I think of the task of systematic theology as one of showing how all things in reality relate to the one God of grace.

The very fact that you and I experience meaning now is indirectly testimony that a whole to history is anticipated in our very experience of meaning. In fact, the whole of history is the condition for the possibility that you and I experience meaning in the moment. In your and my subjectivity, the objectivity of God's promised consummation of all things is proleptically present.

"God" is not merely interchangeable with "the totality of reality," to be sure. Even so, avers Pannenberg, "speaking about God and speaking about the whole of reality are not two entirely different matters, but mutually condition each other."[17] The whole and the part mutually condition one another. Does it follow that God and creation mutually condition one another?

How might this affect our question regarding feeling at home in the cosmos? Might there exist intelligent civilizations on exoplanets within the Milky Way with their own respective histories? Do those extraterrestrial histories also contribute fragments of meaning to what will yet be the consummate history of the cosmos? Will Earth's histories converge with off-Earth histories so that the angels will tell only one story about the totality of God's creation?

CAN BIG HISTORY DO THE JOB WITHOUT GOD?

Big History attempts to unite all cultural histories into a single natural history and to do so without God. And without eschatology. Will this suffice?

If you don't know what Big History is, let me introduce you. According to the International Big History Association, "Big History seeks to understand the integrated history of the Cosmos, Earth, Life, and Humanity, using the best available empirical evidence and scholarly methods."[18] One big historian, Ken Gilbert, tries to emphasize how truly *big* Big History can be. "The cosmos itself, beginning with the Big Bang, has now come to be seen, not as an inert or static backdrop for the planet, but an ever-changing manifestation in which everything is essentially historical and developmental."[19]

What's relevant for our discussion here is this: big historians assume that "the history of the universe [is] a single process."[20] In short, nothing in physical reality is excluded from the cosmic story the big historian tells. Might Big History's future include the confluence of Earth's past with the pasts of exoplanets within the Milky Way?

Our friends in Big History stop after eating their salad. They never taste the entreé let alone the desert to come. They stop short of asking about the whole of reality. They stop short of asking about the meaning of history. They stop short of asking about God.

If Pannenberg's cosmological argument based on the expanding context of meaning is sound, then what might be the implications for Big History? My answer is this. If Big History is to become big enough, it will have to incorporate—or fuse with—the many histories of other civilizations appearing on extraterrestrial planets. One can easily speculate that we will soon face the challenge of parallel histories meeting, exchanging interpretations, converging, and finally fusing.[21] But, if we fail to understand ourselves on Earth as fully historical, the prospect of fusing histories with our extraterrestrial neighbors may be postponed or even precluded.[22]

LOVING OUR EXTRATERRESTRIAL NEIGHBORS

In a recent book, Ryan McAnnally-Linz and Miroslav Volf list four defining qualities of a home: (1) resonance, (2) attachment, (3) belonging, and (4) mutuality.[23] Might contact and communication with ETI—should that day ever come—count as resonance? On the basis of what we have learned so far, it is not unrealistic to expect some level of interaction or resonance through SETI (Search for Extraterrestrial Institute) or METI (Messaging Extraterrestrial Intelligence International) via an as-yet-to-be-developed medium of communication.[24]

Shortly after alien contact, we'll clean the church basement and welcome strangers from afar to a covered dish pot luck dinner.

FROM ASTROETHICS TO PUBLIC POLICY

The cosmos is too vast to be understood by science alone. Certainly, space exploration including plans to establish settlements on the Moon and Mars require extra-scientific societal input. In short, science needs ethics to formulate public policy. Might creation theologians become public theologians and contribute to the discussion of public policy? Might providing sound ethical deliberation become the first concrete step we take up the path toward loving our space neighbors?[25]

The field we are talking about here is called *astroethics* or *astrobioethics* or *space ethics*. Of the many issues already being debated is the question: does life off-Earth possess intrinsic value? How the space community answers this question will be decisive when formulating public policy regarding exploration and exploitation of other worlds.

Astrobiologists tell us that it is quite possible that we will soon discover microbial life within our solar system, most likely on Mars or a moon orbiting either Jupiter or Saturn. For life similar to *Homo sapiens,* we must look beyond our solar system. The prospect of ETI is very high for exoplanets within the Milky Way. Almost every one of the perhaps four hundred billion stars in our galaxy has planets, some of which are rocky earthlike planets within the habitable zone.[26] With these prospects in mind, right now is the time for ethicists to consider what contact might be like and what moral posture our scientists should adopt.

A few years ago, I published an article in *The International Journal of Astrobiology,* "Does Extraterrestrial Life Have Intrinsic Value? An Exploration in Responsibility Ethics."[27] Because public policy was at stake, I could not simply appeal to so-called sectarian religious foundations. So, I appealed to responsibility ethics to ground my assertions.

The key to making such a responsibility ethic viable, I argued, is the simple logic of the good. Because the good is self-defining and is presupposed in all moral discourse, and because living creatures can participate in the good and appreciate the good better than non-living things, it follows that life should be treated as possessing intrinsic value. We *Homo sapiens,* then, are morally responsible to respect, protect, and even enhance life.

Now, suppose such a justification for human responsibility toward life wherever it is found would become persuasive. Then, perhaps we could also provide a persuasive argument for the intrinsic value of life as we find it on Earth and elsewhere in the Milky Way.

Could we find support for such an argument from SCT? Of course. "Scandinavian creation theology wants to highlight the intrinsic value of the created world" says Jacob Wolf in, "At Home in the Universe?" If the good is already present within creation due to God's grace, then the good within creation could provide foundational axioms for public ethics.[28]

Where do I go to take this step? To Knud Ejler Løgstrup. First, as a philosopher in the traditions of Martin Luther and Martin Heidegger, Løgstrup could recognize that responsibility is built right into our fundamental relationships. Our responsibility is inescapable. "By our very attitude to one another we help to shape one another's world. By our attitude to the other person we help to determine the scope and hue of his or her world, we make it large or small, birght or drab, rich or dull, threatening or secure."[29] In sum, space explorers already have a responsibility to the regions in our cosmos where they become present.

Second, our responsibility toward creatures like us requires love. Further, such love implies a form of treating the other creature as having intrinsic value. In Kantian language, our default position would be to treat an off-Earth creature like us as a moral end, not merely a means to a further end.

Such a categorical imperative is incorporated within Løgstrup's notion of the primal ethical demand. We can easily imagine applying Løgstrup to first contact communication that would take place between terrestrials and extraterrestrials. "Regardless of how varied the communication between persons may be, it always involves the risk of one person daring to lay him or herself open to the other in the hope of a response. This is the essence of communication and it is the fundamental phenomenon of the ethical life."[30]

Hans Fink, commenting on Løgstrup, recognizes how communication already implies an ethical demand to be trustworthy, to be loving, to treat the alien as a moral end and not merely as a means.

> It is a fact that we have power over the life committed to us in trust. To have this power is to be faced with the choice between either taking care of the life thus placed at our mercy, or destroying it. There is no third and neutral option, and the responsibility for what we choose is our own. . . . If we take advantage of the trust of others and use it against them for our selfish purposes, we shall have failed them. . . . Løgstrup uses the term 'ethical' exclusively to refer to the demand to act unselfishly for the best of each of the other persons who trust in us.[31]

In sum, I believe the resources exist within SCT to prepare for communication with new space neighbors and to invite extraterrestrials to our hometown for a covered dish potluck dinner.

CONCLUSION

We know we're home when we feel centered, connected, and comforted. If we love one another as God loves, then we will invite neighbors and even strangers into our home so that they can feel at home. Might this apply to strangers on a planet orbiting Proxima Centauri?

If Scandinavian Creation Theology follows the synoptic Gregersen model and reads both the Bible and the Book of Nature, we could rightfully speculate that future neighbors in space could become part of our known world. And, if the entire world is graced by its creator God, that grace will apply to extraterrestrial creatures as well as terrestrial creatures. We will have to ask: How do we think of "home" when considering space strangers becoming neighbors?

NOTES

1. This is the recurrent theme in Niels Henrik Gregersen, Bengt Kristensson Uggla, and Trygve Wyller, editors, *Reformation Theology for a Post-Secular Age: Løgstrup, Prenter, Wingren, and the Future of Scandinavian Theology* (Göttingen: Vandenhoeck und Ruprecht, 2017).

2. Ted Peters, "The Eye of Faith and the Eye of Science: Regin Prenter and Niels Henrik Gregersen on God's Creation," *Dialog* 57:2 (June 2018) 126–32; https://doi .org/10.1111/dial.12393.

3. Ian G. Barbour, *Religion and Science: Historical and Contemporary Issues* (New York: Harper, 1997) 84–89; Ted Peters, *Science, Theology, and Ethics* (Aldershot UK: Ashgate, 2003), 18–19.

4. Regin Prenter, *Creation and Redemption,* tran. Theodore J. Jensen (Minneapolis, MN: Fortress, 1967) 226.

5. Niels Henrik Gregersen, "Is the Universe a Sacrament? Denis Edward's Contribution to Sacramental Thinking," *God in the Natural World: Theological Explorations in Appreciation of Denis Edwards,* eds., Ted Peters and Marie Turner (Adelaide: ATF Press, 2020) 25–42, at 40.

6. Niels Henrik Gregersen, "The Creation of Creativity and the Flourishing of Creation," *Currents in Theology and Mission,* 28:3–4 (June–August 2001), 400–10, at 400.

7. Other SCT scholars similarly respect the value of science for theology. Finnish-American Veli-Matti Kärkkäinen, for example, forcefully asserts that "dialogue with sciences must be had." It is demanded by the inner thirst of creation theology itself in an era where the worldview is "dynamic, interrelated, evolving, in-the-making." Veli-Matti Kärkkäinen, *Creation and Humanity* (Grand Rapids, MI: Eerdmans, 2015), 10–11. Norwegian Pentecostal Knut-Willy Sæther finds traces of God in nature as viewed by science. Knut-Willy Sæther, *Traces of God: Exploring John Polkinghorne on Theology and Science* (Trondheim: Tapir Academic Press, 2011). Jan-Olav Henriksen writes, "Theology is not an attempt to explain the world scientifically. It is a way of interpreting human experiences from all possible sources in the best way possible and building on the sources of tradition as well as the sciences." Jan-Olav Henriksen, "Distinct, Unique, or Separate? Challenges to Theological Anthropology and Soteriology in Light of Human Evolution," *Studia Theologica* 67:2 (2013) 166–83, at 168.

8. Antje Jackelén, *Time and Eternity: The Question of Time in Church, Science, and Theology* (Philadelphia: Templeton Foundation Press, 2005), 221.

9. Ted Peters, *For the Love of Children: Genetic Technology and the Future of the Family* (Louisville, KY: Westminster John Knox, 1996).

10. Edward O. Wilson, "Ethics, Evolution, and the Milk of Human Kindness," in *The Sociobiology Debate,* edited by Arthur Caplan (New York: Harper & Row, 1978), 313.

11. According to Don Browning and Carol Browning, "The Central Ethic of Christian love should be 'equal regard,' and the primary task of families (and hence of the church in supporting families) is raising children to take their place in the kingdom of God." Cited by Betty Vos, "Practicing a Love Ethic for All Families," *Christian Century* 108:33 (January 1, 1991) 1060–62, at 1060.

12. Browning's emphasis on *caritas* or mutuality-in-community by no means precludes self-sacrificial *agape* love. "Christian love defined as a strenuous equal-regard for both other and self also requires sacrificial efforts to restore love as equal-regard when finitude and sin undermine genuine mutuality and community." Don S. Browning, "Love as Sacrifice; Love as Mutuality; Response to Jeffrey Tillman," *Zygon* 43:3 (September 2008), 557–62, at 557.

13. Browning thought Thomas Aquinas and evolutionary psychology taught the same thing. "Aquinas believed this natural interweaving of self-regard and other-regard in kin relationships extends to siblings, parents, and other kin. The insight that Aquinas had is consistent with contemporary evolutionary psychology and its doctrine of inclusive fitness." Ibid., 559. Finally, I find inclusive fitness, even if an accurate category scientifically, falls well short of what Christians include in *agape.* They are not equivalent, even if the comparison is illuminating.

14. Ibid., 559–60.

15. Ted Peters, "Truth in History: Gadamer's Hermeneutics and Pannenberg's Apologetic Method," *The Journal of Religion,* 55:1 (January 1975), 36–56; and Ted Peters, "Clarity of the Part versus Meaning of the Whole," *Beginning with the End: God, Science, and Wolfhart Pannenberg,* eds., Carol Rausch Albright and Joel Haugen (Chicago: Open Court, 1997), 289–301.

16. Wolfhart Pannenberg, *Basic Questions in Theology,* 2 volumes (Minneapolis MN: Fortress, 1970–1971), 1:1.

17. Ibid., 1:156. "Home is to be considered as an eschatological reality directed towards the future and based on the power of *promise,*" says Uggla elsewhere in this volume.

18. International Big History Association, http://www.ibhanet.org/. This definition derives in part from the work of Walter Alvarez, who has been teaching Big History at the University of California at Berkeley since 2006. See http://eps.berkeley.edu/people/walter-alvarez/.

19. Ken Gilbert, "The Universal Breakthroughs of Big History: Developing a Unified Theory," in *Teaching and Researching Big History: Exploring a New Scholarly Field,* ed. Leonid Grinin, David Baker, Esther Quaedackers, and Audrey Korotayev (Volgograd: Uchitel, 2014), 122–46, at 128–29.

20. Barry Rodrigue, Leonid Grinin, and Andrew Korotayev, "Introduction," *Our Place in the Universe, Volume I,* 1–16, at 10.

21. The fusing of historicized horizons of understanding (*Horizontverschmelzung*) is a Gadamerian term. Hans Georg-Gadamer, *Wahrheit und Methode* (Tübingen: J.C.B. Mohr / Paul Siebeck, 1965).

22. Ted Peters, "The Future Fusion of Terrestrial and Extraterrestrial Big Histories," *Theology and Science* 19:1 (2021), 18–32.

23. Miroslav Volf and Ryan McAnnally-Linz, *The Home of God: A Brtief Story of Everything* (Grand Rapids, MI: Brazos, 2022), 16.

24. SETI is passive. METI is active. SETI "searches are considered passive searches in that they are not aiming to elicit contact, but instead are merely listening for the presence of others. METI projects, however, intentionally aim to elicit a response tour own signals and are thereby considered active searches." Chelsea Haramia and Julia DeMarines, "An Ethical Assessment of SETI, METI, and the Value of Our Planetary Home," in Octavio A. Chon Torres, Ted Peters, Joseph Seckbach, and Richard Gordon, eds., *Astrobiology: Science, Ethics, and Public Policy* (Hoboken, NJ: John Wiley & Sons and Scrivener Publishing, 2021), 271–91, at 273.

25. Before asking whether the ETI we meet might be benign or hostile, we need to ask whether we *Homo sapiens* will be benign or hostile. "In contrast to ETI's

demonstrated sophistication, humankind often is deluded about the degree of its own intelligence. To ETIs, however, human beings must appear profoundly immature in their impulses and outbursts, particularly those that hurt and kill other human beings, eradicate other species, and damage the environment." Jensine Andresen, "Mind of the Matter, and Matter of the Mind," in Jensine Andresen and Octavio A. Chon Torres, eds., *Extraterrestrial Intelligence: Academic and Societal Implications* (Cambridge, UK: Cambridge Scholars Press, 2022),281–330, at 305.

26. "Yes, life is out there. Based on our current scientific knowledge, it is highly unlikely that we are alone. Just because we haven't communicated with anyone yet, does not change the end result that there ais other life in the galaxy." Heidi Manning, "Yes, We'll Meet Them: The Drake Equation Tells Me So," in Ted Peters, Martinez Hewlett, Joshua M. Moritz, and Robert John Russell, eds., *Astrotheology: Science and Theology Meet Extraterrestrial Life* (Eugene, OR: Cascade, 2018), 133–45, at 144.

27. Ted Peters, "Does Extraterrestrial Life Have Intrinsic Value? An Exploration in Responsibility Ethics," *International Journal of Astrobiology* 17:2 (2018), 1–7; https://www.cambridge.org/core/journals/international-journal-of-astrobiology/article/does-extraterrestrial-life-have-intrinsic-value-an-exploration-in-responsibility-ethics/5DCA161726CE8F4FC9E58EE8E6D04B81. See University of Lund astroethicist Erik Persson, "The Moral Status of Extraterrestrial Life," *Astrobiology* 12:10 (2012), 976–85.

28. I think the ethicist's category of "intrinsic value" imputes to a human person dignity. Dignity means being regarded as having intrinsic value rather than practical value for someone else's end. "Act so as to treat humanity, whether in your own person or in that of another, at all times also as an end, and not only as a means." Immanuel Kant, *Groundwork of the Metaphysics of Morals,* 2nd Section. Might this apply to microbial life or intelligent life with a second genesis off-Earth?

29. Knud Ejler Løgstrup, *The Ethical Demand* (Notre Dame, IN: University of Notre Dame Press, 1997), 18.

30. Ibid., 17.

31. Hans Fink, "The Conception of Ethics and the Ethical in K.E. Løgstrup's *The Ethical Demand*" in *Concern for the Other: Perspectives on the Ethics of K.E. Løgstrup,* edited by Svend Andersen and Kees van Kooten Niekerk (Notre Dame, IN: University of Notre Dame Press, 2007), 15.

Chapter 13

Embodying Creation and Gospel

Thinking With and After Gustaf Wingren

Lois Malcolm

Contemporary life has often been associated with a loss of belonging or a loss of "home" or "space."[1] But, as Paul Tillich has observed, to have or to lose space does not just have to do with physical locations, like having a body or a homeland; it also has to do with having or losing "social space," like having a vocation and a sphere of influence, or being in places "in remembrance and anticipation" or "within a structure of values and meanings."[2]

The contemporary loss of social space has more recently been analyzed in terms of the "acceleration" of modern life—that modern capitalist societies continually are "expanding, growing and innovating, increasing production and consumption as well as options and opportunities for connection."[3] However, as Byung-Chul Han has argued, in a fashion reminiscent of Tillich in the previous century, the deeper issue at stake in this acceleration is what he calls "dyschronicity," a sense that time itself is "whizzing without a direction" precisely because of the "atomization" of our lives and our identities since, for the most part, we are no longer "embedded in any ordering structures or coordinates that would found duration"—such as the myths and narratives found in previous epochs, along with social practices like promising and forgiveness—which could locate us in relation to one another, the world around us, and to time itself.[4]

As scholars have observed, religious beliefs and practices have had an ambiguous relationship to these dynamics of modern life. On the one hand, they have been associated with reactionary forces, as exemplified by their influence on the rise in recent decades of forms of ethnic and racial nationalism.[5] At the same time, they have been associated with the very roots of modernity itself and its link with secularizing processes.[6] Indeed, Martin Luther's theological legacy has been associated with both reactionary movements, such as Nazi socialism, on the one hand,[7] and with values associated with modernity, such as individual freedom and the value of everyday life, on the other.[8]

In view of these divergent appropriations of Luther, Scandinavian creation theology provides an intriguing counterpoint. With Lutheran roots, it puts forward a creation theology that seeks to address the atomization of modern life, even as it also affirms the positive aspects of modernity.[9] In this chapter, I examine the theological proposal of one of its major exemplars, Gustaf Wingren, in order to explore whether, in the same way that his theological proposal provided an incisive critique and constructive response to the modern theologies and practices of his day, it could also be relevant—if appropriated in fresh ways—for a time when the "dyschronicity" associated with contemporary life has only intensified.

In the first part of the essay, I "think with" Wingren, providing an analysis of his major theological themes that focuses on how, in view of his reading of Irenaeus and of scripture, he reworked a commonplace understanding of Luther's two kingdoms theory in order to address the lack of attention to creation and law in much of the modern theology of his day. In the second part, I "think after" Wingren, situating his work in relation to other sources that can help us interpret his theological proposal for our own time—from twentieth-century philosophers whose work provides insight into his phenomenological and hermeneutic approach to more recent scholarship that helps us appropriate his work in situations beyond the particular Swedish ecclesial and cultural ethos he addressed. Throughout the essay, I make the case that Wingren's distinctive approach for embodying not only our inherent embeddedness in creation and the "demand" it imposes on us, but also the "newness" of the gospel, which turns us ever again to our neighbors' needs in fresh ways, is indeed uniquely apposite for a time when our belonging in social spaces with one another and the world around us is being rendered ever more problematic.[10]

THINKING WITH WINGREN

Rethinking the Two Kingdoms Doctrine

As noted in the introduction, Martin Luther's legacy has been evaluated in a variety of ways. During and after the Second World War, Karl Barth associated him with an atavistic two kingdoms theology that preserved archaic, and even demonic, structures without a moral voice, and thus could, indeed, be linked with the rise of Nazism in Germany.[11] By contrast, a century earlier—even before Max Weber had associated John Calvin with the "spirit of capitalism"—Karl Marx had observed analogies between Luther's stripping of the naked soul from all external religious trappings and Adam Smith's stripping of individual agency, and its capacity for economic expansion, from the bonds of communal life in which it had been embedded.[12]

At the heart of these varied evaluations was an understanding of Luther's two kingdom doctrines (with a "worldly" kingdom on the left and "spiritual" kingdom on the right), which was associated, in turn, with a sharp distinction between law and gospel. This was precisely what Wingren wanted to rethink. He sought to avoid reducing the complex relationship between judgment and promise in scripture and theology to the simplistic formulas of either "gospel and law" or "law and gospel." On the one hand, the "law and gospel" formula loses the dynamic aspect of God's creative activity in the world and the transformative character of proclaiming Christ as gift, which also entails proclaiming Christ as an example to imitate.[13] Instead, Wingren countered any notion of the kind static "orders of creation" theology associated with Lutheran orthodoxy and its support for the status quo, including Nazi socialism prior to and during the Second World War. On the other hand, the "gospel and law" formula loses the sense of God's ongoing work in creation and the law outside of the gospel. It diminishes any possibility of a natural law within creation and God's sustaining and governing work through this law's demand for good works, and thus it loses the sense to which God's work in creation is the hidden source of the law, which comes to us not only as creative life but also incorporates death as judgment over our lives.[14] With this stance, the gospel becomes a kind of special Christian ethics that runs the danger of becoming either legalistic or a political tool used for conservative or revolutionary ends.[15]

In contrast to these two positions, Wingren argued that Luther's two kingdoms doctrine could only be interpreted meaningfully if read in context, that is, as counteracting either the bishops' assumption that their worldly power was divinely sanctioned or the Anabaptists' attempt to govern worldly events according to the Sermon on the Mount.[16] Instead, he found it helpful to read Luther alongside Irenaeus, the anti-Gnostic father of the church. Of course, Irenaeus and Luther had different emphases and responded to different contexts: the former spotlighted the restoration of creation in the face of demonic forces within a pre-Constantinian world; the latter proclaimed the gospel as liberation from the enslaving power of the law within Christendom. Nonetheless, in spite of these differences they both attended carefully to "the doctrines of Christ, the Gospel, the sacraments, and eschatology," even as they carried out their interpretation of these doctrines with an astonishingly "bold" interpretation of the first article of the creed (i.e., the doctrine of creation).[17] Indeed, in the same way that Irenaeus countered a gnostic and Marcionite rejection of creation and law, and emphasized instead that salvation is to be the restoration of this creation, so Luther also emphasized creation and law, giving the call to worldly vocations a place of honor, in lieu of a monastic vocation, since it was precisely within the everyday world of work and family life that one could serve one's neighbor and live in the imitation of Christ.[18]

Creation and Law

If Irenaeus and Luther provided Wingren with a grounding in historical theology, then it was his engagement with contemporary developments in Sweden and Germany that would shape his methodological concerns. In *Theology in Conflict* (1954/1958), he criticized three theologians in particular—Karl Barth, Rudolf Bultmann, and Anders Nygren—for too narrow an emphasis on Christology.[19] He had different criticisms for each: Barth tended to reduce theology to Christology, while Bultmann and Nygren, respectively, tended to reduce it either to a general philosophy of religion or to a historical motif. Nonetheless, by primarily emphasizing God's "revelation" in Christ at the expense of other emphases, all three had lost the robust conviction, found in both Irenaeus' and Luther's theologies, that God is active in all aspects of life. Of course, their concentration on Christology was understandable, especially because all three came into prominence after the First World War, which had undermined liberal theology's overly optimistic reliance on a "modern and trivialized idea of creation" that had its roots in the Enlightenment.[20] In addition, they had lived through the Second World War, which had raised critical questions regarding Lutheran orthodoxy's support of a static theology of the orders of creation. Nonetheless, Wingren maintained, it was only against the backdrop of God's ongoing work in creation, which always preserves life against chaos and destruction, that the uniqueness of the good news of Christ's death and resurrection could be made explicit.[21]

This methodological critique was followed by the constructive case in *Creation and Law* (1958/1961) for the importance of the first article within the context of the rest of theology.[22] There, Wingren develops, in line with Irenaeus and Luther, the creedal affirmation of creation presupposed in Christ's incarnation, death, and resurrection, and the coming of the Spirit to form the church as we await the last judgment and the resurrection of the dead. He begins, therefore, with a concrete starting point—the human body—which, he maintains, also anticipates the resurrection of this body. As bodily creatures, we cannot live without already being "wholly permeated" by the life God breathes into us (19). In truth, God is continually creating us anew, both in our personal lives, as in our birth, and in the midst of our engage-ment with the rest of life, which is also continually being created anew. Life, therefore, is a gift. We always find ourselves in a world and amidst neigh-bors already given to us. At the same time, from this continual creation and bestowal of life flows an "unexpressed demand" or claim upon us, since our every encounter with others and the world around us invokes a call to be responsive to their needs; thus, to receive life also means to be implicated in a "reciprocity of demand" with those around us (31).

The creedal affirmation of creation, in turn, presupposes the epic and anthropomorphic forms of narration found in scripture, thus affirming not only the Christian scripture's reliance on the Hebrew Bible, but also the unity of the two testaments. The two testaments depict a humanity created by God, but which has turned away from God in idolatry and injustice, and thus is now represented by a particular people, Israel, chosen by God to witness to God's law and promise of redemption for the human race and, indeed, for the entire world. This same humanity—precisely as both created good by God and yet subject to the law's disciplines—now awaits the coming of the Spirit; and it is into this same humanity that the Spirit comes in the present time through the gospel and the church. In making explicit these links not only between creed and canon, but also between the Christian scripture and the Hebrew Bible, Wingren aims to root the Christian faith not only in creation and law, but also in the story of Israel in contrast either to an anthropology rooted in philoso-phy, as exemplified by Bultmann, or a purely theoretical form of Christianity, which Wingren identifies with the revelation- or information-oriented theol-ogy of Barth and his followers.[23]

Gospel and Church

If Wingren provided an account of the demand or claim that comes to us in creation and law, then he also depicted the newness of the gospel that the church proclaims—developing what he called a "double-phenomenological" approach.[24] Thus, in spite of his criticism of Barth and Bultmann, he was also deeply influenced by their kerygmatic approach, and in *Living Word* (1949/1960) spotlighted the ways biblical texts were meant to be performed in a repetition of the spoken word throughout the liturgical year. Telling the story of an individual's journey through life, the four Gospels have an epic character that invites us to have our lives reconfigured around Jesus as we "follow" him from birth to death, identifying not only with him, but also with the figures around him (the blind, the lame, sinners, etc.) who exemplify aspects of what it to be human (as "Adam" or "Eve"). Through the Spirit's activity, the Gospels' epic events become "good news" for us as we join in the communion that Jesus had with those around him through our performative narration.

Wingren developed these themes more fully in *Gospel and Church* (1960/1964), which alongside *Creation and Law,* forms his first dogmatics.[25] This book also begins with the body, that is, with the bodily enactment of preaching, baptism, and the eucharist—self-involving events that enact the gifts of the gospel in our lives (3–5).[26] Through the Spirit's work, we become "more fully human" together as these events reconfigure our lives after the pattern or image of Jesus' death and resurrection (11).[27] Nonetheless, since the two sides of Wingren's phenomenological approach interpenetrate each other, the "newness" the gospel offers does not take place in abstract from the actual "demands" we experience in our everyday lives amidst "love, birth, labor, disease, suffering, and death" (4).

In developing these themes, Wingren's starts with the second article of the creed, centering his discussion of it on the depiction of Jesus' baptism in the four Gospels—with the voice speaking of the "beloved son," the overshadowing spirit, and the way each of the four Gospels is structured around this initial event as an anticipation (with allusions to the Servant in Isaiah) of Jesus' suffering and death (7). Resonant with these Gospel accounts are Paul's statements about our being baptized into Christ's life and death—the life and death of the one in whom God's image comes to full expression precisely because of his self-giving in our humanity, even to the point of death, in sharp contrast with the first Adam who exalted himself and, in so doing, was debased (8–10). These links between God's image, on the one hand, and Jesus' crucifixion and resurrection, on the other, are significant because they establish, in line with existing apocalyptic literature, a connection between the incarnate Word and Wisdom through whom God created, and continues to create, the world, on the one hand, and the crucified Messiah whose death and resurrection would usher in the future eschaton, on the other.[28]

Given this connection between creation and eschatology, Wingren's *Christology*, centered as it is in Jesus' baptism, has a backward and forward movement. Its backward movement is toward *recapitulation:* Christ restores humanity and all of creation by reversing the consequences of Adam's sin, a theme developed in early church theologies that integrate Christ's incarnation and atonement with his victory in the resurrection that liberates us from sin, death, and demonic forces. Its forward movement is toward *eschatology*: Christ's resurrection on the third day, as presented in Paul's letters, not only brings about a new creation, but is eschatologically linked both to the last day, when all will be raised, and to our daily dying and rising in Christ this side of the eschaton.

When Wingren moves to the third article of the creed, he begins with *eschatology*. After Christ's ascends and sends the Spirit, the Spirit proclaims—as an "eschatological event" through the church's preaching and sacraments—that Christ, raised from the dead, is God's creative word and wisdom who brings not only justification amid condemnation, but also life amid death and healing amid disease. In this way, the Spirit publishes to all that everyone is called into the promises given to Abraham so that they might become, with Israel, a living witness to God's reign of mercy and justice throughout the world.

In turn, Wingren portrays the Spirit's work of *recapitulation* through the church's "world mission and diaconate," which involves not only the forgiveness of sins but also—in line with Jesus' own messianic ministry—healing, exorcism, and raising the dead (154). In this way, the church remains "open" to the rest of the world through its practice of baptism. In addition to being the gateway and entry into Christ's life and death, baptism is the means by which we become "truly human," as we live our everyday lives sharing in Christ's humanity, which, in turn, Christ shares with everyone else, both within and outside the church (11).

Life in Christ means dying daily to our old, false identities so that we can embody the "new activity" or "new creation" that the Spirit enacts within us, which is not some lofty spiritual state, but rather the "heightening of the demand" that comes from those around us—from infants and children, the sick, the defrauded, the dying, and those treated unjustly (172). Indeed, in view of Christ's resurrection, we now can live with the eschaton—"the resurrection of the dead" (191) and with it "the last judgment" (207)—as the criterion for all our actions, not as a utopian ideal but as the way God uses our distinctive gifts and resources to bestow goodness and life amidst the forces of destruction and death that are often at play in our everyday lives.

But this side of the eschaton, sin and death remain within us and around us; thus, if Wingren related baptism to recapitulation, then he linked the eucharist with *christology*, since it is in our communion with Christ, and thus also with God and with one another, that we receive again and again the forgiveness of sins, which frees us from our self-preoccupation so that we can, indeed, imitate Christ in his service for others. Accordingly, if Wingren used baptism to signify the church's "openness" to the world (countering, e.g., sectarian groups that would shun the world outside the church) then he used the eucharist to signify our "communion" with Christ and with one another (in response, e.g., to a folk church that tended to be assimilated with the surrounding culture) (222).

Just as baptism signifies our union with Christ's resurrection life, which is worked out in our daily dying and rising in Christ, then the eucharist signifies our fellowship with Christ's betrayal and death, which brings about the reconciliation of all things. Moreover, if our baptism into Christ's life makes us vulnerable to our neighbors' demands, then our eucharistic union with Christ's death enacts within us the profound freedom that comes with the proper stewardship of our humanity. Such freedom empowers us to use creation's gifts wisely as we sift through the "multitudinous demands" placed upon us—discerning, for example, whether to accept our conditions, remaining faithful amidst diversity, or to alter them, actively changing, for example, unjust laws or resisting tyrannical powers (228). But we do not do this sifting alone, or in a disembodied fashion; rather, such sifting is enacted (drawing on an image from Irenaeus) as the "bodily fruit" of our eucharistic communion with God and one another—in our "prayer and praise" together, as we "groan" with the rest of creation awaiting the full redemption of our bodies and, indeed, of the entire world (241).

THINKING AFTER WINGREN

A Practical Wisdom

In a series of lectures he gave in Canada in 1979, Wingren reflected on the fact that much of his work up to that point had addressed what he called the "serious loss of substance" in modern theology.[29] Modern theologians like Barth, Bultmann, and Nygren had tended to divorce the life of faith from the realities of everyday life with its work and needs, such as "illness, friendship, health, deceit, love, and death."[30] They had lost the sense, which had existed in the "classical epochs" represented by Irenaeus and Luther, that "it was impossible to speak of anything as good without viewing it as received from the hand of God"—from food and sunshine to caring for the sick, health, and friendship.[31] In fact, one could say that the very epistemological and information-oriented approach of this modern theology was itself a kind of secularization of Christianity—whether or not it sought to limit itself to revelation (e.g., Barth) or draw on an existing philosophical anthropology to interpret the Christian faith (e.g., Bultmann).

In view of this censure, I take as a starting point Bengt Uggla's recommendation that Wingren be associated with the turn to practical knowledge as found, for example, in Martin Heidegger's focus on how we are always-already present in the world or Ludwig Wittgenstein's attention to the life-forms that shape our existence.[32] Read as a "practical wisdom," his theology—especially in its censure of much modern theological method—provides a critique of the kind of "modern subjectivity" (associated, e.g., with Descartes) that defines itself primarily by attention to epistemology, theorizing, and the transmission of knowledge and information, as opposed to what takes place in our lived experience.[33]

In his endeavor to develop an alternative, Wingren found K. E. Løgstrup, the major representative of the Danish tradition influenced by N. F. S. Grundtvig, to be of special interest because he portrayed creation and law in the Christian life as nothing other than the "secular life" human beings already share with one another and the world around them.[34] As Niels Gregersen has noted, Løgstrup appropriated a Heideggerian phenomenology of being-in-the-world (*Dasein*) as a being-with-others (*Mitsein*) as a way to counter the individualism and subjectivizing tendencies of thinkers like Immanuel Kant and Søren Kierkegaard; at the same time, he distanced himself from Heidegger's political philosophy, lack of ethical concern, and rejection of humanist values.[35] By way of a phenomenological analysis of creation, Løgstrup sought to depict how, prior to any deliberation or act of the will, we experience what "builds up" life—what he called "the sovereign manifestations of life," such as mercy, sincerity, and trust—even as these supports become apparent only through forces that "destroy" life.[36]

However, Wingren aimed at a 'double-phenomenological' approach that included the interpretation of scripture and the creeds. Thus, following another of Uggla's recommendations, we can use Paul Ricoeur's philosophical hermeneutics as an interpretive lens for understanding how Wingren related his phenomenology, as influenced by Løgstrup, to his hermeneutics of scripture.[37] For one thing, Ricoeur's mediation of the debate between Hans-Georg Gadamer and Jürgen Habermas over the respective merits of a philosophical hermeneutics versus a critique of ideology provides insight into the way Wingren relates a phenomenology of creation to his rendering of Israel's call within history.[38] Recall that Wingren assumed that within the gift of creation's bestowal of life in which we already find ourselves, there is always an "unexpressed" demand that comes to the fore in our every encounter with others and the natural world. In a related vein, Ricoeur contended that even though Gadamer's hermeneutics presupposed—drawing on Heidegger's notion of the "pre-understanding"—that we could never ultimately rid ourselves of our "prejudice," we still do have at least some possibility of distancing ourselves from our presumptions within the "fusion of horizons" that takes place in any dialogue we might have with a text—or another person, for that matter.[39]

Furthermore, if we found parallels between Wingren's treatment of creation and Gadamer's philosophical hermeneutics, then we can also find correspondences between his construal of Israel's calling and Habermas' critical theory, which was informed by Marx and the Frankfurt School. In his rendering of God's calling of Israel to witness to God's judgment and promise in the face of the nations' idolatry and injustice, Wingren spotlighted the way that this call was not only embodied in a historical people (rather than simply being an ideal, versus Bultmann), but also that they wrestled with it in the midst of actual sin, suffering, and protest (rather than its simply being a theory of revelation, versus Barth). In some intriguing parallels, Habermas' critique of ideology, like biblical judgment, attempts to bring to light ways communication is distorted through the hidden exercise of power; in turn, his invocation of a regulative ideal of unrestricted and unconstrained communication, like biblical promise, does not precede us but rather guides us into the future. But perhaps what is most interesting for our comparison with Wingren is the way Ricoeur points out that this critique and regulative ideal had nonetheless already been embodied and wrestled with in the earlier biblical traditions of emancipatory action, such as Israel's Exodus and Jesus' resurrection.[40]

In yet another thought-provoking parallel, we can find correspondences between Wingren's paradoxical christological and anthropological claims and Ricoeur's arbitration of Heidegger's and Emmanuel Levinas's contrasting conceptions of conscience. In *Oneself as Another*, Ricoeur juxtaposes "self-attestation" (employing Heidegger's depiction of Dasein's call to one's "ownmost possibilities") and "injunction" (referring to Levinas' portrayal of the call or command that comes from the face of the other).[41] Similarly, Wingren speaks of the profound tension and unity between the cross and death, and victory and joy. If Christ's divinity secures victory for us by his self-giving in his humanity, even to the point of death, then the victory he secures for us puts us, as humans, in the way of the cross.[42] Thus, we could say that the "self-attestation" we receive in being justified and united with Christ is precisely what enables us to hear and respond to the "radical demand" coming from our neighbors, even as our response to that "injunction" is only attested as we sift through and discern how best to respond to the multifarious demands placed upon us in freedom.

Contextual Changes and a Social, Even Ecological, Vision

These comparisons with twentieth-century philosophers help us to locate Wingren's double-phenomenological approach in relation to philosophical work that sought to "overcome" the focus on epistemology and knowledge abstracted from life in much modern western philosophy.[43] However, by the time he gave his lectures in Canada, Wingren had already begun to focus on issues within the wider world—such as links among global capitalism, secularization, the ecological crisis, and economic inequality between rich and poor nations.[44] And, instead of aiming to reform an existing Christianity (albeit a modern Christianity rather than the medieval one Luther sought to reform), he was now beginning to realize that Sweden was rapidly becoming secularized—as evidenced not only by the official state-church's loss of status and the sharp decline of its active and committed members, but also by the loss of traditional village life given urbanization patterns.[45] The Church of Sweden, in his view, was beginning to have more in common with the early church than with either the Christendom established by Constantine the Great or the other European state-churches that were formed after the reformation.[46]

Indeed, Wingren welcomed the church's existence as a minority group within the wider culture, even arguing for the dissolution of Sweden's state-church before it was dissolved in 2000. At the same time, he urged the church to reject the temptation to exist as a sectarian group focused only on the "supernatural" or having a "special morality with special norms"—pointing out that the early church held fast to its creedal affirmation of creation and God's being the God of the entire world, in spite of martyrdom and its realistic recognition of the powers of evil, death, and destruction.[47] Instead, he encouraged the church to embrace both "creation and gospel" in a threefold movement—in "mission" towards all of humanity, with an "eschatology" that embraces a future for all, and with a "diakonia" (or service) that strives to address and bear humanity's creaturely needs and burdens.[48]

In the remaining sections of this paper, I endeavor to appropriate Wingren's counsel for a time and for places beyond his own Swedish ecclesial and cultural context. In so doing, I presuppose that the patterns of "dyschronicity" discussed in this essay's introduction, which he himself was beginning to observe in his later years, have only intensified. Thus, I will expand our discussion of Wingren's proposal as a form of practical reason with a treatment of the social, and even ecological, vision it offers—and will do so by setting his depiction of baptism and the eucharist in conversation with emphases in recent literature that attend to analogous concerns.

Baptism and a New Time

In recent decades some philosophers, many of them atheists and Marxists, have found the apostle Paul to be a fruitful resource for addressing two mutually implicating dynamics.[49] On the one hand, the forces of global capitalism increasingly affect both cultural and political processes, possibly bringing about the "supreme danger" that we may no longer recognize the claims of others—from human beings to the natural world itself—because everything and everyone will have become so "fully metabolized by the perpetual motion of capital."[50] On the other hand, these economic forces also spur on the emergence of new tribal identities and conflicts among them—such as when ethnic and religious nationalisms recreate lost heritages in the face of a perceived "displacement," often pitting themselves against the claims to full humanity of previously oppressed groups.[51] As Susan Nieman has observed in a recent book, we now live in a world where we are left only with tribal identities instead of universals, power instead of justice, and despair in place of hope.[52]

Given these mutually implicating dynamics, Alain Badiou has drawn on Paul's apostolic logic in order to develop a "truth procedure" by which individuals from different backgrounds can be grounded in a shared, indeed universal, truth.[53] He begins with the premise that Paul's missionary proclamation centers on a singular event that has the power of universal address: "one died for all; therefore all have died" (2 Cor 5:14). On the one hand, as an event, it is *singular*. It cannot be reduced to any kind of law, legal, economic, or religious; it is wholly gratuitous. On the other hand, its power of address is *universal*. It cannot be limited by any pre-existing condition; it is open to everyone, regardless of ethnicity, gender, class, age, wealth, and so on.

Nonetheless, the actual truth of this event only occurs as it declared and trusted with faith or conviction (Gal 2:16). And yet, as Paul also makes clear, such faith is empty without love (1 Cor 13:1–3). Thus, for this event to be true, there also needs to be fidelity to the Christ-event, and all that it entails (2 Cor 5:14–17). In other words, it only counts as truth when lived out as "faith working through love," that is, from the standpoint of the address' completed character—"the hope of righteousness" (Gal 5:6).

We can note correspondences between this contemporary philosophical portrayal of Paul's apostolic logic and Wingren's depiction of baptism within the context of the church's "world mission and diaconate" to the ends of the earth.[54] Baptism enacts bodily our union with Christ's death and resurrection; in so doing, it reconfigures all the incidental factors that shape our identities (Gal 3:28), enabling us to be "truly human" by sharing the humanity Christ shares with everyone, regardless of their background.

In addition, as Wingren continually reiterates (as a good Lutheran), such baptismal reconfiguration takes place not only at the beginning of the Christian life, but also throughout our lives, as we are daily put to death, as members of Christ's body in the world, amid the multitudinous demands in our everyday lives. This keeps the church continually "open" to the rest of the world, with its focus on the needs and claims of its neighbors rather than on its own "identity" as yet another sectarian enclave attempting to establish its superiority over and against others—as has, unfortunately, been so much a part of Christianity's history with its legacy of anti-Semitism, colonialism, tolerance of slavery, oppression of groups based on gender or sexuality, and the like.

The Eucharist and New Places

If Wingren contrasted baptism and its "openness" to the world with sectarian tendencies, then he also juxtaposed the eucharist and its "communion" with a betrayed Messiah with a folk church that was indistinguishable from the wider culture. Thus, in addition to emphasizing the church's openness to the world, he also sought to spotlight its eucharistic communion with Christ's death and resurrection, which grounds its members in relationship with God and with one another.

Yet how might this communion be lived out, especially in places beyond Sweden, which, as Wingren himself noted in 1979, was also rapidly changing? Like other countries in northern Europe, Sweden had for centuries presupposed a state-church and a relatively intact and homogeneous cultural ethos. Indeed, Luther himself had presupposed the "modality" of the territorial church established centuries before by Constantine, even as he had sought to reform it, and he had assumed a shared German culture in which one could live out one's vocation, even as he had abolished the "sodalities" that the monasteries provided.[55]

But how might we appropriate Wingren's portrayal of the church's communion when it exists as a minority group within the broader society, consisting of people from divergent backgrounds who do not have much in common aside from their baptism into Christ's body and their being brought together by the Spirit of Pentecost? And how might this church be tangibly embodied in a world increasingly characterized by the "dyschronicity" of contemporary life, where enduring institutions and shared practices of any kind are increasingly difficult to sustain over time? Finally, what form might it take without succumbing either to the temptation of becoming yet another closed, sectarian group intent only on securing its own identity in a competitive spiritual marketplace, or that of becoming yet another humanistic organization that does the good work of caring for the poor or advocating for the oppressed, but without reference to its communion with Christ's death and life?[56]

As a postcolonial Brazilian theologian, Vítor Westhelle proves to be a helpful resource for addressing these questions.[57] Not only does he share many of Wingren's theological assumptions, but he also ventures to "transfigure" them for a "planetary" context—one that includes the "global South" where an ever-increasing number of Lutherans now live," in addition to the "North Atlantic axis" of the historic domains of Lutheranism (241–246). To aid him in this task, Westhelle holds to a premise that is also central in Wingren's theology: Luther's understanding of the three modes of Christ's real presence as the historical Jesus, in the bread and cup of the eucharist, and perhaps most importantly "everywhere according to his humanity," which means, according to Westhelle, that "there is no presence without materiality, that is bodily permanence and resilience in time and space" (159).[58]

The third mode of Christ's presence—his being "everywhere according to his humanity"—enabled Westhelle to claim two things, especially within the context of his engagement with Latin American liberation theology (226–240). On the one hand, he maintained that a theology of the cross radicalizes liberation theology's "preferential option for the poor"—especially when the ubiquity of Christ's cruciform presence throughout the world is highlighted (234–236). Drawing on Regin Prenter—in a fashion that also echoes Wingren—he maintained that "the cross of Christ is one with the cross we carry," noting not only the personal relevance of this statement but also its social and even ecological significance, since it identifies God with the suffering of humanity and the earth, and even with death itself (158–160).[59] Indeed, "there is one cross and it is plural" (160), and as such, "one incision" that crosses all the world's "schemes" as an "eternal moment (*ewiger Augenblick*)" that breaks into time as a "now" that is in time yet "breaks through time" (158). In this way, he upheld that "God is present in the very stuff of the world, in the living and nonliving, in the animate and inanimate, wherever pain and death are at stake and the resurrection is a promise, a new creation" (247).

On the other hand, the assumption of Christ's presence "everywhere according to his humanity" provided Westhelle with a means for appropriating liberation theology's critique of the overly individualistic understanding of sin and grace found in much Lutheranism (236–238). He found especially problematic the way an individualistic "piety" could be linked with a "politics" that identified the atomistic individual as its irreducible component and an "economics" focused solely on accumulating wealth, thereby turning all human labor and the natural world itself into a commodity for exchange (140–144). Indeed, he contended that in our time, Christ's redemption does not address a corrupt penitential system as it had in Luther's day. Rather, in a manner resonating with Wingren's attention to the forces that destroy life, he insisted that it addresses what Paul Tillich called "the demonic-tragic structures of individual and social life" that arise out of the disruption, conflict, and despair of much contemporary life and are manifest not only in forms of personal and interpersonal estrangement, but also in economic and political cleavages of various kinds (237).[60]

Thus, just as Wingren sought to relate resurrection hope to an existing hope—without thereby trivializing hope or identifying it with a utopia—so Westhelle depicted how "new creation" as a counter to the "structures of evil" might be manifest both as apocalyptic vision (238) and as response to creaturely need (259–261).[61] On the one hand, the inbreaking of God's reign enacts a *novum* that cannot measured by old scales, an "irruption of divine presence" that "happens against all hope that structures itself as a system, a scheme" (238). On the other hand, this hope is not unrelated to our "quotidian hopes, about health, food, shelter, security, friendship, love, and so many everyday signs of good news" in and through which God creates space for human belonging, even if they are not equated with the "ultimate values of the kingdom" (260). When God's eschatological future for all is divorced from our mundane creaturely needs—and vice versa—both Wingren and

Westhelle would aver that Christianity becomes either legalistic or collapses into politics, with even the most well-intended and righteous causes devolving into yet another form of the will-to-power.

Finally, in a manner that resonates with Wingren's proposal that the church embrace "creation and gospel" in a threefold movement (encompassing mission, eschatology, and diakonia), Westhelle proposed an appropriation of Luther's use of the three estates as a way to envision the church's role in a "planetary" context. Specifically, he posited that the church (*ecclesia* or public assembly) stand in a third space between "politics" (*politia,* concerned with public affairs) and the "economy" (*oikonomia*, which in the ancient world was linked with family life and work)—taking the form of both, without being reduced to either. In this view, the church is to seek neither political authority nor economic expansion; rather, it simply exists to give witness to the gospel and its eschatological vision of a "messianic politics" for all, even as it attends in a rather mundane fashion to the "resurrection of bodies"—individual and corporate—as they are healed and cared for this side of the eschaton with the goodness and life that flows from the Messiah's life, which overcomes all destruction and death.[62]

CONCLUSION

We have only skimmed the surface in our discussion of Wingren's theological relevance for our contemporary situation. In this chapter, I have simply sought to analyze his constructive theological proposal so as to appropriate it as a form of practical wisdom that also offers a social, and even ecological, vision for a time when the modernizing and reactionary forces that he addressed in his work have only intensified. Indeed, we might say that these forces have increasingly eroded the very enduring ecclesial and cultural patterns that he himself presupposed, at least implicitly, throughout much of his life. But if, in fact, as he suggests, our time is analogous to that of the early church, then we might be precisely in the place we need to be in order to interpret a New Testament metaphor central to his work—that when a grain of wheat dies, it bears much fruit "*for others.*"[63]

NOTES

1. For varied analyses of this loss of belonging, see, among others, Charles Taylor, *A Secular Age* (Cambridge, MA: Harvard University Press, 2018); Hartmut Rosa, *Resonance: A Sociology of Our Relationship to the World* (Cambridge, UK: Polity Press, 2020); Byung-Chul Han, *The Scent of Time: A Philosophical Essay on the Art*

of Lingering, trans. Daniel Steuer (Cambridge, UK: Polity Press, 2017); Mark Featherstone and Thomas Kemple, eds., *Writing the Body Politic: A John O'Neill Reader* (London: Routledge, 2020); and John O'Neill, *Five Bodies: The Human Shape of Modern Society* (Los Angeles: Sage Publications, 2004).

2. Paul Tillich, *Systematic Theology,* vol. 1 (Chicago: University of Chicago Press, 1951), p. 194.

3. Rosa, *Resonance,* 1.

4. Han, *The Scent of Time,* vi.

5. See, e.g., Pankaj Mishra, *Age of Anger: A History of the Present* (New York: Farrar, Straus and Giroux, 2017).

6. See, e.g., Taylor, *A Secular Age.*

7. Christine Helmer, *How Luther Became the Reformer* (Louisville, KY: Westminster John Knox Press, 2019), 80–82.

8. Heinz Schilling, *Martin Luther: Rebel in an Age of Upheaval,* trans. Rona Johnston (New York: Oxford University Press, 2017), 523–44.

9. See, e.g., Niels Gregersen, "K. E. Lögstrup and Scandinavian Creation Theology," in *Reformation Theology for a Post-Secular Age: L*ögstrup, Prenter, and Wingren, and the Future of Scandinavian Creation Theology (Göttingen: Vandenhoeck & Ruprecht, 2017), 44.

10. See, e.g., Gustaf Wingren, *Gospel and Church* (Philadelphia: Fortress, 1964), 189.

11. See, e.g., William Lazareth's discussion of "Karl Barth versus Luther's Law-Gospel Quietism," in *Christians in Society: Luther, the Bible, and Social Ethics* (Minneapolis, MN: Fortress, 2001), 10–18.

12. See John O'Neill's discussion in *Sociology as Skin Trade: Essays towards a Reflexive Sociology* (New York: Harper & Row, 1972), 25, in which he quotes a passage from Karl Marx's *Economic and Philosophical Manuscripts* in *Karl Marx: Early Writings,* trans. and ed. T. B. Bottomore (London: C. A. Watts and Company, 1963), 147–48.

13. Gustaf Wingren, *Creation and Law,* trans. Ross Mackenzie (Philadelphia: Muhlenberg Press, 1961), 125.

14. Wingren, *Creation and Law,* 125–26.

15. Wingren, *Creation and Law,* 126.

16. Gustaf Wingren, *Creation and Gospel: The New Situation in European Theology* (Toronto: Edwin Mellen Press, 1979), 12.

17. Wingren, *Creation and Gospel,* 6.

18. Wingren, *Creation and Gospel,* 13–15.

19. Gustaf Wingren, *Theology in Conflict,* trans. Eric H. Wahlstrom (Philadelphia: Muhlenberg Press, 1958).

20. Wingren, *Creation and Gospel,* 77.

21. Wingren, *Creation and Gospel,* 77–78.

22. In the rest of this section, page numbers from Wingren's *Creation and Law* will be given in the body of the text.

23. See, e.g., Wingren's comparison of Rudolf Bultmann and Oscar Cullmann in *Creation and Law,* 68–72, 83–84, and 86–88.

24. See, e.g., Wingren, *Theology and Conflict*, 161.

25. In addition, *Credo: The Christian View of Life and Faith,* trans. Edgar M. Carlson (Minneapolis: Augsburg, 1981) is yet his second dogmatics.

26. In the rest of this section, page numbers in the body of the text are from *Gospel and Church*, unless otherwise indicated.

27. See Bengt Kristensson Uggla, *Becoming Human Again: The Theological Life of Gustaf Wingren,* trans. Daniel M. Olson (Eugene, OR: Cascade Books, 2016), 150–53.

28. Lois Malcolm, "No Wisdom, No Trinity: Why (the Biblical Figure of) Wisdom Matters for Interpreting and Confessing the Trinity," *Word and World* 41, no. 3 (Summer 2021), 221–30.

29. Wingren, *Creation and Gospel*, 7.

30. Wingren, *Creation and Gospel*, 8.

31. Wingren, *Creation and Gospel*, 7.

32. Uggla, *Becoming Human Again*, 116–18.

33. See Charles Taylor, "Overcoming Epistemology," in *Philosophical Arguments* (Cambridge, MA: Harvard University Press, 1995), 1–19; see also Richard Bernstein, *Beyond Objectivism and Relativism: Science, Hermeneutics, and Praxis* (Philadelphia: University of Pennsylvania Press, 1983).

34. Wingren, *Creation and Gospel*, 130.

35. Gregersen, "Løgstrup," 41–45.

36. Gregersen, "Løgstrup," 45. See also K. E. Løgstrup, *The Ethical Demand* (Notre Dame, IN: Notre Dame University Press, 1997).

37. Uggla, *Becoming Human*, 134–35.

38. Paul Ricoeur, "Hermeneutics and the Critique of Ideology," in *Hermeneutics and the Human Sciences: Essays on Language, Action and Interpretation. Cambridge Philosophy Classics,* ed. John B. Thompson (Cambridge, UK: Cambridge University Press, 1981), 63–100.

39. Ricoeur, "Hermeneutics," 64–78.

40. Ricoeur, "Hermeneutics," 78–87.

41. Paul Ricoeur, *Oneself as Another,* trans. Kathleen Blamey (Chicago: University of Chicago Press, 1992), 350–51.

42. Wingren, *Gospel and Church*, 16, 17.

43. See Taylor's "Overcoming Epistemology," 1–19.

44. Wingren, *Creation and Gospel*, 69–100.

45. Wingren, *Creation and Gospel,* 14; see also *Gospel and Church*, 254–56, and Uggla, *Becoming Human Again*, 152.

46. Wingren, *Creation and Gospel*, 14.

47. Wingren, *Creation and Gospel,* 15, 154.

48. Wingren, *Creation and Gospel,* 158–59.

49. See Alain Badiou, *Saint Paul: The Foundation of Universalism*, trans. Ray Brassier (Palo Alto, CA: Stanford University Press, 2003) and Ward Blanton and Hent de Vries, eds., *Paul and the Philosophers* (New York: Fordham University Press, 2013).

50. L. L. Welborn, *Paul's Summons to Messianic Life: Political Theology and the Coming Awakening* (New York: Columbia University Press), p. xii.

51. Robert P. Jones, "The Challenge of Pluralism after the End of White Christian America," in *Out of Many Faiths: Religious Diversity and the American Promise*, ed., Eboo Patel (Princeton, NJ: Princeton University Press, 2018), 113–32.

52. Susan Nieman, *Left Is Not Woke* (Cambridge, UK: Polity Press, 2023).

53. Badiou, *Saint Paul*, 15.

54. Wingren, *Gospel and Church*, 154.

55. Ralph D. Winter, "The Two Structures of God's Redemptive Mission," *Missiology*, 2, no. 1 (January 1974), 121–39.

56. Wingren, *Creation and Gospel*, 152–54.

57. In the rest of this section, page numbers in the body of the text are from Vítor Westhelle's *Transfiguring Luther: The Planetary Promise of Luther's Theology* (Eugene, OR: Cascade Books, 2016), unless otherwise indicated.

58. In discussing this "third mode" in *Transfiguring Luther*, 122, Westhelle refers not only to Regin Prenter's *Luther's Theology of the Cross* (Philadelphia: Fortress, 1971), but also to Niels Gregersen's "Deep Incarnation: The Logos Became Flesh," in Karen Bloomquist, ed., *Transformative Theological Perspectives* (Minneapolis, MN: Lutheran University Press, 2010), 167–82.

59. Regin Prenter, *Theology of the Cross*.

60. Paul Tillich, *Systematic Theology*, vol. 1 (Chicago: University of Chicago Press, 1951), 49.

61. Wingren, *Creation and Gospel*, 156.

62. See Robert Gibbs' discussion of these themes from a Jewish perspective in "Seven Rubrics for Jewish Philosophy," in *Correlations in Rosenzweig and Levinas* (Princeton, NJ: Princeton University Press, 1992), 255–60.

63. Uggla, *Becoming Human Again,* 165–66, (John 12:24; cf. I Cor 15:37).

Index

209

About the Contributors

Svein Aage Christoffersen is Professor Emeritus of Theology at the University of Oslo. He is the author of numerous articles on K. E. Løgstrup and the philosophy of religion, as well as a number of works on aesthetics. He served for many years as the editor of *Norsk Teolokisk Tidsskrift*.

Mary Emily Briehl Duba is Assistant Professor of Theology at University of Dubuque Theological Seminary. Her work responds to theological questions raised by human displacement and ecological collapse. Before earning her PhD from the University of Chicago, she and her husband lived for year in Cochabama, Bolivia, in community with displaced people and with members of the Maryknoll order.

Elisabeth Gerle served for many years as Professor of Ethics at Lund University and at the Church of Sweden Research Department. Her recent books deal with religion and politics, Luther and the erotic, and contemporary idiots, seduced by an ideology claiming that we do not belong to society and the world. Recent books are *Passionate Embrace. Luther on Love, Body, and Sensual Presence.* (2017) Cascade; and *Vi är inte idioter. Klimat, ekonomi, demokrati* (Korpen 2023).

Niels Henrik Gregersen has served since 2004 as Professor of Systematic Theology at the University of Copenhagen. He is the author or editor of numerous books, notably *Incarnation: On the Scope and Depth of Christology* (Fortress, 2015) and *Information and the Nature of Reality: From Physics to Metaphysics* (Cambridge University Press, 2010).

Allen G. Jorgenson is Assistant Dean, Professor of Systematic Theology, and the William D. Huras chair in ecclesiology and church history at Martin Luther University College at Wilfrid Laurier University, Ontario, Canada.

He is the author of the recent book *Indigenous and Christian Perspectives in Dialogue: Kairotic Place and Borders* (Lexington, 2020).

Lois Malcolm is Professor and Olin and Amanda Fjelstad Registad Chair for Systematic Theology at Luther Seminary in St. Paul, Minnesota. She is the author of *Holy Spirit: Creative Power in Our Lives* (Fortress, 2009).

Ryan McAnnally-Linz is a systematic theologian and serves as Associate Director of the Yale Center for Faith and Culture. He co-authored *Public Faith in Action* (Brazos, 2014) and *The Home of God: A Brief Story of Everything* (Brazos, 2022) with Miroslav Volf.

Derek R. Nelson is Professor of Religion and Stephen S. Bowen Professor of Liberal Arts at Wabash College in Crawfordsville, Indiana. He has published a number of books and articles in contemporary and historical theology, including *Sin: A Guide for the Perplexed* (Bloomsbury, 2011) and co-edited, with Paul Hinlicky, the Oxford Research Encyclopedia of Martin Luther (Oxford University Press, 2017).

Ted Peters is Distinguished Research Professor in Theology and Science at the Graduate Theological Union in Berkeley, California. He is the author or editor of over thirty books, including the influential *God—The World's Future: Systematic Theology for a Postmodern Era* (Fortress, 2015).

Sasja Emilie Mathiasen Stopa is a postdoctoral researcher at the University of Aarhus in Denmark and a fellow at the University of Edinburgh. She is the author of *Honour and Glory in the Theology of Martin Luther* (LIT Verlag, 2021).

Bengt Kristensson Uggla is Amos Anderson Professor of Philosophy, Culture, and Management at the Swedish-speaking Abo Akademi University in Turku, Finland. He is the author of ten books, including *Ricoeur, Hermeneutics, and Globalization* (2010) and *Becoming Human Again: The Theological Life of Gustaf Wingren* (Cascade, 2016).

Else Marie Wiberg Pedersen is Associate Professor of Systematic Theology at Aarhus University in Denmark. She is the author or editor of several books, including *The Alternative Luther: Lutheran Theology from the Subaltern* (Lexington, 2019).

Jakob Wolf is Associate Professor emeritus at the University of Copenhagen. He co-edited the book *Earth on Fire: Climate Change from a Philosophical and Ethical Perspective* (2009).

Trygve Wyller is Professor emeritus of Contemporary Theology and the Studies of Christian Social Practice at the Faculty of Theology, University of Oslo, and served as Honorary Professor at the School of Religion, Philosophy and Classics at the University of KwaZulu-Natal, South Africa. He has published on migration, ethics, and ecclesiology both from a dogmatical, spatial, and phenomenological perspective.